WALTER BEYERLIN

ORIGINS AND HISTORY OF THE OLDEST SINAITIC TRADITIONS

Translated by
S. RUDMAN

BASIL BLACKWELL · OXFORD

First printed 1961
A translation of
Herkunft und Geschichte der ältesten Sinaitraditionen
(1961) by permission of J. C. B. Mohr (Paul Siebeck), Tübingen

PRINTED IN GREAT BRITAIN
BY ADLARD AND SON LIMITED, DORKING

In gratitude to

Professor Artur Weiser

FOREWORD TO THE ENGLISH EDITION

During the past generation, the renewed emphasis on the tradition of the Exodus as the basis of Israel's faith has been accompanied by vigorous scholarly debate about Pentateuchal origins, and in particular, about the formation in oral tradition of the material which was subsequently embodied in the written sources of the Pentateuch. In this, as in other important areas of Old Testament research, the importance of the cult in the shaping and transmission of the material has been increasingly realized. Much of the pioneering work in these fields has been carried out by German and Scandinavian scholars. The detailed researches of Professor Gerhard von Rad and Professor Martin Noth have been mediated to English readers by translations of the former's commentary on Genesis and the latter's *History of Israel* and commentaries on Exodus and Leviticus. In the present work, using the same critical tools as von Rad and Noth, Professor Beyerlin reaches conclusions which differ from theirs in important ways. In particular, he denies that the traditions of the Exodus and the Conquest of Palestine were originally separate from those of the Sinaitic Covenant. His arguments are based upon a painstaking examination of the biblical texts; and he has also made effective use of the Hittite treaties, to which so much attention has been directed in recent years. The result is a work of first-rate importance in the contemporary debate about the formation of the Pentateuch, the early history of Israel, and the origins of Israelite religion.

Professor Beyerlin, a disciple of Professor Artur Weiser of Tübingen, and successor of Professor H. W. Hertzberg at the University of Kiel, is one of the most outstanding of the younger generation of German Old Testament scholars. I count it a privilege to write this foreword to his work, now made available to English readers in the Revd Stanley Rudman's excellent translation.

G. W. Anderson

University of Edinburgh

CONTENTS

ABBREVIATIONS

AASF	*Annales Akademiae Scientiarum Fennicae, Helsingfors*
AcOr	*Acta Orientalia (Leiden), Kopenhagen*
ALBO	*Analecta Lovaniensia Biblica et Orientalia, Louvain*
ANET	*Ancient Near Eastern Texts relating to the Old Testament, ed. by J. B. Pritchard, 2nd ed., Princeton (NJ) 1955*
AnOr	*Analecta Orientalia, Rome*
AO	*Der Alte Orient, Leipzig*
AOT	*Altorientalische Texte zum Alten Testament, ed. by H. Gressmann, 2nd ed., Berlin-Leipzig, 1926*
ARW	*Archiv für Religionswissenschaft, Leipzig-Berlin*
ATD	*Das Alte Testament Deutsch, ed. by A. Weiser, Göttingen*
BA	*The Biblical Archaeologist, New Haven, Conn.*
BASOR	*Bulletin of the American Schools of Oriental Research, New Haven, Conn.*
BBB	*Bonner Biblische Beiträge*
BFChTh	*Beiträge zur Forderung Christlicher Theologie, Gütersloh*
BGBE	*Beiträge zur Geschichte der Biblischen Exegese, Tübingen*
BH	*Biblia Hebraica, ed. by R. Kittel, 6th ed., Stuttgart 1950*
BHTh	*Beiträge zur historischen Theologie, Tübingen*
Bibl	*Biblica, Rome*
BJRL	*The Bulletin of the John Rylands Library, Manchester*
BK	*Biblischer Kommentar. Altes Testament, ed. by M. Noth, Neukirchen*
BRL	*Kurt Galling, Biblisches Reallexicon, HAT 1/1, 1937*
BSAW	*Berichte über die Verhandlungen des Sächs. Akademie der Wissenschaften zu Leipzig*
BWANT	*Beiträge zur Wissenschaft vom Alten und Neuen Testament, Stuttgart*
BZAW	*Beihefte zur Zeitschrift für die alttestamentliche Wissenschaft (Giessen), Berlin*
CBQ	*The Catholic Biblical Quarterly, Washington*
EF	*Erlanger Forschungen*
EKL	*Evangelisches Kirchenlexicon, Göttingen 1956–59*
EvTh	*Evangelische Theologie, München*
FRLANT	*Forschungen zur Religion und Literatur des Alten und Neuen Testaments, Göttingen*
F1	*J. Friedrich, Staatsverträge des Ḫatti-Reiches . . . , 1st part, MVÄG 1926*

F2 — *J. Friederich, Staatsverträge des Ḫatti-Reiches . . ., 2nd part, MVÄG 1930*
GAG — *W. v. Soden, Grundriss der Akkadischen Grammatik, AnOr 33, Rome 1952*
HAT — *Handbuch zum Alten Testament, ed. by O. Eissfeldt, Tübingen*
HG — *Hebräische Grammatik*
HK — *Handkommentar zum Alten Testament, ed. by W. Nowack, Göttingen*
HThSt — *Harvard Theological Studies, Cambridge*
HUCA — *Hebrew Union College Annual, Cincinnati (Ohio)*
IEJ — *Israel Exploration Journal, Jerusalem*
JAOS — *Journal of the American Oriental Society, New Haven, Conn.*
JBL — *Journal of Biblical Literature and Exegesis, New Haven, Conn.*
JPOS — *Journal of the Palestine Oriental Society, Jerusalem*
JSSt — *Journal of Semitic Studies, Manchester*
JThSt — *Journal of Theological Studies, Oxford*
KAT — *Kommentar zum Alten Testament, ed. by E. Sellin, Leipzig*
KHC — *Kurzer Hand-Commentar zum Alten Testament, ed. by K. Marti (Freiburg, Leipzig), Tübingen*
Kleine Schriften = Kleine Schriften zur Geschichte des Volkes Israel, München
LVTL — *Lexicon in Veteris Testamenti Libros*
LXX — *Septuagint*
LXX-B — *Septuagint according to Codex Vaticanus*
MT — *Massoretic Text*
MVAG — *Mitteilungen der Vorderasiatisch-Aegyptischen Gesellschaft, Leipzig*
NKZ — *Neue Kirchliche Zeitschrift*
OTS — *Oudtestamentische Studiën, Leiden*
PJ — *Palästinajahrbuch, Berlin*
RE — *Realencyklopädie für prot. Theologie und Kirche, 3rd ed., Leipzig 1896–1913*
RHPhR — *Revue d'Histoire et de Philosophie Religieuses, Strasbourg-Paris*
SATA — *Die Schriften des Alten Testaments in Auswahl, 2nd ed., Göttingen 1920–1925*
SD — *Sammlung Dalp, München-Bern*
SGVS — *Sammlung gemeinverständlicher Vorträge und Schriften, Tübingen*

StBTh	*Studies in Biblical Theology*, London
StTh	*Studia Theologica*, Lund
ThBl	*Theologische Blätter*, Leipzig
ThLZ	*Theologische Literaturzeitung*, Leipzig, Berlin
ThR	*Theologische Rundschau*, Tübingen
ThStKr	*Theologische Studien und Kritiken*, Stuttgart-Gotha
ThT	*Theologisch Tijdschrift*, Leiden
ThWBNT	*Theologisches Wörterbuch zum Neuen Testament*, Stuttgart
TrThZ	*Trierer Theologische Zeitschrft*, Trier
UUÅ	*Uppsala Universitets Årsskrift*, Uppsala-Leipzig
VAB	*Vorderasiatische Bibliothek*, Leipzig
VT	*Vetus Testamentum*, Leiden
VTS	*Vetus Testamentum, Supplements*, Leiden
W	E. F. Weidner, *Politische Dokumente aus Kleinasien. Die Staatsverträge in akkadischer Sprache aus dem Archiv von Boghazköi*, Leipzig, 1923
ZAW	*Zeitschrift für die alttestamentliche Wissenschaft* (Giessen), Berlin
ZDMG	*Zeitschrift der Deutschen Morgenländischen Gesellschaft*, (Leipzig) Wiesbaden
ZThK	*Zeitschrift für Theologie und Kirche*, Tübingen

INTRODUCTION

The form-critical and traditio-historical method of enquiry goes beyond the purely literary-critical analysis of the Pentateuch, because it has learned to see the literary growth as simply the final, culminating process of a long history that goes back many years and is for the most part pre-literary. H. Gunkel in his form-critical studies and his source-criticism was the first to draw attention to the pre-literary stage of tradition in the Pentateuch and to raise the question of the *Sitz im Leben* of the traditions embedded in it,[1] a method of enquiry which was subsequently adopted by H. Gressmann in his exposition of the traditions about Moses.[2] Both these scholars, and likewise A. Alt in his studies of Pentateuchal legal material[3] employed the methods of form-criticism to great advantage when dealing with smaller units of tradition. G. von Rad, however—following S. Mowinckel's attempt to derive the Yahwistic-Elohistic account of Sinai from the festival-cult at Jerusalem[4] and J. Pedersen's interpretation of Exodus i–xiv[5]—subjected the whole literary complex of the Hexateuch[6] and its main underlying traditions to a thorough form-critical examination.[7] He came to the following conclusion: the Exodus–Conquest tradition and the Sinai tradition were originally separate and distinct, each with its own particular *Sitz im Leben*. The former tradition was connected with the shrine at Gilgal and grew out of the 'brief historical creed' found there (Deuteronomy xxvi. 5 f.; vi. 20 f.), which was the festival-legend of the Feast of Weeks. The latter was linked with the cult of the renewal of the covenant at Shechem; it grew out of the Shechemite shrine's festival legend and in its basic structure reflects the pattern of the cult there. Only at a later stage, after the two traditions had been separated from their original cultic roots, were they linked together by the Yahwist in his literary composition. M. Noth[8] also considers that such 'leading themes' as the deliverance from Egypt, the entry into Canaan and the revelation on Sinai were originally independent complexes of tradition, which ultimately go back to 'certain specific expressions of faith, rooted in the cult and

[1] *Genesis*, *HK* I/1,[5] 1922.
[2] *Mose und seine Zeit. Ein Kommentar zu den Mose-Sagen*, *FRLANT*, 18, 1913.
[3] *Die Ursprünge des israelitischen Rechts*, 1934 (= *Kleine Schriften* I, pp. 278–332).
[4] *Le Décalogue*, 1927.
[5] 'Passahfest und Passahlegende', *ZAW*, 52, 1934, pp. 161–175.
[6] Whether we should think of a Tetra-, Penta-, or Hexateuch does not concern us here.
[7] *Das formgeschichtliche Problem des Hexateuch*, 1938 (= *Gesammelte Studien*, pp. 9–86).
[8] *Überlieferungsgeschichte des Pentateuch*, 1948.

shaped by its creed'.[9] M. Noth differs from G. von Rad, however, in allowing that the Exodus-Conquest theme might already have been united with the Sinai theme in the common basis (G) presupposed by the Yahwist and the Elohist: as a result of the tribes finally being brought together into the one tribal confederacy of Israel these traditions were also combined. It is no longer possible to recognise what forces contributed to this process and directed it, or to know what factors contributed to the development of the separate complexes of tradition earlier. Only the literary blocks of material can be analysed with any certainty. Thus the attempt of the Yahwist to minimise the cultic basis of the leading themes of the tradition and many of the individual pericopae and to spiritualise and rationalise the tradition at many points is obvious.[10] H-J. Kraus also agrees with G. von Rad that the Sinai tradition and the Exodus-Conquest tradition were originally separate and were associated with different local shrines: the former with Shechem[11] and the latter with Gilgal.[12] But Kraus attributes the union of the two lines of tradition not to the literary initiative of the Yahwist but to an event in the history of the cult: when the cult-centre of the amphictyony was transferred from Shechem to Gilgal the Sinai tradition was given a place alongside the Exodus-Conquest tradition.[13] This shows that Kraus considers that the Sinai tradition retained its cultic context even after leaving Shechem; this is made perfectly clear in his study *Gottesdienst in Israel*, where he expresses the view that the tradition of the Sinaitic covenant constantly succeeded in establishing itself in the Jerusalem state-cult also.[14]

There is no agreement, therefore, as to when or how the union of the two sets of traditions, one dealing with Sinai and the other with Exodus-Conquest, came about. There are different views, too, as to how long the Sinai traditions continued to be closely connected with the cult or when they began to be detached from their original *Sitz im Leben* or what forces governed their further pre-literary form. That is why it is necessary to make a fresh examination of the *Sitz im Leben* of the Sinai traditions which were given their present shape by the Yahwist and the Elohist, of the presuppositions and influences which moulded their pre-literary growth, and of the roots to which

[9] *Ibid.*, p. 48.
[10] Cf. *ATD*, 5, pp. 5 f.
[11] *Gottesdienst in Israel. Studien zur Geschichte des Laubhüttenfestes*, pp. 57 f.
[12] Gilgal. Ein Beitrag zur Kultusgeschichte Israels', *VT* I, 1951, pp. 188 f.
[13] *Ibid.*, pp. 193 f.
[14] Cf. *ibid.*, pp. 77–91.

the separate elements of these traditions go back. But before any traditio-historical examination of these questions can be undertaken the text of the Sinai pericope must be subjected to literary-critical analysis and the separate traditions of J and E defined.

I

TRADITIO-CRITICAL AND LITERARY-CRITICAL ANALYSIS

The present investigation is limited to the Sinai traditions in the Yahwistic and Elohistic strata of the Pentateuch. The first task, therefore, is to separate and define these older strata within the Sinai pericope, Exodus xix. 1–Numbers x. 10,[1] by subtracting what belongs to the Priestly Source (I. 1). Secondly, the Book of the Covenant has also to be detached, because it has nothing to do with the actual Sinai tradition and was only brought into a loose connection with it later (I. 2). Finally, the remaining text will be analysed by the methods of traditio-critical[1a] and literary-critical analysis (I. 3–11).

1. The Sinai Pericope in the Priestly Source

At the present time a great deal of Pentateuchal criticism is in flux[2] and uncertainty again, but by and large there is a great deal of agreement[3] concerning the parts of the Pentateuch which belong to the Priestly Source[4] or have been worked into it[5] and have been handed down from the beginning in priestly circles.[6] In the Sinai pericope this is undoubtedly true of the following parts:

(a) Exod. xix. 1–2a.[7] The reference to the itinerary which is repeated here is a continuation of Exod. xvii. 1abα, a passage which also belongs to P and which, together with Exod. xix. 1–2a, belongs

[1] On the definition of this section cf. G. von Rad, *Das formgeschichtliche Problem des Hexateuch* (= *Gesammelte Studien*, p. 21 f.); M. Noth, *Überlieferungsgeschichte des Pentateuch*, pp. 151 f.

[1a] The term 'traditionskritisch' refers to a complex of different *traditions*, which are united by one literary context, whereas 'literarkritisch' and 'quellenkritisch' refer to a *literary* complex, composed of different literary sources (*Tr. note*).

[2] Cf. C. R. North, 'Pentateuchal Criticism', *The Old Testament and Modern Study*, pp. 48–83; see also U. Cassuto, *The Documentary Hypothesis and the Composition of the Pentateuch*, (1941), 1953.

[3] This is also true on the whole in respect of I. Engnell, *Gamla Testamentet. En traditionshistorisk inledning* I, pp. 209 f. Cf. C. R. North, op. cit., pp. 68, 77–8.

[4] There is no need to discuss the earlier or later history of the text of P here. Cf. on this R. Rendtorff, *Die Gesetze in der Priesterschrift*, *FRLANT*, 62; K. Koch, *Die Priesterschrift von Exodus 25 bis Leviticus 16*, *FRLANT*, 71; G. von Rad, *Die Priesterschrift im Hexateuch*, *BWANT*, IV, 13; and P. Humbert, 'Die literarische Zweiheit des Priester-Codex', *ZAW*, 1940/41, pp. 30 f.

[5] According to M. Noth (*Überlieferungsgeschichte des Pentateuch*, pp. 8 f.) these insertions may have taken place after P was received into the Pentateuch.

[6] Cf. for instance M. Noth, *op. cit.*, pp. 7 f. or any Introduction to the O.T.

[7] Perhaps in reverse order prior to the traditions being combined. For further detaiis consult B. Baentsch, *HK*, 2/1 p. 172 or M. Noth, *Überlieferungsgeschichte des Pentateuch*, pp. 14, 18, n. 32, 55.

to the framework of P as the text now stands. The chronological note in xix. 1abα, which was once even more precise,[8] as the expression *bayyôm hazzeh* reveals, is characteristic of P,[9] like the designation of the month[10] by a numeral[11] and the expression *midbar sinay*, which only occurs in such passages as are generally ascribed to the P stratum.[12] Exod. xix. 2b, however, must belong to another source, since its contents are a doublet of xix. 2aβ.

(b) The section Exod. xxiv. 15b–xxxi. 18a also belongs to the P stratum.[13] This section breaks up the obvious and fairly generally recognised connection between Exod. xxiv. 12–15a (18b) and Exod. xxxii (the story of the Golden Calf). It is not in itself a unity, apart from the fairly compact unit Exod. xxv. 1–xxxi. 17ab,[14] where the institution of the Tent and the ordination of the priests are described. Exod. xxiv. 15b–18a rounds off the Priestly version of the Sinai-theophany, to which xxxi. 18a also belonged originally. When the account of the theophany was linked with the description of the institution of the Tent and the ordination of the priests,[15] xxxi. 18a (together with 18b) was separated from its context because of the giving of the Law referred to in xxv. 16, 21; in its present position at the end of the legal section this half verse describes the fulfilment of what was predicted earlier in xxv. 16, 21. In other words, Exod. xxv. 1–xxxi. 17 has been inserted between Exod. xxiv. 15b–18a and Exod. xxxi. 18a: Moses goes into the cloud; Yahweh gives him oral instructions about the Tent and the ordination of the priests etc.; afterwards he hands Moses the two Tables of the Law. If the theophany is not to seem like a mere appendage it is necessary for the above block of material to be introduced after Exod. xxiv. 15a at the latest. At the same time the conclusion, Exod. xxxi. 18a, which refers to the two Tables of the Law, acts as a transition to Exod. xxxii–xxxiv, where these two Tables are again prominent.[16] At any rate, xxxi. 18a seems to have displaced xxiv. 18b from its position directly before xxxii. 1. What else could 'Moses delayed to come down from

[8] Further discussion in B. Baentsch, *HK*, 2/1, p. 171.

[9] Cf. C. Steuernagel, *Lehrbuch der Einleitung in das Alte Testament*, p. 231.

[10] *Pace* A. B. Ehrlich and B. D. Eerdmans, to whom W. Rudolph (*Der 'Elohist' von Exodus bis Josua*, *BZAW*, 68, pp. 41 f.) refers.

[11] Cf. C. Steuernagel *op. cit.* p. 234, and S. Mandelkern, *Veteris Testamenti Concordantiae* (2nd ed.) p. 372.

[12] Cf. S. Mandelkern, *op. cit.*, pp. 289f.

[13] With the exception of Exod. xxiv. 18b. Cf. what follows.

[14] For this and what follows cf. K. Koch, *Die Priesterschrift von Exodus* 25 *bis Leviticus* 16, *FRLANT*, 71, especially p. 32.

[15] This link is meant to authorise the new instructions about the Sinai-theophany.

[16] Cf. M. Noth, *Überlieferungsgeschichte des Pentateuch*, p. 14.

the mountain' (xxxii. 1a) refer to, if not to the forty days and nights which Moses spent on the mountain (xxiv. 18b)? On the other hand, xxiv. 18b originally followed xxiv. 15a quite well. In its present position verse 18b provides a satisfactory chronological framework for the following oral advice in the matter of the Tent, the ordination of priests, altars, sacrifice etc. Exod. xxiv. 15b–18a; xxv. 1–xxxi. 17; xxxi. 18a, therefore, belong to P. These Priestly passages are embedded in another layer of tradition to which Exod. xxiv. 12–15a, 18b; xxxii. 1 f. belong and which will be examined later.

(c) Finally, the whole concluding section of the Sinai-pericope, from Exod. xxxiv. 29 to Num. x. 10, should be assigned to P. This section, too, is not a unity, a point which does not need developing in the context of the present work. The first serious break occurs just before xxxv. 1: chap. xxxiv. 29–35[17] is very different in form and content from the section Exod. xxxv.–xl, which even in detail offers a clear parallel to Exod. xxv–xxxi in describing how the instructions to build the Tent-shrine, the altars etc. were carried out. Obviously these two sections must stem from the same source. Lev. viii f. continues the account of Exod. xxxv–xl by describing how the regulations of Exod. xxix relating to the ordination of priests were put into effect. The detailed correspondence with Exod. xxix is another indication that the passage belongs to the P stratum. Chap. ix with its description of the first Israelite sacrificial worship constitutes a further Priestly passage. It is characteristic of the Priestly theology that sacrifice cannot legitimately begin until *after* the revelation on Sinai.[18] Lev. x. is also the outcome of definite priestly interests and interpretations[19] and belongs to P. Lev. xvi. 1 is linked explicitly with x. 1–7 (the story of Nadab and Abihu), so that even apart from the similarity of the subject-matter (the ritual of the great Day of Atonement) and the fact that in several places the Priestly giving of the Law in Exod. xxv–xxxi is presupposed it is demonstrably a part of P.[20] The following legal corpora, also belonging to the P tradition,

[17] In its *present* form, at least, this passage belongs to P: in verse 32 the reference is probably to the giving of the Law in Exod. xxv. 1 f. The phrase 'mount Sinai' (v. 29) is characteristic of P, as is the mention of 'Aaron and all the people of Israel' (v. 30) and 'all the leaders (*neśi'îm*) of the congregation' (v. 31). There is no proof that any constituent of this tradition previously belonged to another context (cf. M. Noth, *Überlieferungsgeschichte des Pentateuch*, p. 33, n. 118). It is easier to assume that Exod. xxxiv. 29–35 originally continued the Priestly narrative of Exod. xxiv. 15b–18a; xxxi. 18a, while 'the glory of the Lord was like a devouring fire' (xxiv. 17) could form the background of xxxiv. 29 f.

[18] Cf. M. Noth, *Überlieferungsgeschichte des Pentateuch*, pp. 262 f.; O. Eissfeldt, *Einleitung in das Alte Testament*, 2nd ed., pp. 219 f.

[19] Cf. M. Noth, *op. cit.*, p. 205.

[20] Cf. B. Baentsch, *HK*, 2/1, pp. 379 f.

have been inserted in the above Priestly narrative: the collection of *toroth* about sacrifice in Lev. i–vii,[21] laws about purification in Lev. xi–xv,[22] the Holiness Code in Lev. xvii.–xxvi and the regulations about vows and tithes which were added later in Lev. xxvii. As for the remaining section, Num. i. 1–x. 10, it is perhaps sufficient in the context of the present work to note that there is no dispute about it being assigned to P.

In short, Exod. xix. 1–2a; xxiv. 15b–18a; xxv. 1–xxxxi. 17; xxxi. 18a; xxxiv. 29–35; xxxv–xl; Lev. i–vii; viii–ix; x; xi–xv; xvi; xvii–xxvi; xxvii; Num. i. 1–x. 10 belong to P in a broad sense. That P constitutes the latest source in the Pentateuch may be taken as proven. It originated in the 5th or at the earliest in the 6th cent. B.C.[23] The above passages, therefore, in their present literary form, at any rate, belong to this late period of Israelite–Jewish history. The possibility that these late literary passages embody much older traditions in certain cases is not to be discounted, of course.

If the above passages are removed from the Sinai-pericope, Exod. xix. 1–Num. x. 10, we are left with the following passages which bear witness to an older tradition: Exod. xix. 2b–xxiv. 15a, 18b; xxxi. 18b; xxxii. 1–xxxiv. 28. The first passage in this collection includes the Book of the Covenant (Exod. xx. 22–xxiii. 33). We shall now demonstrate briefly that this was originally an independent legal corpus which was added to the Sinai tradition later.

2. Exodus xx. 22–xxiii. 33

It has been well-known and widely appreciated for a long time that 'the book of the covenant'[24] in Exod. xxiv. 7 refers primarily to the Ten Commandments,[25] not the whole Book of the Covenant. 'Ordinances' in xxiv. 3a was a later addition inserted because of the addition of the Book of the Covenant. Accordingly verse 3b takes no notice of the addition. *Kol dibrê yhwh* (xxiv. 3, 4; similarly 7 and 8) must obviously mean the same as *Kol hadd*ᵉ*bārîm* in xx. 1, which refers to the Ten Commandments.[26] Since the Ten Commandments were not announced to the people directly, in spite of the appearance

[21] Cf. R. Rendtorff, *Die Gesetze in der Priesterschrift*, *FRLANT*, 62, pp. 4 ff.

[22] *Ibid.*, pp. 38 f.

[23] Cf. any Introduction to the O.T.

[24] Cf. S. Mowinckel, *Le Décalogue*, p. 31.

[25] For its analysis cf. A. Jepsen, *Untersuchungen zum Bundesbuch*, *BWANT*, III, 5 and A. Alt, *Die Ursprünge des israelitischen Rechts* (= *Kleine Schriften* I, pp. 278 f.).

[26] It is difficult to say, therefore, whether this is a definite technical term. Cf. A. Alt, *op. cit.*, p. 323, n. 1.

of the present context, but only through the mediation of Moses, the request of the people in Exod. xx. 18–21 for such mediation only makes sense if it was expressed *before*, not after, the proclamation of the Ten Commandments; this suggests that Exod. xx. 18–21 originally preceded xx. 1–17.[27] The reversal of the order of these two passages was brought about by the later insertion of the Book of the Covenant,[28] which was then related to the Ten Commandments by means of xx. 18–21. Consequently the Decalogue was displaced from its earlier rôle as the Book of the Covenant and relegated to the position of '*hors d'oeuvre*'[29] in relation to the Book of the Covenant.[30] There is no doubt, at any rate, that the Book of the Covenant was originally independent of its present context,[31] particularly since it is detached from its present surroundings both by form-criticism and tradition-history. At a later stage, but *before* the insertion of the Book of the Covenant in its present position in the Sinai-story, the section xxiii. 20–33, which is best understood as a sort of peroration in the manner of Deut. xxvii f. and Lev. xxvi, was gradually added to this legal corpus (xx. 22–xxiii. 12),[32] to which the cultic regulations in xxiii. 13–19 (parallel to xxxiv. 14–26)[33] were attached. Although xxiii. 20–33, which reveals unmistakable Deuteronomistic touches,[34] is connected with the material transmitted in Exod. xxxii–xxxiv,[35] it cannot be fitted into the context of these chapters;[36] it has only a loose connection with the Sinai tradition.

[27] First recognised by Kosters, Kuenen and Jülicher—according to H. Holzinger, *KHC*, 2, p. 69, and R. Smend, *Die Erzählung des Hexateuch*, p. 160. This view is opposed by W. Rudolph, 'Der Aufbau Exod. xix–xxxiv' (*Werden und Wesen des Alten Testaments* ed. by J. Hempel) p. 42; he refers to Exod. xix. 19a, where it is stated the aim of the theophany is the divine attestation of Moses in the eyes of the people; this would rule out any idea of God addressing the people directly. It is questionable, however, whether this *one* strand of the tradition (the attestation of Moses) excludes a strand of tradition which interprets the theophany as the prelude to the public proclamation of his will. Both could have found a place next to each other in the tradition quite well; in fact, they would have balanced each other: Yahweh's aim of attesting Moses as the mediator and the desire of the people, who were afraid of the phenomena accompanying the theophany, for Moses to act as mediator in view of the imminent self-revelation of Yahweh. To this extent the assumption that xx. 18–21 preceded xx. 1–17 seems quite probable.

[28] On its probable earlier position cf. A. Weiser, *Introduction to the Old Testament*, pp. 121 f., on the date of its composition A. Jepsen, *op. cit.*, pp. 97 f.; M. Noth, *Exodus*, p. 173.

[29] Cf. B. Baentsch, *HK*, 2/1, p. 177.

[30] Cf. O. Eissfeldt (*op. cit.*) for further evidence about the later addition of the Book of the Covenant.

[31] There is no connection with the following passage as the word-order at the beginning of xxiv. 1a proves. Cf. M. Noth, *Überlieferungsgeschichte des Pentateuch*, p. 39, n. 139.

[32] Cf. further below, I. 10 and II. 7 for the evidence cf. M. Noth, *Exodus*, p. 173, 192 f.

[33] Cf. further below, I. 10 and II. 7.

[34] Cf. M. Noth, *ibid.*; A. Weiser, *Introduction to the Old Testament*, p. 171 (cf. n. 49).

[35] Cf. xxiii. 20 with xxxii. 34; xxiii. 24 with xxxiv. 13 f.; xxxiii. 32 f. with xxiv. 12.

[36] With W. Rudolph, *Der 'Elohist' von Exodus bis Josua*, *BZAW*, 68, p. 61; *contra* O. Eissfeldt, *op. cit.*, p. 255; *Hexateuch-Synopse*, p. 58.

If we exclude the Book of the Covenant and its accretions from the Sinai pericope of the Yahwist, we are left with the following passages: Exod. xix. 2b–xx. 21; xxiv. 1–15a, 18b; xxxi. 18b; and xxxii. 1–xxxiv. 28. We shall now examine these by means of tradito-critical and literary-critical analysis.

3. Exodus xix. 2b–25

(a) According to these verses Moses climbed Mount Sinai at least three times in one day, although no good reason for this is given in the instructions he received.[37] It is most unlikely that a single unit of tradition spoke of Moses exerting himself in this way without giving any adequate explanation. It seems much more probable that at least three different traditions have been combined in this chapter. The first reference to Moses going up to God[38] occurs in xix. 3a which follows on xix. 2b without a break. This is at variance with the statement in xix. 3b that Yahweh[39] called to him out of the mountain.[40] There is certainly no implication here that Moses had in fact gone up. Clearly xix. 3b is the beginning of a fresh tradition, which, on the evidence of style alone, must reach as far as verse 6.[41] Nor is there any reason to separate vv. 7 and 8. In view of xix. 6b *Kol hadd*ᵉ*bārīm* in xix. 7 must undoubtedly refer to the words of Yahweh in xix. 3b.[42] They were spoken by Yahweh 'out of the mountain', it is said. According to this statement Yahweh is already on Sinai. But this does not harmonise with what is said in verse 9 ('Lo, I am coming to you in a thick cloud . . .')[43] . . . at least, not readily.[44] Verse 9 is further distinguished from the preceding passage (xix. 3b–8) by the fact that Yahweh's epiphany is not so much the prelude to his addressing the house of Jacob as to his divine attestation of

[37] Cf. also J. Wellhausen, *Die Composition des Hexateuchs*, p. (553) 83; and E. Auerbach, *Moses*, p. 163. Further oddities are mentioned by M. Noth, *Exodus*, p. 153.

[38] The almost unanimous reading of the *LXX eis to oros tou theou* probably goes back to the attempt to counteract the anthropomorphism of the *MT*, although it should not be considered impossible in view of xxiv. 13. Cf. E. Stauffer, *theos*, *ThWBNT*, p. 110.

[39] The different names for God should be disregarded to begin with. The weakly attested variant *hā'*ᵉ*lōhîm* should be rejected, even if for no other reason than the remarkable way in which the *LXX* refuses on several occasions to countenance this alteration. Cf. xix. 8, 18, 21, 23, 24; xxiv. 2, 3, 5, 16.

[40] The *LXX* reading 'from heaven' was probably intended to prevent anthropomorphism and is, therefore, to be rejected, particularly since it is only attested by Codex Vaticanus (and a minuscule). Possibly, too, being influenced by such motives, the translator thought the *ek tou orous* of his text was a mistake for *ek tou ouranou*.

[41] Cf. A. B. Ehrlich (*Randglossen zur hebräischen Bibel* I) on Exod. xix.

[42] For a different view cf. H. Gressmann, *Mose und seine Zeit*, *FRLANT*, 18, p. 181.

[43] Futurum instans.

[44] Cf. R. Smend, *Die Erzählung des Hexateuch*, p. 165, and, differently, W. Rudolph, *Der 'Elohist' von Exodus bis Josua*, *BZAW*, 68, p. 43.

Moses in the eyes of the people. It seems reasonable to assume, therefore, that xix. 3b–8 embodies a distinct unit of tradition.

Only the first half of xix. 9 is original, however, for 9b repeats 8b in almost the same words, although there has been no further news to give to Yahweh in the meantime. With verse 10 the theme changes; but this could hardly be a reason for making another unit of tradition begin here, especially since it is impossible to distinguish any break in diction between 9a and 10. (Even after the excision of 9b the introductory formula of verse 10 is not unusual as the introduction to a new section within the same speech.)

11a is undoubtedly the continuation of 10. 11b, on the other hand, which speaks abruptly of Yahweh in the third person, does not fit into its present context in which Yahweh addresses Moses directly: 11b is obviously a gloss. It is not difficult however, to find the continuation of Yahweh's speech in xix. 12–13a. Verse 13b is clearly at variance with its position in chap. xix, from the point of view of content. Whereas the main body of the chapter nowhere reckons with anyone having to climb the mountain apart from Moses, according to 13b an unspecified number of Israelites[45] were to climb Mt. Sinai when the trumpet[46] sounded. 13b probably contains an older fragment of tradition which might belong to the tradition preserved in Exod. xxiv. 1a, 9–11.[47] xix. 13a is picked up without any difficulty by verses 14–15, which describe the fulfilment of the instructions given to Moses in 10–11a. If the instructions and their fulfilment are compared in detail it appears questionable whether 15b, which is only loosely connected, formed part of the original text. It could well be a later accretion. 15a concludes the preparations for the theophany. The obvious sequel to 15a and the immediate introduction to the description of the theophany is formed by 16aα. There is no doubt that 16aβ.b and 17 belong together and are obviously linked to verse 18. The 'thick cloud' of xix. 16a is parallel to the 'smoke' of xix. 18 which covers the whole mountain. On the other hand, there are differences between verses 16aβ–17 and 18: whereas there is no mention of God

[45] On the assumption that we are dealing with a fragment which does not really belong to its present context, *hēmāh* need not refer to the whole people, which is certainly not ordered to climb Mt. Sinai anywhere in the Sinai-story. The pronoun might originally have referred to the people spoken of in Exod. xxiv. 1a, 9–11. There is no need to have recourse to W. Rudolph's explanation of the passage ('Der Aufbau von Exod. 19–34', p. 41).

[46] 13b also differs from its surroundings in the use of *yôḇēl* for 'trumpet', whereas 16a and 19a use *šôpār*.

[47] Cf. S. Mōwinckel, *Le Décalogue*, p. 44.

descending in the first passage, and verse 17, to all appearances, assumes that God is already on the mountain (a striking parallel, incidentally, to the view expressed in xix. 3a), verse 18 gives a picture of Yahweh's descent. Moreover, the phenomena accompanying the theophany are infinitely more vivid and colourful than in the former passage. It seems that xix. 18 was part of the continuation of xix. 16a, while xix. 19, which certainly does not need to be divided,[48] follows very well after verses 16a–17: the loud trumpet-blast of 16a grows louder in 19a after the Israelites have been drawn up at the foot of the mountain. The same word is used on both occasions.

According to verse 20 Yahweh descends on Sinai once more and Moses ascends the mountain again, only to be sent down to the people again in verse 21 with a message which could be described as a sort of midrash on vv. 12–13a: at a later date the question was asked in priestly circles whether the prohibition to come near to Yahweh applied also to the priests, who, as consecrated persons, had the right to approach him.[49] At any rate it is clear that the whole section xix. 20–24 is a later gloss, which has possibly severed an original connection between xix. 19 and xix. 25. These two verses would go together quite well, for the dialogue between God and Moses in 19b leads one to expect some message for the people. What this could have consisted of is open to conjecture, as the account breaks off in the middle of verse 25.[50] The continuation of the verse was presumably displaced by the reversal of xx. 18–21 and xx. 1–17 already referred to,[51] which was caused by the introduction of the Book of the Covenant and which enabled the announcement of the Decalogue to follow directly on chap. xix. The possibility that xix. 25 is a continuation of the gloss in verses 20–24 and a realisation of the command in 24a that Moses should descend is not to be ruled out altogether. Verse 25b would then introduce the announcement of further prohibitions affecting the priesthood. But it does not seem very probable that such a later addition could have been mutilated in this way by the reversal of xx. 18–21 and xx. 1–17. It seems more likely that there was some connection between xix. 19 and xix. 25.

Summary. Exod. xix. 3b–8 contains a special unit of tradition. In

[48] *Contra* R. Smend, *Die Erzählung des Hexateuch*, p. 165.

[49] Cf. W. Rudolph, *op. cit.*, p. 41; and *Der 'Elohist' von Exodus bis Josua*, *BZAW*, 68, p. 41.

[50] According to Gesenius–Buhl, *Hebräisches und aramäisches Handwörterbuch*, p. 50 *'mr* can never be used by itself in the sense of 'tell'.

[51] Cf. section I. 2.

xix. 13b an older, fragmentary piece of tradition has been preserved. xix. 20–24 is a later accretion, a sort of midrash. Verses 9b and 11b (perhaps also 15b) are interpolations. For the rest, two substantially continuous traditions appear to have been woven together. One tradition consists of the following verses: 9a, 10–11a, 12–13a, 14–15a (15b), 16aα, 18. The other comprises verses 2b–3a, 16aβ–17, 19 and 25.

(b) In which strata of the Pentateuch did the traditions just delimited find written expression? As far as xix. 13b is concerned, this question can only be answered within the context of an analysis of chap. xxiv. For the moment we shall turn to those two broadly continuous traditions which are interwoven in the present text. After the exclusion of the Priestly stratum, the broad choice is between the Yahwistic and Elohistic strata.[52] The use of different names for God in the texts under discussion does not afford any definite criterion for deciding which stratum they belong to, since the Elohist also uses the name Yahweh for God after it has been revealed in Ex. iii 15. Nevertheless it is striking that all the passages containing *'elōhîm*[53] belong to one and the same unit of tradition. Hence verses 2b–3a, 16aβ–17, 19, 25 might be considered as belonging to E.[54] It is certainly true that *'elōhîm* reminds us of the way in which God and man stand over against each other, and has overtones of *mysterium tremendum.*[55] Might not this emphasis, however, have led the Elohist to refrain from using the name of Yahweh at this point although the name had been revealed and was at his disposal? A marked awareness of the distance between God and man is undoubtedly a recognised characteristic of the Elohist.[56] Another factor which also tells in favour of ascribing this tradition to E[57] is the fact that other influences are at work in the context of the same tradition, namely the fear of the people who are brought to the foot of the mountain to meet God (xix. 16aβ–17), whereas according to the other tradition (xix. 12–13a) the same people have to be held back by strict, prohibitive measures. The idea that God dwells on the mountain and

[52] For further discussion about the independence of the E-source, apart from introductions to the Old Testament, see P. Volz and W. Rudolph, *Der Elohist als Erzähler Ein Irrweg der Pentateuchkritik? BZAW*, 63, 1933; W. Rudolph, *Der 'Elohist' von Exodus bis Josua, BZAW*, 68, 1938.

[53] Exod. xix. 3a, 17, 19. On xix. 3a cf. above, p. 10, n. 2.

[54] See also M. Noth, *Exodus*, p. 153.

[55] So W. Rudolph, *Der 'Elohist' von Exodus bis Josua*, p. 42.

[56] Cf. O. Eissfeldt, *Einleitung in das Alte Testament*, 2nd ed., p. 218; A. Weiser, *Introduction to the Old Testament*, p. 114.

[57] Cf. O. Eissfeldt, *op. cit.*, p. 219; M. Noth, *Exodus*, p. 153 f.

does not just descend on it is also characteristic of the Elohist.[58] In the context of chap. xix. this idea only reappears in those verses which are thought to be Elohistic.[59] The absence of the name Sinai in these verses also points to E. All this taken together confirms the suspicion that the tradition in Exod xix. 2b–3a, 16aβ–17, 19, 25 belongs to the Elohistic stratum.[60]

On the other hand, the context of the tradition represented in verses 9a, 10–11a, 12–13a, 14–15a, (15b), 16aα, 18 proves to be Yahwistic. As we have said, nothing is proved by the fact that only 'Yahweh' is used here. In favour of J, however, is the fact that several characteristics peculiar to the Yahwistic source appear in the above verses. Yahweh does not dwell on the mountain but has to descend on it.[61] The term 'mount Sinai' likewise occurs in the same verses.[62] The people are not afraid of the theophany but have to be restrained by command.[63] The vivid description of the phenomena accompanying Yahweh's epiphany in verse 18 is characteristic of the Yahwist.

The section xix. 20–24 is distinct both in content and diction from the Yahwistic tradition just discussed. Verse 20 speaks of Yahweh's descent on Mt. Sinai in the same way as vv. 18, 9a, (and 11b). Verses 21–24, as we have said, comment on vv. 10, 12–13a from a fresh standpoint. This section, which grew out of the Yahwistic tradition, was probably not added till later, when the J and E sources had already been combined. Otherwise it would be difficult to understand why verses 20 and 24, which express the aim of the section, were not placed directly next to vv. 12–13a, to which they refer.[64] It should be noted that verse 11b, which was added later, also has a clearly marked Yahwistic character.

The passage xix. 3b–8, because of its numerous affiliations with the language and style of Deuteronomy,[65] has been held to be a later addition in the Deuteronomic style[66] or an Elohistic passage reworked by the Deuteronomist.[67] It is true that the affinities of

[58] Cf. O. Eissfeldt, *Hexateuch-Synopse*, p. 46.
[59] Cf. especially verses 3a, 17.
[60] Cf. on 2b G. Beer *HAT*, 1/3, p. 96 f. also.
[61] Cf. Exod. xix. 18, 9a. See Eissfeldt on this.
[62] Exod. xix. 18. Cf. *ibid.*, p. 47.
[63] Cf. O. Eissfeldt, *Einleitung in das Alte Testament*, 2nd ed., p. 219.
[64] On the basis of xxiv. 1, verse 24a in chap. xix is to be considered as a secondary insertion within the later complex xix. 20–24. Cf. W. Rudolph, *Der 'Elohist' von Exodus bis Josua*, *BZAW*, 68, p. 41.
[65] Cf. comparison of B. Baentsch, *HK*, 2/1, p. 171.
[66] Cf. A. Kuenen, *Historisch-kritische Einleitung in die Bücher des Alten Testaments*, 1/1 p. 235, 249; O. Procksch, *Die Elohimquelle*, p. 85; M. Noth, *Überlieferungsgeschichte des Pentateuch*, p. 44, n. 112; *Exodus*, p. 157.
[67] Cf. G. Beer, *HAT*, 1/3, p. 96.

language and style with Deuteronomy are unmistakable. Yet it remains an open question how they are to be interpreted; we shall examine this more fully later.[68] As far as substance goes there are no specifically Deuteronomic elements in Exod. xix. 3b–8.[69] Which source this passage really belongs to is difficult to say. There are no good textual reasons for altering, as the LXX does, 'Yahweh' to 'Elohim' in xix. 3b, in view of the marked tendency of the Greek version to replace 'Yahweh' by 'Elohim'.[70] On the other hand, the name Yahweh is not sufficient reason for attributing the passage to the Yahwist. In view of the following words about God having revealed himself to his people (see xix. 4), the Elohist can equally use the name of Yahweh, revealed in iii. 15. The introduction in xix. 3b, which pictures Yahweh as dwelling on the mountain, seems to tell in favour of E.[71] Thus, verse 4 conceives the mount of God as Yahweh's dwelling place.[72] Another pointer to the Elohist is the theologically reflective style of Yahweh's speech: exclusive claims are made upon Israel and its position is defined in relation to other nations.[73]

Summary. The unit of tradition Exod. xix. 3b–8 could most easily belong to the E source. A full discussion of the linguistic and stylistic findings must come later. The tradition represented by xix. 2b–3a, 16aβ–17, 19, 25 also belongs to E. Verses 9a, 10–11a, 12–13a, 14–16aα, 18, on the other hand, are part of the J tradition. The later additions Exod. xix. 20–24 and xix. 11b also stem from the J tradition.

4. Exodus xx. 1, 2–17

The Decalogue is a relatively independent and self-contained unity (xx. 1–17). Before the insertion of the Book of the Covenant into the context of the Sinai-story it stood between Exod. xx. 18–21 and xxiv. 1 ff.[74] Although xx. 1 links the Decalogue as God's *debārîm* with xxiv. 3–8,[75] it is clear from the word-order at the beginning of xxiv. 1 that the section beginning with this verse could not have followed

[68] See below, section II. 6, especially p. 70.

[69] Cf. also G. von Rad, '*Das formgeschichtliche Problem des Hexateuch*' (= *Gesammelte Studien*, p. 47, especially n. 47).

[70] Cf. xix. 8, 18, 21, 23, 24; xxxiv. 2, 3, 5, 16.

[71] For the text *vide supra*, n. 40.

[72] Cf. J. Wellhausen, *Die Composition des Hexateuchs*, p. (562) 93.

[73] Cf. A. Weiser, *Introduction to the Old Testament*, pp. 114 f.; O. Eissefeldt, *Einleitung in das Alte Testament*, 2nd ed., p. 239. J. Muilenburg, 'The form and structure of the covenantal formulations', *VT*, ix, 1959, p. 351, has also argued in favour of the passage belonging to E.

[74] *Vide supra*, section I. 2.

[75] Cf. especially verses 3, 4, 8.

directly on xx. 1–17 originally.[76] Likewise, the connecting verse xx. 1 also gives the impression by its colourlessness that it was only prefixed to the Decalogue later. The definition of Exod. xx. 2–17 as an originally independent unit on grounds of literary criticism is confirmed by form-criticism: the Decalogue contains a whole series of apodeictic sentences[77] of great antiquity,[78] which in any case had their own (pre-literary) history.[79] Exactly when the Decalogue was inserted in its present context in the tradition is difficult to say. It must at any rate have been *before* the insertion of the Book of the Covenant, which, as we have said, displaced the Decalogue in its role as 'the book of the covenant' (xxiv. 7) and at the same time took over its function. We are not thinking of the Decalogue in its present form, of course; in view of the reason given for the Sabbath law in xx. 11 this can hardly be older than the tradition which found expression in the Priestly account of creation.[80] On the other hand, there is nothing to disprove the view that an earlier form of the present Decalogue containing a Sabbath law attracted the Priestly interpretation *after* being inserted in the context of Exod. xx. 18–21; xxiv. 1. This is also true of the present expanded Decalogue. The question as to which source the Decalogue stemmed from can only be answered after its context has been analysed.

5. Exodus xx. 18–21

Between the Decalogue, which ends in Exod. xx. 17, and the Book of the Covenant, which begins in Exod. xx. 22, there is the passage xx. 18–21. Reference has already been made[81] to the fact that originally it must have had its place not here but *before* the Ten Commandments, whereas now it has to fulfil the task of relating the Book of the Covenant, which was added later, to the Decalogue. The first question to be considered at the present juncture is the unity of the passage. Its substantial unity cannot be denied. Nevertheless, knowledge of the two interwoven traditions of Exod. xix provokes the suspicion that in xx. 18a not all the elements which follow in

[76] *Vide supra*, p. 5, n. 31. After the Decalogue had been spoken to *Moses* (this also applies to the Book of the Covenant in its present context) the emphatic position of the words 'and he said to Moses' at the beginning of xxiv. 1 do not make sense if they were a direct continuation.

[77] Cf. A. Alt, *Die Ursprünge des israelitischen Rechts* (= *Kleine Schriften* I, pp. 317 f.).

[78] Cf. *ibid.*, pp. 330 f.

[79] See below, section II. 5.

[80] Cf. Gen. ii. 2.

[81] *Vide supra*, section I. 2.

sequence belong to the same tradition: the smoking mountain in 18a has probably been added because of harmonising tendencies. The only complete correspondence to this is in xix. 18, which belongs to the Yahwistic source.[82] On the other hand, the 'thunderings' and the 'sound of the trumpet' in xx. 18 recur in xix. 16a*β*, 19, which we defined as Elohistic. On the whole, therefore, Exod. xx. 18a is to be attributed to E. Likewise verse 18b, according to which the people feel afraid[83] and keep at a distance from God; both these features are characteristic of the Elohist. There is a similar feeling of fear and sense of distance in vv. 19–21, which are likewise to be attributed to E, therefore. The linguistic findings confirm this view of the sources. The exclusive use of 'Elohim' for God's name is also consonant with this view.

There is no proof that xx. 18–21 is an interpolation. The view[84] that xx. 19 is not foreshadowed by anything in chap. xix is possible only on the basis of a one-sided estimate of the theophany in Exod. xix. 9a. It has already been demonstrated that this particular view of Yahweh's epiphany need not exclude a second interpretation of his appearing—namely, as the prelude to the public proclamation of the divine will.[85] It is not necessary to understand xix. 19 in the the light of xix. 9a; in fact, the findings of source-criticism make such an interpretation very difficult. There is, therefore, a place for xx. 19 alongside xix. 19. Reference has already been made to the points which xx. 18–21 has in common with the Elohistic tradition of chap. xix. There is no reason to conclude, however, that one depends on the other. Nor can one say that xx. 18–21 is to be seen as the continuation of the Elohistic account in chap. xix. But the conversation of the people with Moses in Exod. xx. 19 f., including xx. 21, must have preceded xix. 19b. Exod. xx. 18, however, obviously contradicts such an order, since its account of the reaction of the people to the phenomena accompanying the theophany (18b) would be a repetition of the account in xix. 16b, similar to the repetition of xix. 16a*β*, and 19a by xx. 18a. The passage Exod. xx. 18–21 seems more like a variant on the Elohistic account of chap. xix, in that it gives eloquent expression to the people's fear in the prayer for Moses to act as mediator between God and the people of Israel. It is impossible to suppress the suspicion that the Elohistic tradition

[82] So also M. Noth, *Exodus*, p. 168.

[83] Following the reading *wayyir'ᵉû* attested by the Sam. Pent., the *LXX* and the Vulgate; this also corresponds to the words of Moses in xx. 20a.

[84] So W. Rudolph, 'Der Aufbau von Exodus xix–xxxiv', p. 34.

[85] *Vide supra*, p. 5, n. 27.

consisted less in a continuous narrative than in a collection—possessing order and shape, of course—of traditional material.

6. Exodus xxiv

(a) Chap. xxiv. is no more homogeneous than chap. xix. The opening verse is fragmentary, as appears from the words that are set at the head of the chapter,[86] 'and he said to Moses'. The next break follows immediately afterwards: in the first part of the verse Yahweh himself is speaking, whereas in the speech that follows 'Yahweh' is used in the third person. It is difficult, however, to make this the basis of any conclusions about the source of the tradition. *'el yhwh* should be struck out as a gloss[87] or altered[88] to *'ēlay* on the assumption that the unpunctuated *'ly* has been misunderstood as an abbreviation for *'el yhwh*. But there is a break to be felt between the two halves of the first verse: vv. 1b–2 reverse the sense of v. 1a, which orders Moses, Aaron, Nadab, Abihu and seventy elders to go up the mountain (sc. to God), whereas verses 1b–2 keep them at a distance and permit only Moses to come near.[89] xxiv. 1b–2, therefore, should be treated as a distinct unit of tradition. xxiv. 1a is continued in verse 9, which describes exactly how the divine command in v. 1a was fulfilled. Verse 10, describing the result of the ascent, follows virtually without a break. 11a, however, could be later reflection, which has been attached to the old, original account. It must be older than verses 1b–2, nevertheless; verses 1b–2 soon destroy all ground for the suprising reflection of 11a.[90] 'They beheld . . .', parallel to 'they saw' (v. 10), takes up the train of thought interrupted by the reflection of 11a and describes the covenant-meal before God. There is nothing further in chap. xxiv that would fit this singular, original tradition of verses 1a, 9–11,[91] but the old fragment of tradition in xix. 13b, according to which a number of Israelites ascended the mountain, also seems to belong here.[92]

Quite obviously a new unit of tradition begins with xxiv. 12. The introductory words of verses 1 and 12 repeat each other. xxiv 12, however, in contrast to xxiv. 1a, knows only of a command to Moses

[86] Cf. M. Noth, *Überlieferungsgeschichte des Pentateuch*, p. 39, n. 139; *Exodus*, p. 196.

[87] With H. Gressmann, *Mose und seine Zeit, FRLANT*, 18, p. 181, n. 1.

[88] Cf. M. Noth, *ibid.* p. 196; *Überlieferungsgeschichte des Pentateuch*, p. 39, n. 140.

[89] See now also M. Noth, *Exodus*, pp. 196 f.

[90] The way this half-verse is expressed also points to it being a considerable age. Cf. on this point M. Haelvoet, *La Théophanie du Sinai, ALBO*, II, 39, p. 387.

[91] On its unquestionable antiquity cf. *inter alios* M. Noth, *Überlieferungsgeschichte des Pentateuch*, p. 178; E. Auerbach, *Moses*, p. 167.

[92] Cf. *supra*, section. I 3.

to come up the mountain. Moreover, the ascent has quite a different result from that described in verses 10 and 11. xxiv. 12–15a, 18b[93] are variously reckoned with the unit of tradition beginning in xxiv. 12 and regarded as a unity.[94] This can hardly be right, however. Whereas in v. 12, as we have said, Moses alone is commanded to climb the holy mountain, xxiv. 13a says, 'So Moses went with his servant Joshua'. It is inconceivable that Moses should have taken Joshua with him on his own initiative. Verse 13a, therefore, must belong to a different strand of tradition from v. 12, which is continued to all appearances in v. 13b, where Moses ascends the mountain alone once more.[95] xxiv. 15a seems to pick up 13b after being interrupted by v. 14.[96] Verse 14 assumes Moses was accompanied and thus obviously continues 13a.[97] According to v. 12 Moses has to *remain* on the mountain. This undoubtedly agrees with xxiv. 18b, where Moses' stay on the mountain is given as forty days and nights. According to all appearances, therefore, the following verses belong together; xxiv. 12, 13b (15a), 18b from one source and xxiv. 13a, 14 from another. The whole passage xxiv. 12–15a, 18b, both in its individual component parts and in its totality, introduces the story of the Golden Calf in Exod. 32.[98]

But first let us deal with the remaining verses in chap. xxiv. The passage xxiv. 3–8 is obviously a unity, apart from the phrase 'and all the ordinances' in 3a, which has been added later as a result of the subsequent insertion of the Book of the Covenant.[99] In view of the parallelism of verses 3 and 7, however, it seems that in this unit of tradition two originally parallel versions of the proclamation of the divine will and the subsequent express promise of the people to obey have been combined in an organic unity.[100] A detailed list of com-

[93] Cf. e.g. S. Mowinckel, *ibid.*, p. 45.

[94] So W. Rudolph, 'Der Aufbau von Exodus 19–34', p. 44 (where verses 12–15, 18b are discussed).

[95] The reading of the *LXX* assimilates 13b to 13a, which stems from a different tradition; it should certainly not be given preference over the *MT*.

[96] The *LXX* reading of Codex Vaticanus *kai Iesous* should certainly be regarded as another later assimilation.

[97] Cf. the plural *nāšûb*. The instructions of Moses in xxiv. 14 could hardly have applied to the elders, for, as Nöldeke shows, ' "and he said to the elders" is probably a harmonistic correction for "and he said to the people". Aaron and Hur could only have been appointed as interim judges for the *Israelites* not for the elders, since it is most unlikely that disputes would have broken out among the elders.' J. Wellhausen, *Die Composition des Hexateuchs*, p. (558) 89.

[98] Cf. W. Rudolph, *Der 'Elohist' von Exodus bis Josua BZAW*, 68, p. 48.

[99] *Vide supra*, section I. 2.

[100] To judge by Exod. xix. 7 f. there were obviously other versions of this tradition. Cf. also H. Holzinger, *KHC*, 2, pp. 103 f. on the different interpretations of the parallelism of Exod. xxiv. 3 and 7.

mands has been attached by way of explanation to the tradition of Exod. xxiv. 3–8, where mention was made of 'words' and 'a book of the covenant'; this is to be found in the Decalogue, Exod. xx. 2–17 (i.e. an early form of it). xx. 1 links xx. 2–17 with the tradition in xxiv. 3–8, by referring to the Decalogue as 'words' in view of xxiv. 3, 4, 8.

(b) What sources do the various parts of chap. xxiv which we have separated belong to?[101] As far as the tradition of xxiv. 3–8 is concerned, it should most probably be assigned to the E source in view of the very strongly marked similarities of xxiv. 3, 7b and the Elohistic xix. 7. This also fits with the fact that it is not difficult to see in it the continuation of the Elohistic narrative of Exod. xix, or the parallel section xx. 18–21.[102] Also in favour of E is the fact that the reported erection of the pillars (verse 4) occurs in a similar way in Gen. xxxi. 45, which is also an Elohistic passage.[103] Likewise the unit comprised by xxiv. 12, 13b, (15a) 18b seems to belong to the E source; for behind verses 12, 13b, and 18b there is the idea of God dwelling on the mountain, which seems to be a characteristic of the Elohist. It is difficult to decide the source of xxiv. 13a, 14. We can be fairly confident that this particular tradition is related to the tradition of Exod. xxiv. 1a, 9–11, inasmuch as both passages speak of Israel being led by a group consisting of four men.[104] It is true there is a difference in the composition of the group: xxiv. 1a names Moses, Aaron, Nadab and Abihu,[105] while xxiv. 13a, 14 names Moses, Joshua, Aaron and Hur. The only other occasion on which this latter group is referred to is in the account of the defeat of the Amalekites, Exod. xvii. 8–16.[106] In view of the fact that Joshua, the Ephraimite, is described as Moses' appointed successor in Exod. xvii. 8 f., the linking of the two names in Exod. xxiv. 13a, 14 may be

[101] On the numerous attempted solutions of this cf. R. Brinker, *The Influence of Sanctuaries in Early Israel*, pp. 1 f.

[102] *Vide supra*, section I. 5.

[103] Cf. also A. Weiser, *Introduction to the Old Testament*, pp. 114 f.

[104] The elders in v. 14 probably did not belong to the earliest account, as we have already noted. Cf. p. 15, n. 97.

[105] The hypothesis that Nadab and Abihu were only inserted by the Priestly redactor (cf. for instance, K. Budde in *ZAW*, 1891, p. 223) is hardly correct, since both are disqualified in Lev. x. 1. Their names would have been omitted at such a central point of the tradition as Exod. xxiv. 1a, if their position had not been securely attested from an early date. Further details in M. Noth, *Überlieferungsgeschichte des Pentateuch*, p. 204 f. Cf. also G. Beer, *HAT*, 1/3, p. 125 f.

[106] M. Noth (*op. cit.* p. 196, n. 501) considers it possible that Exod. xxiv. 13a, 14 was written to introduce the story of the Golden Calf (Exod. xxxii) with reference to Exod. xvii. 8–16, whereas from the point of view of Exod. xxxii there is no compelling or intelligible explanation of the balanced juxtaposition of the two names in v. 14a. However this may be, it can be assumed that the two pieces of tradition belong together.

understood correspondingly. This obvious emphasis on northern Israel in the above fragment of tradition points to it being a part of the Elohistic stratum.[107]

The relationship of the broken passages of tradition in xxiv. 13a, 14 and xxiv. 1a, 9–11 (*vide supra*) favours the assignment of the latter to the Elohist. This assumption is strengthened by the observation that the idea of God dwelling on the mountain also lies behind verses 1a and 9 ff. Moreover, the way in which this piece of tradition[108] refers to *hā-'elōhîm* (v. 11b) rather than *yhwh*[109] is in agreement with this view.[110] There is no reason for thinking that the choice of the divine name was intended to express *mysterium tremendum.* This could hardly be reconciled with the meal which the elders of Israel celebrated in God's presence. Everything, therefore, points to the fact that xxiv. 1a, 9–11 belongs to E. The same applies to xix. 13b, which fits the context of *this* tradition.[111]

This provides the answer to the question previously deferred, namely, into which source was the Decalogue (xx. 2–17) inserted.[112] It has been set in the Elohistic source of tradition, where it has been linked with the passage xxiv. 3–8 by means of xx. 1, which was added later.[113] Prior to the insertion of the Book of the Covenant the Decalogue was preceded, as stated, by the passage Exod. xx. 18–21, which we have likewise assigned to the E-source.[114] The Book of the Covenant was embedded in the Elohistic narrative when it was linked with the tradition in Exod. xxiv. 3–8 and took over the function of explaining the 'book of the covenant' in xxiv. 7. This legal corpus is also set within the framework of E: namely, Exod. xx. 18–21, which has been transplanted from its original position, and the complex of tradition represented by Exod. xxiv. 1 ff.

Finally, it should be noticed that within this complex of traditions of divergent content there are traces of harmonising tendencies. On

[107] On the origin of the E-source cf. O. Procksch, *Das nordhebräische Sagenbuch. Die Elohimquelle*, p. 175 ff.

[108] On the various fragments of this tradition cf. H. Gressmann, *Mose und seine Zeit*, *FRLANT*, 18, p. 181 ff.

[109] *Vide supra*, p. 14, n. 87 and n. 88.

[110] M. Noth (*Exodus*, p. 196) also concludes from this that it belongs to the E-source.

[111] *Vide supra*, section I. 3.

[112] Cf. *supra*, section I. 4.

[113] It should be admitted that the reading 'Yahweh', attested by the *LXX* (Targum and Vulgate), is to be taken seriously in view of the otherwise noticeable tendency of the Greek version to replace 'Yahweh' by *elōhîm.* (cf. W. Rudolph, *Der 'Elohist' von Exodus bis Josua*, *BZAW*, 68, p. 46). It is not surprising, however, that 'Yahweh' is named as the speaker, in view of the direct proximity of the declaration 'I am Yahweh'. Exod. xx. 1 cannot be described as Yahwistic simply on account of the divine name that is used.

[114] Cf. *supra*, section I. 5.

the whole, the basis of this harmonization is the theologically reflective Elohistic tradition as it is fixed in Exod. xix; xx. 18–21.[115] Naturally, the very old, original fragment of tradition, Exod. xxiv. 1a, 9–11, was affected by this; verses 1b–2 were added as a theological correction. There can be no doubt that this corrective, with its 'afar off' and 'Moses alone', corresponds to the Elohistic tradition of chapters xix and xx. 18–21. It is also conceivable that in the process of harmonisation xxiv. 13a, 14 was pushed back to its periphery.[116]

7. Exodus xxxi. 18b

It has been established in an earlier context[117] that Exod. xxxi. 18 became separated when the Priestly account of the theophany (xxiv. 15b–18a) was linked with the building of the Tent and the ordination of the priesthood (xxv. 1–xxxi. 17). Whereas the first half of the verse was considered part of P, the source of xxxi. 18b remained an open question at first. It can now be stated quite definitely that xxxi. 18b is very closely connected with xxiv. 12b in the history of tradition; there is no need to examine its content or linguistic usage further.[118] xxiv. 12 is part of the Elohistic tradition, and xxxi. 18b appears in the same light. The choice of the divine name also points to E.

8. Exodus xxxii

It is quite clear that this chapter also is not a unity. But at first the account proceeds without a break and without serious difficulties up to the end of verse 6. Verses 1–4a and 4b–6 can hardly be understood as variant passages.[119] The latter verses nowhere say that the people made the calf. According to the present text the people simply

[115] Cf. also S. Mowinckel, *Le Décalogue*, p. 45, on Exod. 19–20: 'c'est là la version la plus récente et elohistique proprement dite.'

[116] Considerations of textual criticism just referred to are not necessarily affected by this. Cf. p. 15, n. 95 and 96.

[117] *Vide supra*, I. 1b.

[118] Cf. also M. Noth, *Exodus*, p. 247.

[119] Against H. Gressmann, *Mose und seine Zeit*, *FRLANT*, 18, p. 199, n. 4. The proposal of S. Lehming ('Versuch zu Exod. xxxii', *VT* x, 1960, pp. 22, 24 f.) to interpret Exod. xxxii. 2–4a as a late insertion which supplanted an older version of the tradition in which a *wooden* calf was referred to, should probably be rejected. Verse 20, which certainly does not permit any definite conclusion that the calf-image was made of wood (as Lehming himself admits, p. 20, n. 2), offers no satisfactory basis for a conjecture of such far-reaching implications (cf. also M. Noth, *Exodus*, p. 249). Nor do vv. 7–8 permit the conclusion that underlying them must be a tradition which knew only of a *wooden* image. The view that these verses must be a gloss which sought to interpret an older tradition in the sense of a metal image need not be examined.

accept the cult-image with the words, 'This is your God, O Israel . . .'; 'Aaron saw this' refers to the people's reaction. It is conceivable, however, that the tradition which found expression in Exod. xxxii. 1–6 assessed Aaron's part in the making of the Golden Calf differently at different periods of its history.[120]

In analysing the rest of the chapter it will help if we observe the following pointers: Moses learns of the apostasy of Israel in two basically different ways (cf. xxxii. 7 f. with xxxii. 15 f.), there are two accounts of Moses' intercession (cf. xxxii. 11 f. with xxxii. 30 f.), and the text gives several irreconcilable answers to the question of a possible punishment of the people (cf. xxxii. 14 with xxxii. 25–29, 34, 35).[121]

Accordingly the following passages of tradition can be separated from one another: xxxii. 7–14; 15–20; 21–24; 25–29; 30–34; 35. On the whole each of these groups is a unity, apart from xxxii. 15–20, where vv. 17–18 seem to stem from a different tradition.

Of the two passages 7–14 and 15–20, both of which are linked with vv. 1–6 and run parallel to each other, the latter is obviously more original and older. It was probably separated from xxxii. 1–6 at a later date by vv. 7–14, which stand out from their present context by their distinct style.[122] It will be shown later that xxxii. 20 is not dealing with any 'water of cursing'.[123] Accordingly v. 35 cannot be understood as a continuation of xxxii. 15–20. Rather, this verse appears to be a later accretion.[124] It is equally impossible to understand vv. 30–34 as a continuation of vv. 25–29: according to v. 34 the sin of the people is not avenged; the punishment is postponed. The action of the Levites in exacting vengeance is not presupposed. The report of this was obviously inserted later. A comparison of the two intercessory prayers of Moses (xxxii. 11–14, 30–32) does not give the impression that they were closely related. Everything goes

[120] Cf. the textual tradition of vv. 4b–6 and W. Rudolph, *Der 'Elohist' von Exodus bis Josua*, *BZAW*, 68, p. 49. See especially vv. 21–24. To what extent the originality of Aaron's appearance in vv. 1b–4 can be questioned on the ground of this section which was added later, I am not sure (cf. M. Noth, *Exodus*, p. 244). As stated, the formulation of verse 5 does not imply that Aaron was not involved in what had happened previously.

[121] Cf. H. Holzinger, *KHC*, 2, p. 108; B. Baentsch, *HK*, 2/1, p. 268 f.; G. Beer, *HAT*, 1/3, p. 153; O. Eissfeldt, *Hexateuch-Synopse*, p. 50; M. Noth, *Exodus*, p. 245; S. Lehming, 'Versuch zu Exod. xxxii.', *VT*, x, 1960, pp. 21 f.; on the other hand, B. D. Eerdmans *Exodus, alttestamentliche Studien*, 3, pp. 73 f.; R. Smend, *Die Erzählung des Hexateuch*, pp. 169f., and W. Rudolph, *op. cit.*, p. 51.

[122] Cf. pending fuller discussion M. Noth, *Überlieferungsgeschichte des Pentateuch*, p. 33, n. 113, and section II. 11 below.

[123] Cf. section II. 11 below.

[124] See also M. Noth, *Überlieferungsgeschichte des Pentateuch*, pp. 158 f., n. 415.

to suggest that underlying them are different arrangements of a *single* motif.

(b) Which sources, then, do the separate pieces of tradition in chap. xxxii belong to? An old, northern Israelite tradition, it will be demonstrated[125], lies at the basis of vv. 1–6; probably, therefore, the *Elohist* handled this material. At any rate, there is nothing to necessitate the assumption that the polemic against the cult of the calf-image was sponsored only by Judaean-Jerusalemite circles. In the E source, corresponding to the religio-political situation in the northern kingdom, traces of conflict with foreign religious traditions frequently occur.[126] According to the present text, at least, xxxii. 1 f. contains a direct reference to the tradition represented by xxiv. 12a, 13b, (15a), 18b, in which Moses has to spend forty days and nights on Mt. Sinai; these verses we previously assigned to E.[127] For this reason also, therefore, xxxii. 1–6 seems to belong to the E-source.[128]

Verses 15–16 and 19–20, in which the story of xxxii. 1–6 was probably continued at first, obviously refer to these Elohistic elements of tradition in chap. xxiv and are also to be allotted to E, therefore. The position of the camp at the foot of the mountain (xxxii. 19a) also corresponds to the Elohistic tradition (cf. xix. 16b–17). On the other hand, xxxii. 17–18 undoubtedly belongs to the same tradition as the fragment preserved in xxiv. 13a, 14 and the source underlying Exod. xvii. 8–16.[129] The view that this tradition must be Elohistic because of its emphasis on northern Israel may also be applied to Exod. xxxii. 17–18. Thus, this account in chap. xxxii which is composed of different variants of tradition, corresponds to and continues the work of the Elohist in chap. xxiv.

xxxii. 21–24, in view of the words it borrows from xxxii. 1–6,[130] must be considered a later accretion, which arose out of E-material and attached itself to the E-source. Exod. xxxii. 25–29, simply because of its close connection with the passage about Levi in the Blessing of Moses (Deut. xxxiii. 8 f.)[131] which is probably of northern

[125] Cf. section II. 11 below.

[126] Cf. pending fuller discussion A. Weiser, *Introduction to the Old Testament*, pp. 114 f.; see also R. Baentsch, *HK*, 2/1, p. 269.

[127] *Vide supra*, section I. 6b; further, the versions of Deut. ix. 9.

[128] Cf. also R. Smend, *op. cit.*, p. 169 and O. Eissfeldt, *op. cit.*, p. 51. *Contra* S. Lehming, *op. cit.*, p. 28, who wishes to assign xxiv. 18 entirely to P and would refer xxxii. 1a–xxxiv. 28a to J.

[129] Cf. O. Eissfeldt, *op. cit.*; 'Auf die nur Exod. xvii. 8–16 and xxxii. 17 in dem hier gemeinten Sinne vorkommenden Wortstämme *gābar* und *chālasch*, "siegen" und "niederwerfen", hat man immer schon geachtet und aus dieser Beobachtung eine engere Zusammengehörigkeit der beiden Stellen gefolgert.'

[130] Cf. M. Noth, *Exodus*, p. 244.

[131] Cf. S. Lehming, *op. cit.*, p. 42 f., *inter alios*.

Israelite origin,[132] is nearer to the Elohistic tradition than the Yahwistic. Moreover the nuance of that section is best understood against the background of the historical circumstances of the northern kingdom after the time of Jeroboam I,[133] which is a further reason for seeing in the tradition of vv. 25–29 an extension of the Elohistic tradition. But Exod. xxxii. 30–34 also belongs to E: the idea of God dwelling on the mountain obviously lies behind xxxii. 30–31a and the linguistic evidence also supports the allocation of the passage to E.[134] Finally, xxxii. 35 is to be regarded as a later gloss on the Elohistic narrative, brought about perhaps by the strange fact that the traditions of chap. xxxii, apart from the passage xxxii. 25–29 which was obviously inserted later, nowhere describe the actual punishment of the people. The general remark in verse 35 that Yahweh punished the people because of their sin seeks to repair this deficiency.

As already mentioned, the unit of tradition in Exod. xxxii. 7–14 was inserted at a later date between xxxii. 1–6 and xxxii. 15 f. It is often regarded as an addition in the Deuteronomic style;[135] this, as we shall show,[136] can hardly be right.[137] In subject-matter, at any rate, there are no specifically Deuteronomic elements in vv. 7–14. In so far as Moses is represented as exercising the prophetic function of intercession, as in Exod. xxxii. 30–34 which belongs to the E-source, it would be better to think of vv. 7–14 as belonging to E, since E displays a definite closeness to the prophetic movement on different occasions.[138] In addition there are some other points of similarity with the Elohistic tradition.[139] There is, therefore, a great deal in favour of the view that Exod. xxxii. 7–14 should be assigned to E.

Summary. Chap. xxxii. embodies Elohistic tradition. xxxii. 1–6

[132] Cf. O. Procksch, *Die Elohimquelle*, p. 178; A. Weiser, *op. cit.*, p. 117.

[133] Cf. pending fuller discussion H. W. Wolff, 'Hoseas geistige Heimat', *ThLZ*, 81, 1956, p. 91; S. Lehming, *op. cit.*, pp. 44 f. See below section II. 11, especially p. 132, n. 564.

[134] Cf. R. Smend, *op. cit.*, pp. 169 f.

[135] So e.g. by O. Procksch, *Die Elohimquelle*, p. 90; M. Noth, *Überlieferungsgeschichte des Pentateuch*, p. 33, n. 113.

[136] See below, section II. 11.

[137] Verse 9, at any rate, which is parallel to vv. 7 and 8 and is not attested in the *LXX*, apart from a few minuscules, will have been added later from Deut. ix. 13. This is the best explanation of the verbal agreement between the two passages.

[138] Cf., for instance, Gen. xx. 7, 17(E), where Abraham is described as a *nābî'*. See also G. von Rad, 'Die falschen Propheten', *ZAW*, 1933, pp. 114 f.

[139] In v. 13 the well-attested reading of the Sam. Pent. and the *LXX*, 'Jacob', is to be preferred. This would then be another factor telling in favour of assigning the passage to E, since it is most unusual to use the name 'Israel' alongside 'Jacob', Cf. C. Steuernagel, *op. cit.*, p. 215.

contains an old, northern Israelite kernel of tradition which has been taken up and reworked by E. xxxii. 15 f. continues the Elohistic complex of Exod. xxiv. 12 f. Exod. xxxii. 7–14 also seems to belong to the E-source; the stylistic features reminiscent of Deuteronomy in this passage still await explanation. xxxii. 25–29 seems to be of northern Israelite origin and, therefore, to be an accretion of the E-source. Other later accretions in E are xxxii. 21–24 and xxxii. 35.

9. Exodus xxxiii

This chapter as a whole is very complex; this is particularly true of its introductory section Exod. xxxiii. 1–6, which in the present arrangement of the text is separated by both its theme and form from the following passage Exod. xxxiii. 7 f. The first big break occurs after xxxiii. 3a: as generally observed, the preceding verses are words of promise, whereas the following verses are merciless and hard. The caesura is also marked by a change of person addressed: in 3b it is the people and no longer Moses that is addressed.[140] From this point of view it also becomes clear where the next break, which is obviously not quite so great, comes, namely between vv. 4–5. The two parts which are so divided run parallel. Both contain hard words from Yahweh. In 3b–4, however, as the result of Yahweh's speech the people take off their jewels spontaneously, whereas in 5–6 they are specifically commanded to do so by Yahweh. All things considered there can be no doubt that these two parts which we have just distinguished represent variants of the same tradition, especially since the same expressions occur in both. Over against this tradition stands the rather different tradition of vv. 1–3a, which is by no means an unbroken unity in itself, however: as frequently observed, v. 2 breaks the connection of 1 and 3a. Since xxxiii. 2 is not presupposed by xxxiii. 12, which, it will be shown later, belongs to the same stratum of tradition as xxxiii. 1 and 3a, verse 2 must clearly have been added at a later date.

In comparative isolation from the complex of tradition we have just discussed (xxxiii. 1–6) and similarly isolated from what follows (xxxiii. 12 ff.) stands the tradition about the Tent of Meeting, xxxiii. 7–11, a tradition which again is not from one source.[141] We

[140] Cf. also W. Rudolph, *op. cit.*, p. 53 f.; M. Noth, *Exodus*, p. 253.

[141] Cf. otherwise section II. 10. The absence of any noun to refer *lo-* (in xxxiii. 7) to arises from the fact that there has been an omission in the text preceding this verse. The *LXX* has smoothed over this awkwardness and should certainly not be preferred to the *MT*.

shall discuss this later.[142] The section which begins with Exod. xxxiii. 12 runs without break to the end of verse 17, apart from a caesura after the first half-verse which we shall not examine further at this stage.[143] Even if there is no question about xxxiii. 14b[144] there is no need to conclude from the changed course of conversation in v. 16 f. that this is a fresh unit of tradition; v. 16 simply varies and develops the argument of v. 13b with regard to other nations.[145] It is clear that the whole conversation between Moses and Yahweh is favourably disposed to the people of the covenant. If this is so, however, xxxiii. 12 ff. must follow xxxiii. 1–3a[146] rather than xxxiii. 3b–4 or xxxiii. 5–6. Verse 2, as already mentioned, must be later than the tradition of xxxiii. 12–17; otherwise, Moses' words in xxxiii. 12 would be meaningless.

Separated by a slight thematic displacement from the previous verses, the section Exod. xxxiii. 18–23 introduces chap. xxxiv. Since the section is not a unity, as shown, for instance, by the thrice repeated introduction of God's words in verses 19, 20 and 21,[147] it is most probable that it grew up gradually as a result of reflections which were obviously inspired by Exod. xxxiv. 5–6. Verse 19, at any rate, undoubtedly refers to xxxiv. 5 f. in the manner of a later commentary.[148]

(b). To which strata of the Pentateuch, therefore, do the elements of tradition just distinguished in chap. xxxiii belong? The two variants xxxiii. 3b–4 and xxxiii. 5–6 go best with the Elohistic verse xxxii. 34, of which they are clearly a direct continuation. Yahweh remains on the mount of God; he does not journey with them. The people are punished for their apostasy by dismissal from Yahweh's dwelling.[149] This latter conception, as we have already indicated on several occasions, is characteristic of the Elohist. xxxiii. 7–11 also belongs to the E source: the camp of the Israelites is referred to again, as in xix. 16b–17 (E). The place of God's revelation is *har-ḥēḳ mīn-hammaḥaneh* (xxxiii. 7), which corresponds to the *mērāḥēḳ* in xx. 18, 21 (E). Moreover, in xxxiii. 11 Moses is clearly described as a prophet, which is another characteristic of E.[150] It is inconceivable

[142] See section II. 10.
[143] See section II. 9.
[144] Cf. O. Eissfeldt, *Hexateuch-Synopse*, p. 157; W. Rudolph, *op. cit.*, p. 56, *inter alios*.
[145] So with the *LXX*, Syriac and Vulgate.
[146] So J. Wellhausen, *op. cit.*, p. 94, n. 1 (563, n. 2).
[147] With M. Noth, *Exodus*, p. 257.
[148] Cf. W. Rudolph, *op. cit.*, p. 57, n. 2.
[149] Cf. J. Wellhausen, *op. cit.*, p. 93 (562).
[150] Cf. A. Weiser, *Introduction to the Old Testament*, pp. 113 f. See also section 8b above.

that xxxiii. 1, (2), 3a, which goes with xxxiii. 12 ff., should belong to the same source as xxxiii. 3b–4, 5–6, (where the atmosphere is so different) or the other traditions just mentioned. Exod. xxxiii. 1, (2), 3a, 12–17, 18–23 are, therefore, usually allocated to the Yahwist. Also in favour of this is the connexion of xxxiii. 18–23 with xxxiv. 5 f., which is clearly Yahwistic in its description of Yahweh coming down and in its agreement with xix. 9a, 18. But xxxiii. 18–23 and a large part of xxxiii. 12–17, as will be shown below,[151] come from a late portion of J. *Summary.* Exod. xxxiii. 3b–4, 5–6, and 7–11 belong to E; xxxiii. 1, 3a belong to J. Later parts of the J source are to be found in xxxiii. 12–17, 18–23.

10. Exodus xxxiv

(a) The first twenty-eight verses do not belong to P.[152] The last verse of this section enables us to see that a decalogue must have directly preceded it.[153] Instead of this, however, there is now a series of commands (Exod. xxxiv. 10–26) which broadly corresponds to Exod. xxiii. 12–19. In their present context (cf. xxxiv. 1, 4) these commands are *d^ebārîm repeated* in *place of* the first table of commandments given to the Israelites which has been destroyed. There is no doubt that this reference to Exod. xxxii bears the stamp of a later addition[154] and presupposes the fusion of Elohistic and Yahwistic tradition. Accordingly the words from *kārī' šōnîm* to *šibartā* in xxxiv. 1 and the expression *kārī' šōnîm* in xxxiv. 4 are recognised and acknowledged as additions. Apart from them xxxiv. 1–8 is, on the whole, a unity. Verse 9, however, presupposes the combination of Elohistic and Yahwistic tradition, insofar as it refers to Exod. xxxii by its request for forgiveness, to the J–E complex of Exod. xxxiii by its diction and to the later Yahwistic tradition of Exod. xxxiii. 12–17 by its request for God to accompany them on their departure from Sinai.[155] Everything points to Exod. xxxiv. 9 being a later addition. There can be little doubt that old tradition lies behind xxxiv. 27. If xxxiv. 1a and 4 record Yahweh's command to prepare two stone tables, the tradition may well have recorded the command to write down the *d^ebārîm* (words), for only so would the restoration of the tables make

[151] See below, section II. 8.

[152] Cf. above, section I. 1c.

[153] For the proof of this cf. section II. 7. See provisionally W. Rudolph, *op. cit.*, p. 59, especially n. 1.

[154] Cf. J. Wellhausen, *op. cit.*, p. 84 f. (553 f.); O. Eissfeldt, *Hexateuch-Synopse*, pp. 55 f.; W. Rudolph, *op. cit.*, pp. 58 f.

[155] Cf. in detail below, section II. 8.

sense. It should also be noted that xxxiv. 27–8 in which *Moses* is thought of as the writer are only at variance with xxxiv. 1b (*added later*) which makes Yahweh himself the writer. There is no reason why xxxiv. 27b which tells of the making of a covenant should be a later addition. What is possible in one tradition (xxiv. 7) should not be considered impossible in the tradition parallel to it. Undoubtedly Exod. xxxiv. 28 contains a kernel of old tradition, which includes, it is clear, the words *'ᵃśereṯ had-dᵉbārîm* which are at variance with the later insertion xxxiv. 10–26 and which could not have been derived from that passage (see below, p. 81, n. 280 and 281.)

(b) The Elohistic verses xxiv. 12b; xxxi. 18b and xxxii. 15 f.[156] make Yahweh himself write the commandments. In this respect they are closely paralleled by the later accretion xxxiv. 1b, but not by the verses we have just mentioned, xxxiv. 27–8, which, as stated, make Moses the writer. We must ask, therefore, whether the complex of tradition to which xxxiv. 27 f. belongs should not be separated from the E-source. The linguistic differences between xxiv. 12b; xxxi. 18b and xxxiv. 1a (*luḥōṯ hāʾeḇěn and luḥōṯ' ᵃḇānîm*) might suggest this. Moreover, it has long been recognised[157] that the tradition in xxxiv. 5 of Yahweh's descent agrees with xix. 18. Exod. xxxiv. 2 and xix. 18 both refer to 'mount Sinai'. The expression *hāyāh nāḵôn* also occurs in both xxxiv. 2 and xix. 11a. Finally, xxxiv. 3 and xix. 12–13a mention the same safeguards to keep back the people (who were obviously more forward than fearsome), and their animals from the area of revelation. All the above-mentioned passages in chap. xix, however, have been shown to belong to the J-source.[158] According to all the evidence, there can be no doubt that Exod. xxxiv. 1a (*kārī' šōnîm*), 2–8, 27–28 belong to the Yahwistic source of the Pentateuch. These verses are not so much a continuation of the J-tradition of Exod. xix as a variant of it; their theophany, at any rate, is fuller than that of Exod. xix. Into this Yahwistic complex of tradition have been inserted firstly the predominantly legal passage xxxiv. 10–26 and later xxxiv. 9 which is a combination of J and E.

11. Results of the Traditio-Critical and Literary-Critical Analysis

The following traditions dealing with the Sinai-covenant and its conclusion belong to the Elohistic source of the Pentateuch:

[156] Cf. above, sections I. 6b, 7, 8.
[157] Cf. J. Wellhausen, *op. cit.*, p. 84 (553).
[158] *Vide supra*, section I. 3b.

Exod. xxiv. 1a, 9–11 (+ xix. 13b), 3–8, 12–15a, 18b (+ xxxi. 18b); xix. 3b–8. Additional E material is to be found in xx. 2–17 (the Decalogue, which is linked with xxiv. 3–8), in the complexes of tradition Exod. xix. 2b–3a, 16aβ–17, 19, 25 and xx. 18–21,[159] which find their climax in the theophany on Sinai, and in the interpolation xxiv. 1b–2. Parts of the later gloss in xxxiv. 9, together with the passage xxxiii. 3b–4, 5–6 and the attached unit xxxiii. 7–11, are also Elohistic. Finally, Exod. xxxii. 1–6, 15–20 with the passages which were added later, xxxii. 7–14, 21–24, 25–29, 30–34, 35, also belong to E. The Yahwistic source comprises the account of the covenant being made in Exod. xxxiv. 1, 4, 10–28, parts of the later interpolated verse xxxiv. 9, the tradition cited in xxxiii. 12–17 and the fragment xxxiii. 1, 3a, together with the passages dealing with the theophany on Sinai, xix. 9a, 10–11a, 12–13a, 14–16aα, 18; xxxiv. 2–3, 5–8; and the later accretions xix. 20–24 and xxxiii. 18–23.

159 With the exception of the last part of xx. 18a, which is Yahwistic.

II

TRADITIO-HISTORICAL INQUIRY

Following the preceding statement of our assumptions in the matter of literary-criticism and traditio-critical analysis, the second part of the work will be concerned with an examination of the roots of the separate elements of the Elohistic and Yahwistic traditions, of the assumptions and influences which moulded them in their pre-literary stage, and of their *Sitz im Leben.*

1. Exodus xxiv. 1a, 9–11

There are three principal elements of tradition which have left their mark on the fragmentary E-tradition in Exod. xxiv. 1a, 9–11;[1] (a) Alongside Moses, Aaron, Nadab and Abihu on the holy mountain there is a deputation of the *elders of Israel*, representing the people of the covenant. (b) *God's presence* on the mountain is presupposed by the narrative and is portrayed and described in a particular manner (cf. especially vv. 10 f.). (c) Israel's representatives hold a *meal* in God's presence (v. 11b). In what follows we shall investigate where these elements of tradition stem from and in what context they took shape and were handed down.

(a) The institution of the *elders* has its origin in the patriarchal tribal system of the still unsettled groups who were later to form Israel.[2] Exod. xxiv. 1a, 9, however, speaks of the 'elders of *Israel*';[3] this presupposes the constitution of the sacral tribal union of 'Israel'. According to Joshua xxiv[4] the tribes included in this union are represented at the assembly at Shechem[4] primarily by the 'elders of Israel'. They appear in the war against the Philistines as a body that makes decisions for the tribal confederacy (1 Sam. iv. 3). Saul would like to be honoured before them (1 Sam. xv. 30).[5] They negotiate with Samuel for the institution of a king in Israel (1 Sam. viii. 4). David is made king of Israel by means of a covenant with them (II Sam. v. 3). The last time the elders of Israel appear as the representatives of the whole Israelite amphictyony is at the dedication of Solomon's Temple (1 Kings viii. 1, 3). After that they are only

[1] On the questions of age, demarcation and source of the tradition, see section I. 6.

[2] Cf. for instance M. Noth, *The History of Israel*, p. 108; G. Bornkamm, *presbus*, *ThWBNT* VI, p. 655; R. de Vaux, *Ancient Israel*, p. 8.

[3] On the number 70 cf. M. Haelvoet, *La Théophanie du Sinai*, *ALBO* II. 39, p. 388 f.

[4] In Joshua xxiv. 1, 25 the reading of the *MT*. 'Shechem' is preferable to the reading of the *LXX* 'Shiloh' on both textual and historical grounds. Cf. also J. Muilenburg in *VT*, ix, 1959, p. 357.

[5] Cf. on this A. Weiser, I Sam. xv, *ZAW*, 1936, p. 15.

mentioned as representatives of individual groups or cities (1 Kings xx. 7 f; xxi. 8, 11; 2 Kings x. 1, 5); they declined in importance as a result of the growing civil service under the kings.[6] On the whole, therefore, the history of the premonarchic amphictyony and the earliest period of the monarchy stand out as the time when the elders of Israel possessed concrete reality in the sense that they represented all Israel. It must have been during this period, therefore, that the tradition that the elders of Israel represented the covenant-people on Sinai originated.[7] This, then, is the first indication that the tradition which is contained in Exod. xxiv. 1a, 9–11 took shape in the historical period of the tribal confederacy before Israel became a state.

(b) The same block of tradition takes *God's presence* for granted. This raises the question of the source(s) of those elements which the tradition uses to describe God's appearance. Exod. xxiv. 10a uses the phrase *'ᵉlōhê yiśrāēl*. There is no doubt that this name for God was a well-established formula.[8] As numerous texts (especially late pre-exilic ones) make clear, this formal name for God was distinctive of the worship of the Jerusalem Temple.[9] The name did not *originate* here, however. As Gen. xxxiii. 20; Joshua viii. 30; xxiv. 2 indicate, the description of (*yhwh*) *'ᵉlōhê yiśrāēl* had its place in the cult at Shechem[10] before Israel became a state.[11] At the same time it cannot be said to belong exclusively to the shrine at Shechem. God is described as above—but without any reference to Shechem—both in the Song of Deborah, which comes from the early period before Israel became a state (Judges v. 3, 5), and in connection with the temple at Shiloh (1 Sam. i. 17). There is only *one* explanation for this: the shrines at Shechem and Shiloh and the Song of Deborah are all connected with the sacral tribal union of Israel. This amphictyony was set up at Shechem; it was there that it had its first central shrine

[6] With G. Bornkamm, *op. cit.*, p. 657. Cf. also R. de Vaux, p. 138.

[7] It is doubtful, therefore, whether *they* are to be ascribed to the oldest block of tradition, while Moses is first mentioned only at a later stage of tradition. *Contra* M. Noth, *Überlieferungsgeschichte des Pentateuch*, pp. 172 f.; *Exodus*, p. 195.

[8] Cf. C. Steuernagel, 'Jahwe, der Gott Israels', *BZAW*, 27, pp. 329 f. The formula may occur both with and—as here—without the name of Yahweh. Cf. on this the survey in C. Steuernagel, *op. cit.*, pp. 332 f.

[9] See 1 Kings viii. 15 f.; 2 Chron. vi. 4 f.; 1 Chron. xv. 12, 14; 1 Chron. xxiii. 25; 2 Chron. xi. 16; xxix. 7; xxx. 1, 5; xxxiii. 16; Ezra viii. 35; Ezek. viii. 4; ix. 3; x. 19, 20; xliii. 2; xliv. 2. Cf. C. Steuernagel, *op. cit.*, pp. 338 f., 334 f.

[10] The shrine on Mt. Ebal (Joshua viii. 30) is probably identical with that at Shechem. With C. Steuernagel, *op. cit.*, p. 344.

[11] It is not clear on what grounds M. Haelvoet (*La Théophanie du Sinai*, *ALBO*, II. 39. p. 389) doubts the existence of this name in the oldest part of the Pentateuch. C. Steuernagel, *op. cit.*, has established that the divine name in Joshua viii. 30 cannot go back to deuteronomistic revision but must belong to an old tradition. On the text of Joshua xxiv. 1, see J. Muilenburg, *op. cit.*

and its first cult.[12] Later the temple at Shiloh took over the rôle of the central cult-place of the amphictyony.[13] Finally, the Song of Deborah is simply a cultic liturgy of the same Israelitic tribal union.[14] All this means, therefore, that the name 'God of Israel' belongs to the institution of the tribal union of 'Israel'.[15] It retained this connection when it moved from Shechem to Shiloh and finally to Jerusalem.[16] The tribal union which was included under the name 'Israel' recognised Yahweh, *its own* God, as the 'God of Israel'. From the very beginning to confess one's faith in him meant to reject 'other gods'.[17] In opposition to them Yahweh, the jealous God, is the sole *'elōhê yiśrāēl* (cf. Joshua xxiv. 19 f.). Corresponding to the renunciation made at the assembly at Shechem Israel continued periodically to renounce the sway of foreign gods in the covenant-cult[18] at Shechem,[19] and to renew its trust in its God, the God of Israel. It is clear that the divine name *'elōhê yiśrāēl* had its original *Sitz im Leben* here in the context of the amphicytonic covenant-cult before Israel became a state. If the tradition of Exod. xxiv. 10a uses this very name to describe the God who makes himself known, this reveals—like the appearance of the elders of Israel in xxiv. 1a, 9—its connection with the pre-monarchic amphictyony. The tradition makes use here of a concept which originated in the context of the tribal union of Israel and was given shape and force by its cult, especially by the rite of renunciation.

According to the narrative of Exod. xxiv. 10b God's appearance was accompanied by the brightness as of a jewel, 'like the very heaven for clearness'.[20] It is probable that the tradition is following a well-established picture here also. Yahweh's appearance is linked

[12] Cf. M. Noth, *History of Israel*, p. 92 f.

[13] Cf. M. Noth, *op. cit.*, pp. 95 f.

[14] Cf. A. Weiser, 'Das Deboralied. Eine form- und traditionsgeschichtliche Studie.', *ZAW*, 71, 1959, pp. 67–97.

[15] Cf. also M. Noth, *Das System der zwölf Stämme Israels, BWANT*, IV. 1, pp. 94 f.

[16] Cf. M. Noth, *Die Gesetze im Pentateuch* (*Gesammelte Studien*, pp. 44 f.); 'Jerusalem und die israelitische Tradition' (*Gesammelte Studien*, pp. 174 f.); 'Gott, König, Volk im Alten Testament' (*Gesammelte Studien*, pp. 224 f.); H.-J. Kraus, *Gottesdienst in Israel*, pp. 77 f.; A. Weiser, 'Theophanie in den Psalmen und im Festkult', *Bertholet-Festschrift*, p. 527. Cf. for a different view L. Rost, 'Sinaibund und Davidsbund,' *ThLZ*, 1947, pp. 129 f.

[17] So also C. Steuernagel, *op. cit.*, pp. 345 f.

[18] Cf. for instance A. Alt, *Die Ursprünge des israelitischen Rechts* (*Kleine Schriften* I, pp. 325 f.); E. Sellin, *Geschichte des israelitisch-jüdischen Volkes* I, 2nd ed., p. 101; G. von Rad, *Das formgeschichtliche Problem des Hexateuch, BWANT*, IV. 26 (*Gesammelte Studien*, p. 44).

[19] Cf. also Gen. xxxv. 2–4, for which see A. Alt, 'Die Wallfahrt von Sichem nach Bethel' (*Kleine Schriften*, I, pp. 81 f.).

[20] If by 'sapphire' the semi-precious lapis lazuli is meant, then when it is compared to the heaven simply in respect of its clearness, it is its brightness rather than its colour which is being emphasised, which is also the case in Ezek. i. 4–28.

with the shining of light in numerous other texts of ancient tradition (cf. for instance Exod. xiii. 21 f. J; Exod. xxxiv. 29 f. P;[21] Deut. xxxiii. 2;[22] Ps. xcvii. 4, 6.). If the divine *k̲āb̲ôd̲* is made visible by the theophany,[23] then in spite of different expressions in detail (thunder, lightning:[24] Ps. xxix; xcvii. 4, 6; consuming fire: Exod. xxiv. 15b f. P; the brightness of a human form; Ezek. i. 28,[25] etc.) light generally lies at the root of them.[26] Moreover, Ezekiel, to whom the *k̲āb̲ôd̲* presented itself with the brightness of crystal (i. 22–28; x. 1–4), used or presupposed the expression *k̲ᵉb̲ôd̲ 'ᵉlōhê yiśrāēl* no less than seven times (viii. 4; ix. 3; x. 19; xi. 22; xliii. 2; cf. x. 20; xliv. 2).[27] As the prophet uses the name 'God of Israel' exclusively in this connection, whereas he has other names for God elsewhere, it may be assumed that he did not coin the formula but that it was in use long before him and happens to have been preserved by him.[28] By his return to this expression Ezekiel seems to be appealing to an old tradition according to which the *'ᵉlōhê yiśrāēl* was surrounded by light and brightness. Perhaps it is this or a related picture which influenced the Sinai tradition in Exod. xxiv. 10 to make the God of Israel appear accompanied by the brightness of crystal.[29] However that may be, the combination of theophany and light corresponded to an ancient and widely-held view.

As the call-vision of Ezekiel, in which Yahweh's *k̲āb̲ôd̲* becomes visible in crystal brightness (i. 4–28) and which includes the picture of cherubim and throne (cf. x. 1), was witnessed in connection with the *Ark*, and as, moreover, Ps. xxiv. 7–10; xcvii. 1–6[30]; 1 Sam. iv.

[21] Behind the late literary account may be old Priestly tradition. Cf. G. von Rad in *ThWBNT* II, p. 242, col. 3.

[22] On the dating of the Blessing of Moses cf. for instance O. Eissfeldt, *Einleitung in das Alte Testament*, 2nd ed., p. 272.

[23] Cf. for instance G. von Rad, *op. cit.*, pp. 240 f.; F. Hesse, 'Herrlichkeit Gottes', *RGG*, 3rd ed., III, p. 273 f.

[24] A. von Gall (*Die Herrlichkeit Gottes*, 1900) seeks to limit the whole idea of light to lightning. He is opposed by M. Dibelius, *Die Lade Jahwes*, 1906, pp. 50 f.; cf. G. von Rad, *op. cit.*, p. 242, col. 32 f.

[25] Cf. further W. Zimmerli, *Ezechiel, BK* 13, pp. 57 f.

[26] This is different from Isa. vi. 3 where the glory of God which is hidden to the human senses but revealed to the heavenly beings is meant. Cf. further F. Hesse, *op. cit.*, p. 274.

[27] Cf. C. Steuernagel, 'Jahwe, der Gott Israels', pp. 334 f.

[28] With C. Steuernagel, *op. cit.*, pp. 334 f.

[29] The literary origins of Ezek. i can hardly be dependent on Exod. xxiv. 10. On the other hand, M. Haelvoet, *La Théophanie du Sinai, ALBO* II. 39, p. 387 (' . . . la description de la vision divine dans Ezek. s'est inspirée d'Exod. xxiv. 10b . . . '). More probably the connection arose in the history of tradition. This also makes the 'série de différences de vocabulaire entre les deux textes', to which Haelvoet refers, more intelligible.

[30] There is no doubt that the psalm is connected with the Jerusalem Temple and the Ark (especially in view of v. 8). On the pre-exilic application of the royal enthronement psalms cf. *inter alios* H. Schmid, 'Jahwe und die Kulttraditionen von Jerusalem', *ZAW* 67, 1955, pp. 185 f.

21 f.; and 1 Kings viii. 11 also point to a connection of Yahweh's *kāḇôḏ* and the Ark,[31] the question arises whether the tradition of Exod. xxiv. 10, which makes a crystalline brightness accompany God's appearance, could have originated under the influence of and in connection with the theophany of the Ark. This is a distinct possibility, seeing that it is the ephiphany of *'elōhê yiśrāēl* before the assembled elders of the pre-monarchic tribal union that is referred to. The divine name which was customary in the context of the amphictyony's shrine at Shechem (*vide supra*) can hardly have come to Shiloh (1 Sam. i. 17) and finally to Jerusalem except in connection with the Ark.[32] Thus Ezekiel's expression *keḇôḏ 'elōhê yiśrāēl* describes Yahweh's appearances of glory which take place in the Holy of Holies in the Jerusalem Temple (i.e. in connection with the shrine of the Ark), as in ix. 3; x. 18 f.; xi. 22 f.; xliii. 1 f.[33] particularly. This divine name, therefore, appears to have been closely related to the Ark.

But it is not only this description of God which makes it probable that the theophany associated with the Ark forms the background of the tradition in Exod. xxiv. 10. The general description of God's appearance also points in this direction: only his feet are mentioned.[34] They are also emphasised on other occasions (cf. for instance 2 Sam. xxii. 10/Ps. xviii. 10; Neh. i. 3; Mic. i. 4; and Isa. vi. 1)[35]. Almost everywhere where God's feet are mentioned, however, a theophany is thought of; in most cases, in fact, the reference is to his epiphany above the Ark. The frequently recurring phrase, 'his footstool', a periphrasis for the shrine of the Ark (cf. Ps. xcix. 5; cxxxii. 7; Lam. ii. 1; 1 Chron. xxviii. 2),[36] is significant. Moreover, wherever clouds or thick darkness under his feet are spoken of there may be a reference to the cherubim of the Ark, which probably represented the cloud cultically and symbolically.[37] It could be said, therefore, that

[31] See M. Dibelius, *Die Lade Jahwe*, p. 49. Cf. further H. Schmidt, 'Kerubenthron und Lade', *Gunkel—Festschrift 'Eucharisterion'*, *FRLANT* 36, pp. 120 f. Even if it is not possible to derive from that visionary throne a cult object which corresponds to the Ark in every detail, Schmidt's view that the throne-like structure of Ezekiel's vision 'has its origin in the world of the senses' (p. 124) is correct.

[32] Cf. also M. Noth, *Das System der zwölf Stämme Israels*, *BWANT* IV. 1, pp. 94 f.

[33] Cf. also C. Steuernagel, *op. cit.*, p. 335.

[34] Disregarding the later addition xxiv. 11a. Cf. section I. 6a above.

[35] In Isa. vi. 1 mention of God's feet is replaced by reference to the train of his garment.

[36] See also H. Schmidt, 'Kerubenthron und Lade', *Gunkel-Festschrift 'Eucharisterion'*, *FRLANT* 36, pp. 129 f.; A. Klostermann, *Der Pentateuch*, pp. 73 f.; and E. Auerbach, *Moses*, pp. 132 f.

[37] Cf. II. Sam. xxii. 10; Ps. xviii. 10; Neh. i. 3 and on this H. Torczyner, *Die Bundeslade und die Anfänge der Religion Israels*, 2nd ed., pp. 38 f.; A. Weiser, 'Theophanie in den Psalmen und im Festkult', *Bertholet-Festschrift*, p. 520.

whenever 'his feet' are spoken of there is almost always some reference to the Ark. Consequently, it is not unreasonable to assume a connection between the theophany tradition of Exod. xxiv, which mentions God's feet, and the Ark.

'And there was under his feet as it were a slab[38] of sapphire stone, like the very heaven for clearness' (Exod. xxiv. 10b). The account of Ezekiel's call[39] and his vision of God's throne refers to a fixed platform,[40] 'shining like crystal' (Ezek. i. 22) or, as it is said in another place, a fixed platform above which 'there was the likeness of a throne, in appearance like sapphire' (Ezek. i. 26; cf. x. 1). On the other hand, as stated, the throne-like structure of Ezekiel's call-vision probably 'had its origin in the world of the senses'; in fact, it was most probably modelled on the Jerusalem Ark,[41] seeing that the prophet undoubtedly had in mind the cherubim which adorned the Temple when he described his vision.[42] This suggests that Ezekiel's conception of this platform which shone like crystal was based on the covering-lid of the Ark described in Exod. xxv. 17 f.[43] This covering was certainly not peculiar to the 'tabernacle' of P; there was probably some corresponding object in Solomon's temple, which may have provided the model for the 'tabernacle'.[44] But if Ezekiel was influenced by this picture there is also reason to suspect that the Sinai-tradition, which is related in subject matter, namely, in its similar description of a platform which shone like crystal and above which God was enthroned, was influenced by the picture of the Ark and its covering lid.

Summary. As the shining appearance of Yahweh's *k̲āḇôḏ* seems to have arisen in close connection with the Ark and the name *'elōhê yiśrāēl* must have been linked with the Ark, and since, moreover, Yahweh's feet are thought of chiefly in connection with the Ark, while the crystalline platform for God's feet, according to the evidence of Ezekiel, seems to be modelled on the covering lid of the Ark-shrine, there are good grounds for believing that the tradition of God's appearance in Exod. xxiv. 10 was influenced by the ideas

[38] On the translation cf. Koehler-Baumgartner, *LVTL*, p. 472, with reference to the Akkadian word *libittu*.

[39] On this type of call-narrative cf. W. Zimmerli, *Ezechiel*, *BK*. 13, pp. 18 f.

[40] Hebr. *rky'*, derived from the verb *rk'*, to crush, to tread down, to flatten (in metalwork).

[41] See H. Schmidt, *op. cit.*, p. 124; cf. above p. 38, n. 1.

[42] Cf. W. Zimmerli, *op. cit.*, p. 54.

[43] Cf. K. Koch, *Die Priesterschrift von Exodus 25 bis Lev. 16. Eine überlieferungsgeschichtliche und literarkritische Untersuchung*, *FRLANT* 71, pp. 11 f.

[44] Cf. K. Koch, *op. cit.*, pp. 16 f., and differently J. Wellhausen, *Prolegomena to the History of Ancient Israel*, pp. 37, 43; H. Schmidt, *op. cit.*, p. 138 (especially n. 2).

which were connected with the theophany above the Ark. Bearing in mind that this piece of tradition, in which the elders of Israel make their appearance and in which the expression *'elōhê yiśrāēl* is used to describe God, took shape in the historical period of the pre-monarchical tribal confederacy (*vide supra*), we should not be surprised if the Ark of Yahweh, as the central shrine of the amphictyony, has in fact left its mark on this tradition. At any rate, it is certain that Exod. xxiv. 1a, 9–11 involves a tradition which presupposes the old Israelite amphictyony, both in the matter of its sociological structure and of its cultic confession of faith in the one God of Israel.

(c) A third element which has made its mark on this part of the Sinai tradition is to be seen in the *meal* which Israel's representatives hold in God's presence (xxiv. 11b): '. . . they beheld God and ate and drank'. Undoubtedly, there is something special about this meal: it is *for this purpose* clearly that the God of Israel orders the representatives of his people to ascend the mountain (v. 1a, 9),[45] and subsequently the meal takes place in God's presence (v. 10, 11b). This can hardly mean anything but a covenant-meal here.[46] Also in favour of this view is the fact that the tradition represented by vv. 9–11 has been placed immediately after the account of the covenant in Exod. xxiv. 3–8 when the various traditions were combined. Obviously those who transmitted this tradition regarded the making of the covenant and the sacrificial offering in xxiv. 3–8 as the self-evident and essential presupposition of the account in xxiv. 9–11. They were probably not mistaken. Everything points to Exod. xxiv. 11b involving a sacrificial meal in which the covenant between *'elōhe yiśrāēl* and his people was realised and made effective.

There is no doubt, however, that the tradition was not establishing anything new in this respect, but was reflecting previous sacral usage. The sharing of a sacrificial meal was observed in the ratification of a treaty or covenant among Israel's patriarchs,[47] just as it was among the ancient Arabs:[48] thus, according to Gen. xxxi. 44, 54 (E), Jacob seals his pact (*b^erîṯ*) with Laban by sharing a sacrificial meal. Again, according to Gen. xxvi. 26–31 (J) Isaac ratifies his

[45] E. Auerbach (*Moses*, p. 166) also regards the meal as the climax of the scene.

[46] So also for example, M. Noth, *Exodus*, p. 196.

[47] Cf. also J. Pedersen, *Israel: Its Life and Culture* I-II, p. 305 f.; L. Köhler, *Theology of the Old Testament*, § 52.3.

[48] Cf. W. Robertson Smith, *The Religion of the Semites*², pp. 269 ff. See further G. van der Leeuw, *Religion in Essence and Manifestation*, pp. 357 f.

covenant (*b^erîṯ*) with Abimelech of Gerar by preparing him a meal (v. 30). There is evidence also for the period of the conquest of 'Israel' that eating and drinking together was one of the rites involved in making a covenant: according to Joshua ix the covenant (*b^erîṯ*) which the Gibeonites obtained by their cunning was ratified by the fact that the Israelites ate and drank from the provisions they carried for their journey (v. 14 f.). The Sinai tradition in Exod. xxiv. 11b obviously refers to this ancient, sacral rite of eating and drinking together, which is attested for the period of the patriarchs and the conquest and which was used to ratify the terms of treaties between human partners in the cases quoted: the God of Israel makes a covenant with his people, insofar as he lets Israel's representatives eat and drink in his presence. It is perhaps not accidental that Exod. xxiv. 11b describes the completion of this covenant-rite in the same words as Gen. xxvi. 30b: 'and they ate and drank'. On the other hand, there is an interesting parallelism in an Arabic poet: 'There was a sworn covenant between Liḥyân and Muṣṭaliḳ: they used to eat and drink together'.[49] This raises the consideration whether or not this 'eating and drinking' could be used simply as a technical term for making a covenant. In that case the words 'and they ate and drank' in Exod. xxiv. 11b (and Gen. xxvi. 30b) could be a formal expression which was immediately understood in ancient Israel from its connection with that rite. This would also explain the pithiness and brevity of the tradition in Exod. xxiv. 11b which sounds so mysterious.[50] But, whatever the truth of this may be, there is no doubt that this old fragment of the Sinai tradition goes back to a sacral custom of covenant-making, which is attested several times in the period of the patriarchs and the conquest of Israel. Thus, the third element of tradition which has contributed to the distinctiveness of Exod. xxiv. 1a, 9–11 points to it having originated in Israel's early history. The tradition of the meal on the mountain is determined by ancient sacral usage. The term 'God of Israel' belongs to the tribal union 'Israel': it was given its full weight in its cult, in the constantly renewed rejection of foreign gods. The deputation of elders also presupposes the pre-monarchic tribal union and its organisation. Moreover, there seem to be references in Exod. xxiv. 10 to the Ark of Yahweh, the central shrine of the amphictyony. It may be said to be established, therefore, that the tradition of Exod. xxiv. 1a, 9–11

[49] Diwân of the Hudhailites, no. 87, ed. by Kosegarten, p. 170; quoted from W. Robertson Smith, *op. cit.*, p. 268.
[50] Cf. for instance M. Noth, *op. cit.*, p. 196.

originated in the context of ancient Israel's amphictyony and that it presupposes the amphictyony in several respects.

2. Exodus xix. 13b

The fragment of tradition Exod. xix. 13b is separated from its context by the fact that it represents not only Moses but a number of Israelites being summoned to Sinai: 'when the trumpet sounds a long blast *they* shall come up the mountain'. According to Exod. xxiv. 1a, 9–11 also not only Moses but a larger delegation of the people of Israel was privileged to meet God on the mountain. In so far as both of these traditions are based on the same assumption they are probably related.[51] For this reason the fragment Exod. xix. 13b is to be examined in connection with Exod. xxiv. 1a, 9–11.

This piece of tradition mentions the blowing of the trumpet. The Sinai tradition as a whole refers to the trumpet exceptionally often (Exod. xix. 16, 19; xx. 18).[52] This is probably because Yahweh's voice was thought to be heard in the 'voice' of the horn, as indicated in Exod. xix. 19 (cf. Isa. lviii. 1). Understood in this way the blowing of the trumpet was obviously another way of representing Yahweh's cultic epiphany dramatically:[53] according to 2 Sam. vi. 14 f. (cf. 1 Chron. xiii. 8; xv. 28) the Ark above which Yahweh was enthroned (cf. 2 Sam vi. 2) was brought up to Jerusalem with the sound of the horn (and with shouting—*t^erû'āh*). Later, in 2 Chron. v–vii which is parallel to 1 Kings viii, the absence of reference to the blowing of the trumpet at the first theophany in the Temple after the Ark had been transferred to the Holy of Holies was apparently missed; this is now to be found in 2 Chron. v. 11b–13a and vii. 6 which were added later. The unison of the temple music, in which the priests had the privilege of blowing the trumpets, invoked the Shekina, the 'glory' of Yahweh concealed in the clouds (v. 13).[54] There is probably a faint reflection, at least, in these additions of the cultic practice of blowing the trumpet during the theophany above the Ark-shrine of the pre-exilic

[51] With S. Mowinckel, *Le Décalogue*, p. 44; M. Noth, *Exodus*, p. 158 *et al.* It is impossible to relate these two fragments of tradition as parts of a clearly defined narrative.

[52] Cf. also section II. 12. By *yôḇēl* and *šôp̄ār* the same instruments are probably meant. Cf. linguistic usage in Joshua vi; on which see M. Noth, *Das Buch Josua*, *HAT* 1/7, pp. 34 f., and also K. Galling, *BRL*, *HAT* 1/1, col. 391 f.

[53] Cf. A. Weiser, 'Theophanie in den Psalmen und im Festkult', *Bertholet-Festschrift*, p. 523.

[54] Cf. W. Rudolph, *Chronikbücher*, *HAT* 1/21, p. 211.

Temple.[55] There are direct reflections of this cultic usage in Ps. xlvii. 6; lxxxi. 4; and xcviii. 6.[56]

It is reasonable to assume, therefore, that the tradition in Exod. xix. 13b, 'when the trumpet sounds a long blast', originated in this way and reflects the pattern and influence of this cultic usage. It is something quite obviously well-known and taken for granted in the expression *bimᵉšōḵ hay-yôḇēl*.[57] When the trumpet sounds a long blast, then Yahweh, as all Israel knows, is present in the cultic community. And in view of the connection between the blowing of the trumpet and theophany above the Ark in the cult of the pre-exilic Temple this means also that, when the trumpet is heard, Yahweh is enthroned above the Ark. By its reference to the trumpet the tradition of Exod. xix. 13b is saying in effect that these representatives of Israel are going up the mountain to meet God.

Our examination of Exod. xxiv. 1a, 9–11, led to the suggestion that the narrative regards the covenant meal as taking place on the holy mountain in the presence of God who is thought of according to pictures drawn from the theophany above the Ark. The conclusion we have just reached, that the tradition in Exod. xix. 13b also clearly refers to God enthroned above the Ark, fits in with this exceedingly well. In Exod. xix. 13b a number of Israelites are ordered to climb the mountain when the trumpet announces Yahweh's epiphany above the Ark. In Exod. xxiv. 1a, 9–11 a larger number of Israel's representatives celebrate a sacrificial meal in the presence of the God who makes his epiphany above the Ark. The close links between the two fragments as well as their relation to closely connected facts about Israel's worship of Yahweh are apparent.

3. Exodus xxiv. 3–8

Handed down in close connection with Exod. xxiv. 1a, 9–11 is the Elohistic unit of tradition, Exod. xxiv. 3–8.[58] In age, the two passages

[55] Along with S. Mowinckel, *Psalmenstudien II*, pp. 109 f., and H.-J. Kraus, *Die Königsherrschaft Gottes im Alten Testament*, *BHTh.* 13, pp. 30–39, it may be accepted that the entry of the Ark into Jerusalem pictured in II Sam. vi.; I Kings viii; 1 Chron. xv. f.; and 2 Chron. v–vii was repeatedly described and celebrated. The blowing of the trumpet at Yahweh's epiphany above the Ark is also to be regarded as a repeated cultic act.

[56] There can hardly be any doubt about the connection with the theophany above the Ark. On the pre-exilic origin of the Enthronement-psalms (xlvii and xcviii) cf. the discussion of H. Schmid, 'Jahwe und die Kulttraditionen von Jerusalem', *ZAW* 67, 1955, pp. 185 f.; and H-J. Kraus, *Die Königsherrschaft Gottes im Alten Testament*, *BHTh* 13.

[57] Cf. also G. Beer and R. Meyer (*Hebräische Grammatik II*, § 96, 4a) on the use of the article in this expression.

[58] Cf. section I. 6.

are about the same. Insofar as Exod. xxiv. 3–8 mentions *conditions* for the covenant[59] it seems to be more detailed than the tradition of xxiv. 1a, 9–11, although this is difficult to judge in view of the fragmentariness of the passage. It cannot be concluded from this, however, that vv. 3–8 are later.[60] Nor do the sacrifices mentioned in Exod. xxiv. 5 and the interpretation of them prove that the tradition of Exod. xxiv. 3–8 as such is later than the tradition of xxiv. 1a, 9–11.[61] The peace-offerings (*zeḇāḥîm*) in xxiv. 5. undoubtedly have their origin in Israel's nomadic past (cf. Exod. xviii. 12);[62] they are attested for the patriarchal period in Gen. xxxi. 54. Burnt-offerings (*'ōlōṯ*) also were sacrificed in Israel's earliest period, though in a simpler form, of course, prior to the conquest (cf. Exod. xviii. 12).[63] Only the words *šelāmîm layhwh*, which stand out as an explanatory comment on *zeḇāḥîm*,[64] come from a later period.[65] Perhaps they are meant to emphasise the ancient communion-offering[66] rather than the gift-offering.[67] Whatever the exact truth, the words of explanation which have been added could represent a particular phase in the history of Israel's sacrificial cult which moulded the tradition. Apart from this gloss, however, there is no reason to suspect that the tradition of Exod. xxiv. 3–8 comes from a later period.[68] The fact that this piece of the Sinai-tradition makes the sprinkling of blood, not the sacrificial meal, the dominant rite in the making of the

[59] Assuming, with M. Noth (*Exodus*, p. 198), that 'Yahweh's words' were reported even in the oldest strata of tradition. On the other hand, the phrase 'and all the ordinances' in xxiv. 3a has been added with reference to the Book of the Covenant which was inserted in the Sinai-pericope later. See section I. 2.

[60] *Contra.* S. Mowinckel, *Le Décalogue*, p. 45.

[61] The fact that the terms for sacrifice used in v. 5 (*'ōlāh*, *zebāḥ*, and *šlm*) all correspond to terms used in Ugaritic texts (*š'ly*, *dbḥ*, and *šlm/m*) does not permit any conclusion about direct connection of content between sacrifice in Ugarit and Israel, or about the date when the corresponding types of sacrifice were first practised in Israel. Cf. J. Gray, 'Cultic affinities between Israel and Ras Shamra', *ZAW* 62, 1950, pp. 209 f.

[62] See also, for instance, A. Lods, 'Eléments anciens et éléments modernes dans le rituel de sacrifice israélite', *RHPhR* 1928, pp. 405 f.: R. Rendtorff, *EKL* 2, col. 1692 f. For the use of the term 'nomadic' cf. W. F. Albright, *Archaeology and the Religion of Israel*, pp. 97 f.

[63] Cf. R. Dussaud, *Les origines cananéennes du sacrifice israélite*, 1st. ed., p. 72, pp. 155 f., and especially p. 156, n. 3.; cf. A. Lods, *op. cit.*, p. 406.

[64] With L. Köhler, *Theology of the Old Testament*, § 52, section 7, and W. B. Stevenson, 'Hebrew,' Olah and Zebach Sacrifices', *Bertholet-Festschrift*, p. 493.

[65] Cf. also R. Rendtorff, *op. cit.*, col. 1693.

[66] Cf. A. Loisy, *Essai historique sur le sacrifice*, pp. 450 f.

[67] These are not, of course, two completely different types of sacrifice (*contra* L. Köhler, *op. cit.*, § 52, section 5); the gift-offering also involved a force which bound giver and receiver together. (It would be better called 'dedicatory offering'). Cf. G. van der Leeuw, *Religion in Essence and Manifestation*, pp. 350 ff., and A. Bertholet, 'Zum Verständnis des alttestamentlichen Opfergedankens', *JBL* 49, 1930, pp. 218 f. On the gradual suppression of the *zbḥ* cf. also L. Rost, 'Erwägungen zum israelitischen Brandopfer', *Eissfeldt-Festschrift*, *BZAW* 77, 1958, pp. 182 f.

[68] *Contra* E. Auerbach, *Moses*, p. 166.

covenant should not, therefore, be understood as the result of a historical development which has diverged from Exod. xxiv. 1a, 9–11. They should be seen as two rival, variant traditions of approximately the same age, both dealing with the making of the covenant on Sinai.

The antiquity of the tradition in Exod. xxiv. 3–8 is attested by (a) the twofold sprinkling of blood which is peculiar to this tradition and which is not found elsewhere in the O.T., and by (b) the appearance of young men, who are not priests, to offer the covenant-sacrifice,[69] which is also without parallel in the O.T. We shall now investigate the source of these two traditions.

(a) It goes without saying that the twofold sprinkling of blood referred to in Exod. xxiv. 6, 8 did not just come into being on the occasion of the Sinaitic covenant. Seeing that the pre-Islamic Arabs also sought to bind themselves to God by means of corresponding blood-rites,[70] it is probable that the Sinai tradition at this point is modelled on a ritual which originated in the nomadic past of the Yahwistic community.[71] To describe the ratification of the covenant the tradition preserved in Exod. xxiv. 1a, 9–11 draws on the custom of eating and drinking together which was practised in the period of the patriarchs and of the occupation of Canaan; similarly the tradition of Exod. xxiv. 3–8 makes use of a rite from this early period, according to which partners bound themselves together by partaking together of the blood of sacrifice at the same time and in equal amounts.[72] The two variant traditions of the Sinaitic covenant make it clear to what extent old cultic and ritual practices have contributed to the formation and differentiation of the tradition.[73] Finally it should be noticed that the tradition of Exod. xxiv. 6, as can be seen

[69] With C. Steuernagel, 'Der jehovistische Bericht über den Bundesschluss', *ThStK* 72, 1899, pp. 349 f.; M. Buber, *Moses*, p. 114; and M. Noth, *Exodus*, p. 199.

[70] Herodotus (iii. 8) records an occasion when Arabs smeared their own blood on sacred stones. Generally, however, they too seem to have used the blood of animals for sprinkling on the altar, while they themselves ate the flesh of the animals; in older times they probably ate the flesh in the blood. Cf. J. Wellhausen, *Reste arabischen Heidentums*, 2nd ed., pp. 126 f.; W. R. Smith, *The Religion of the Semites*³, pp. 338 f. A. Lods, 'Éléments anciens et éléments modernes dans le rituel du sacrifice israélite' *RHPhR* 1928, pp. 405 & 409. On the interpretation of blood underlying this, cf. for instance J. Pedersen, *Israel. Its Life and Culture I–II*, p. 268.

[71] So also A. Lods, *op. cit.*, p. 409. For the use of 'nomadic' cf. W. F. Albright, *op. cit.*, pp. 97 f.

[72] Cf. M. Buber, *Königtum Gottes*, 3rd ed., p. 97.

[73] If the formula 'to throw the blood against the altar' or a similar formula occurs both in the tradition of Exod. xxiv. 6b, 8a and in the sacrificial ritual of Lev. i + iii, which reflect ritual practices that are considerably older than their literary form (with R. Rendtorff, *Die Gesetze in der Priesterschrift*, *FRLANT* 62, pp. 22 f., 77), this suggests that at this point the Sinai tradition has been influenced in its diction also by an already existing priestly terminology. See the summary in Rendtorff, *op. cit.*, p. 11, n. 4.

from the determinative position of *bā'aggānōt*,[74] presupposes the idea of the sacrificial cult. Moses does not pour the blood into basins of just any sort but into sacrificial basins which, it is assumed, are familiar from prevailing cultic practice (cf. 1 Kings vii. 40, 45).

(b) Further evidence of the antiquity of the tradition preserved in Exod. xxiv. 3–8 is to be found, as stated, in the fact that the (normal) sacrificial acts in Exod. xxiv. 5 are performed by the *na'ᵃrê bᵉnê yiśrāēl* and not by the priests, apart from the ritual connected with the blood which Moses himself performs. There is probably a corresponding cultic practice concealed behind this feature of the Sinai-narrative also: the fact that Israel's young men have an active share in making the covenant and the fact that this is spoken of so naturally are best understood against the background of a custom whereby a new generation of young men were received from time to time into the covenant-people at the annual ceremony for the renewal of the covenant (see below) by being given an active share in making the covenant. The fact that they are called *na'ᵃrê bᵉnê yiśrāēl*, and not simply *nᵉ'ārîm*, in the old tradition, suggests that it is precisely the relationship of these young people to the covenant-community of Israel which is of interest. This would be obviously understandable if the service they performed involved their reception as active, cultic participants into the union of the covenant-peoples of Israel. If Yahweh's undisputed claim to the first-born among the Israelites (cf. Exod. xii. 2, 12 f.; xxii. 29; xxxiv. 20b; Num. iii. 13) had been commuted in various ways (cf. Num. iii. 11 f., 40 f., 46 f.; viii. 16–P; Gen. xxii.–E.), it may be that the divine claim to every new generation in Israel's early history found expression and fulfilment in *this* form. Whatever the exact truth, it is clear, at any rate, that the tradition about the sacrifices offered by the *na'ᵃrê bᵉnê yiśrāēl* originated in the very early history of the cult, like the tradition about the twofold sprinkling of blood. In addition, the appearance of the young men of Israel in Exod. xxiv. 3–8 points to the fact that this tradition, like that of Exod. xxiv. 1a, 9–11, took shape within the tribal confederacy of Israel.[75] The following pages will confirm this impression.

Linked with the sacrificial and blood-rituals of Exod. xxiv. 5, 6, 8 and combined with them are the proclamation of Yahweh's revealed will and the dutiful response of the people. It is striking and revealing that in vv. 3 and 7 Moses' declaration of God's will and the

[74] Cf. Beer-Meyer, *Hebräische Grammatik* II, § 96, 4a.
[75] Cf. for instance H. Holzinger, *KHC* 2, pp. 103 f.

corresponding oath of obedience on the part of the people is described *twice*. On the first occasion God's will is declared *orally*, on the second occasion it is fixed in *writing* and read out. This doublet seems to have arisen through two originally rival versions of the declaration of God's will and the corresponding oath of obedience on the part of the people having been woven into an organic whole, like two related acts of a play. If, in addition, Exod. xix. 7 f., which is equally Elohistic, is quoted, there are obviously three versions of the same act of commitment to compare. It is clear from this that on the whole the same outline and the same evidently formal phrases underlie them all: Moses delivers all Yahweh's words,[76] the whole people answer unanimously, 'All the words which Yahweh has spoken (i.e. everything Yahweh has commanded) we will do (and hearken to)'.[77]

Of itself, the circumstance that there are three versions of this event which to all appearances coincide and have been handed down in almost the same words raises the question whether this event was really a single occurrence or whether it reflects a cultically repeated action with its stereotyped phrases. In favour of the latter, which seems the more likely, there is above all the wide measure of agreement between the tradition of Exod. xxiv. 3, 7 and the declaration of God's will and the people's duty at the covenant-festival celebrated periodically at Shechem[78] according to the evidence of Joshua xxiv; Deut. xxvii; xi. 29 f., and Joshua viii. 30 f. At this festival the tribal confederacy constantly renewed its oath of obedience to Yahweh and his will:[79] law and justice are given to the people at Shechem as covenant-obligations (Joshua xxiv. 25; cf. Deut. xxvii. 9 f., 15 f.). The people bound themselves expressly: Jahweh we will serve, and his voice we will obey (Joshua xxiv. 24). When faced with the decision the people 'answers' with its confession of faith (Joshua xxiv. 16). Moreover, the comparatively late cultic ordinances of Deut. xxxi. 9–13 were attached, obviously shortly before the exile,

[76] xxiv. 3a, 4a, 7a; xix. 7. On xxiv. 3a see section I. 2.

[77] The view that these are fixed formulae finds confirmation in the fact that similar stereotyped expressions occur throughout the Amarna-tablets. Cf. for instance J. A. Knudtzon, *Die El-Amarna Tafeln*, *VAB* 2, no. 64, line 18, p. 355; no. 315, lines 10 f., p. 919, etc.

[78] More details in A. Alt, *Die Ursprünge des israelitischen Rechts* (*Kleine Schriften I*, pp. 325 f.); G. von Rad, *Das formgeschichtliche Problem des Hexateuch* (=*Gesammelte Studien*, p. 44); cf. also M. Noth, *Das System der zwölf Stämme Israels*, pp. 66 f., 144 f.; further H-J. Kraus, *Gottesdienst in Israel*, p. 57; and J. Muilenburg, 'The form and structure of the covenantal formulations', *VT* ix, 1959, pp. 357 f.; in Joshua. xxiv. 'Shechem', not 'Shiloh' should be read, following the *MT* rather than *LXX*.

[79] With E. Sellin, *Geschichte des Volkes Israel* I, p. 101.

to an already existing, or at least still remembered, cultic practice, whereby the commandments were periodically proclaimed.[80] For this proclamation the ordinances of Deut. xxxi. 9–13 were linked with the Feast of Booths (v. 10), with which the festival of the covenant celebrated at Shechem was connected.[81] Moreover, according to Neh. viii there was a reading of God's law at the Feast of Booths and the people promised to obey. It 'answers' with its confession of faith (v. 6). Once more (v. 1, cf. Ezra iii. 1) the unanimity of the people is mentioned; it is especially marked in Exod. xxiv, 3 and xix. 8.

In view of the stereotyped nature of the tradition in Exod. xxiv. 3, 7; xix. 7 f. and considering all the similarities between the covenant-obligations in Exod. xxiv. and in the festival held at Shechem it may be considered practically certain that the event described in Exod. xxiv. 3, 7 corresponds to a cultically repeated proclamation of the law and promise of obedience, such as took place particularly in the worship of Yahweh at Shechem.

There is no reason, however, for supposing that this was *peculiar* to the cult at Shechem or remained *limited* to Shechem: the cultic practice of regularly reciting fixed legal clauses as presupposed in the ordinances inserted in Deuteronomy (xxxi. 9–13) shortly before the exile clearly points to the existence in Israel even during the monarchy of a (more or less) regular cultic proclamation of law at the Feast of Booths. Otherwise there could hardly have been any knowledge of such a custom shortly before the exile. Moreover, the fact that a number of the kings of Judah and Jerusalem—Asa (1 Kings xv. 9 f.), Joash (2 Kings xi. 13 f.), Hezekiah (2 Chron xxix. 10 f.) and Josiah (2 Kings xxiii. 1 f.)—undertook a renewal of the Sinaitic covenant and sought to bind the people to the principles of the amphictyony by their reforms,[82] is further evidence that the proclamation of amphictyonic justice and the response of the cultic community to it had not fallen into complete abeyance in the state-cult of Jerusalem but were still sufficiently alive, in spite of all the temporary neglect and superficiality which the Deuteronomic history suggests existed, to be able to act as starting-points for reform.[83] Josiah's reform makes express mention of a proclamation of law (cf. 2 Kings xxiii. 2).

[80] Cf. A. Alt, *op. cit.*, *Kleine Schriften*, I, pp. 326 f.; S. Mowinckel, *Le Décalogue*, pp. 131 f.

[81] Cf. G. von Rad, *op. cit.*, *Gesammelte Studien*, pp. 42 f.

[82] Cf. H-J. Kraus, *op. cit.*, p. 85.

[83] For a more detailed discussion of the importance of these reforms in the history of the cult see H-J. Kraus, *op. cit.*, pp. 81 f.

A covenant-obligation on the part of the people is referred to in 2 Kings xxiii. 3; 2 Kings xi. 17; 2 Chron. xv. 12, 14. Yet how else could such a covenant-duty have been phrased, except in a way corresponding to the formulae of Exod. xxiv. 3, 7; xix. 7 f.; Joshua xxiv. 24? Finally, the continuance of a cultic recital of law in the Jerusalem cult during the monarchy is attested by the way in which the eschatological pilgrimage to Zion to receive God's law foretold in Isa. ii. 1–4 (Mic. iv. 1–5)[84] obviously presupposes the idea of a cultic recital of law which was still practised at that time.[85] An examination of the traditions found in the preaching of the prophet Micah also enforces the conviction that they could refer to a regular cultic proclamation of law at that time.[86] All in all the assumption seems justified that the cultic usage of Shechem, involving the proclamation of the law and the response of God's people to it was continued—in spite of neglect and superficiality at times—in the cult at Jerusalem under the monarchy. In the light of this cultic institution of the pre-exilic period it also becomes easy to understand the ceremony described in Neh. viii as following the reading of the law. Since not only this post-exilic festival but probably also the pre-monarchic festival of the covenant-cult at Shechem was connected with the Feast of Booths and since, moreover, the cultic ordinances of Deut. xxxi. 9–13, which belong to the late pre-exilic period, also regard the practice of proclaiming the law as connected with the Feast of Booths,[87] it seems natural to assume that on the whole the covenant-festivals during the monarchy were also celebrated at the Feast of Booths.[88]

All things considered, therefore, this much at least is certain: the cultic practice of proclaiming the law and of the people binding themselves to keep it, apparently connected with the Feast of Booths,

[84] On the connection of this passage with the traditions of the Zion-songs cf. H. Wildberger, 'Die Völkerwallfahrt zum Zion', *VT* 7, 1957, pp. 62–81.

[85] Cf. G. von Rad, 'Die Stadt auf dem Berge', *Ev.Th.* 1949, vol. x, pp. 440 f., *Gesammelte Studien*, pp. 216 f. Cf. also H. Wildberger, *op. cit.*, pp. 79 f.

[86] Cf. the work of the author, *Die Kulttraditionen Israels in der Verkündigung des Propheten Micha*, *FRLANT* 72, section II. 2, pp. 42 f.

[87] Cf. H-J. Kraus, *op. cit.*, pp. 83 f. on 2 Kings xi. 13 f.

[88] It can hardly be proved from 2 Kings xxiii. 21–23 that the covenant of 2 Kings xxiii. 1–3 was renewed at a Passover-festival. Rather, it *precedes* all the measures taken by Josiah to fulfil the Deuteronomic law. The Passover-festival belonging to these measures took place *after* the covenant had been renewed (with N. M. Nicolsky, 'Pascha im Kulte des jerusalemischen Tempels', *ZAW*, 45, 1927, p. 181). Since, moreover, this Passover represented an *innovation* in place and time (see 2 Kings xxiii. 22 f.; 2 Chron. xxxv. 18; cf. N. M. Nicolsky, *op. cit.*, pp. 171 f., 180 f.; S. Talmon, 'Divergences in Calendar-Reckoning in Ephraim and Judah', *VT* 8, 1958, pp. 62 f.), it cannot be concluded straightaway from the contiguity of covenant-renewal and Passover in 2 Kings xxiii what was the position of this covenant-festival in Israel's festival-calendar before 621.

cannot be regarded as an exclusively Shechemite tradition.[89] Rather, it moved with the institution of the Israelite tribal confederacy until it was finally planted and nourished in the cult of the Jerusalem Temple. Its links with the tribal confederacy are clearly visible in the way it proves alive and active again in every reform emanating from Jerusalem and recalling the amphictyonic principles. Corresponding, therefore, to the event described in Exod. xxiv. 3, 7 there is not only a scene in the covenant-cult at Shechem but also a scene in the festivals celebrated in the state-shrine at Jerusalem; running parallel is an obviously specific amphictyonic usage, which, as the Deuteronomic history indicates, was sometimes suppressed and disregarded but which managed to survive and to exert its influence from time to time.

So far we have not discussed verse 4 in the unit of tradition represented by Exod. xxiv. 3–8: 'And Moses wrote all the words of the Lord. And he rose early in the morning, and built an altar at the foot of the mountain, and twelve pillars, according to the twelve tribes of Israel.' As far as the writing is concerned, this, too, has correspondences in the cultic sphere: according to Joshua xxiv. 26 the law of God was written down in the assembly at Shechem.[90] The aetiological explanation of a corresponding document in the shrine at Shechem is probably to be found in this particular tradition.[91] It is quite clear that the act of writing, which was linked with the erection of a large stone, represents a precise counterpart to the event described in Exod. xxiv. 4, which likewise includes the erection of pillars. Here again, however, it is doubtful whether the tradition of Exod. xxiv. 4 conceals a state of affairs characteristic only of Shechem.[92] The reference to Deut. xxvii. 3 and Joshua viii. 32—passages which undoubtedly refer to the cult at Shechem—cannot prove this. O. Eissfeldt[93] has shown that Deut. xxvii. 1 f., from which Joshua viii. 30 f. demonstrably derives,[94] did not originally describe the writing of a law on whitened blocks of stone but simply the

[89] *Contra* G. von Rad, *Das formgeschichtliche Problem des Hexateuch* (=*Gesammelte Studien*, p. 46 f.).

[90] On the textual problem of the place-name of. J. Muilenburg, in *VT* 9, 1959, p. 357.

[91] A. Alt ('Josua', *Kleine Schriften*, I, p. 191) also points to the aetiological character of the account in Joshua xxiv.

[92] So H-J. Kraus, *Gottesdienst in Israel*, p. 58.

[93] Cf. 'Die Umrahmung des Mose-Liedes Deut. xxxii. 1–43 und des Mose-Gesetzes Deut. i–xxx in Deut. xxxi. 9–xxxii. 47.' *Wissenschaftliche Zeitschrift der Martin-Luther-Universität Halle-Wittenberg*, 4 Jahrg., Vol. 3, pp. 411–17. 'Das Lied Moses Deut. xxxii. 1–43 und das Lehrgedicht Asaphs Psalm 78 samt einer Analyse der Umgebung des Moseliedes', *Berichte über die Verhandlungen des Sächs. Akademie der Wissenschaften zu Leipzig*, Phil.-histor. Klasse Bd. 104, Vol. 5, Berlin 1958.

[94] Cf. M. Noth, *Das System der zwölf Stämme Israels*, *BWANT*, IV, 1, pp. 143 f.

erection of an altar in conformity with the directions of the Book of the Covenant. It was the redactor, 'who wanted to link Deuteronomy with the older Pentateuchal narrative, who made the altar-stones into inscription-stones'.[95] This, however, suggests that for the compiler who lived shortly before the exile the practice of writing the laws on blocks of stone and corresponding writing tablets was still such an immediate and tangible reality that he could risk modifying and altering the original meaning of the tradition about the stones to make it appear intelligible and credible to his contemporaries. The custom of writing down the law, therefore, must still have been remembered at the end of the pre-exilic period—and, according to all the evidence, at Jerusalem also. Do the passages Deut. xxxi. 9–13, 24–30 also belong, then, to the same period and place? They try to relate what was said originally about the Song of Moses (in E?) to the law of Moses. Of Moses' song it is said, 'Now, therefore, write this song, and teach it to the people of Israel . . . that it may be a witness for me against the Israelites . . . So Moses wrote this song.' (Deut. xxxi. 19–22). This is now said with regard to the law of Moses. Moses writes down the law and then hands over the writing and copying of the words of the law to the Levitical priests who carry Yahweh's covenant-Ark in order that the words of the law might be deposited near the Ark as a witness against the unruly covenant-people (cf. Deut. xxxi. 9, 24 f.). The conclusion suggested by this revision is again that at the end of the pre-exilic period in the life of the Temple at Jerusalem very great importance was attached to a law being written down. The account of how the Levitical priesthood was made responsible for this and for depositing it near the Ark of the covenant probably reflects cultic rites which had in fact been carried out and, correspondingly, existing circumstances.

Everything points to the writing of a law of Yahweh being a living and palpable reality not only at Shechem but also in the Jerusalem Temple during the last few decades before the exile. In both instances the writing of the law belongs to the same cultic context: it is connected with the proclamation of the law (cf. Joshua xxiv. 25 and Deut. xxxi. 10 f.). In both instances it is related to the making of a covenant and in the same way: like the large stone erected at Shechem (Joshua xxiv. 26 f.) it had to act as witness that a covenant had been made; likewise, according to Deut. xxxi. 26 f., Moses' law was written down and deposited near the Ark of Yahweh to act as a witness that a covenant had been made. Since the writing of God's

[95] O. Eissfeldt, *op. cit.*, p. 412; cf. pp. 47 f.

commands by Moses in Exod. xxxiv. 4 is linked with their proclamation (xxiv. 3, 7) and since, as the connection with the pillars demonstrates (xxiv. 4), they were written in order to witness that a covenant had been made, there can be no doubt that this feature of the Sinai tradition also represented a particular aspect of the Israelite covenant-cult. Ultimately this cult, which was independent of any particular local shrine,[96] and yet, as the connection with the Ark of the covenant indicates (cf. Joshua viii. 33; Deut. xxxi. 9, 26), was obviously linked with the institution of the sacral tribal confederacy, was finally transplanted from Shechem to Jerusalem. The tradition of the commands being written down on the holy mountain in Exod. xxiv. 4 could easily be understood as an aetiological explanation of these amphictyonic laws.

According to the tradition of Joshua xxiv. 26 f. Joshua set up a second witness of the covenant at Shechem (i.e. in addition to the writing of the law): '. . . he took a great stone, and set it up there under the oak in the sanctuary of the Lord. And Joshua said to all the people, "Behold, this stone shall be a witness against us, for it has heard all the words of the Lord which he spoke to us" . . . .' Since, as we have seen, the proclamation and writing of the law at Shechem, which was linked with the erection of this stone, had an exact parallel in Exod. xxiv. 3 f., it may be assumed that there was also a close connection between this stone at Shechem and the pillars mentioned in Exod. xxiv. 4. The difference in the number of the stones in the two passages is not a serious objection to this view. The singular *maṣṣēḇāh* in Exod. xxiv. 4 is not so extraordinary in relation to the number twelve that it could prove that originally only *one maṣṣēḇāh* was mentioned and the number twelve was added later.[97] But although the number twelve cannot be shown to be of later origin by means of philology and literary criticism, historical grounds alone rule out any union of the twelve tribes of Israel prior to the assembly at Shechem.[98] Even in the period of the Judges Israel seems to have consisted of only ten tribes.[99] At any rate, only individual tribes were involved in what took place at Sinai; it was

[96] Cf. also the written copy of the previously published royal rights and its deposition by Samuel before Yahwe at the shrine at Mizpah. (1 Sam. x. 25).

[97] With G. Beer–R. Meyer, *Hebräische Grammatik*, II, § 99, 3b (with reference to Ugaritic and Arabic linguistic usage) *contra* H. Holzinger, *KHC* 2, p. 105, whose conjecture is only conceivable in the case of a purely literary transmission of tradition.

[98] Cf. M. Noth, *Das System der zwölf Stämme Israels*, *BWANT*, IV, 1, especially pp. 65 f.

[99] According to S. Mowinckel, 'Rahelstämme', *BZAW* 77, 1958, pp. 137 f.; and A. Weiser, 'Das Deboralied, eine form- und traditionsgeschichtliche Studie', *ZAW* 71, 1959, p. 87.

only later that they came together as Israelite tribes.[100] At the very earliest, therefore, there could have been no mention of the '*twelve* pillars corresponding to the twelve tribes of Israel' until after the tribal union of the twelve tribes had been formed, and there is no doubt that the tradition of Exod. xxiv. 4 in the form it has come down to us must be later than the tradition of the single *maṣṣēḇāh* at Shechem, which, in view of Judges ix. 6,[101] seems to have been of pre-amphictyonic origin. The tradition about the pillar at Shechem in Joshua xxiv. 26 f. is also clearly older than the tradition of Exod. xxiv. 4 in its *interpretation* of the stone: whereas in Joshua xxiv the stone is understood and valued as a witness that a covenant has been made,[102] in Exod. xxiv. the pillars have been robbed of independent importance and interpreted simply as symbols of the twelve tribes of Israel. But in both cases the stones have been put at the service of the amphictyonic cult: in the one case they are related to the making of the covenant, in the other to the members of the tribal confederacy. Thus, it is clear that the traditions of the pillars in Joshua xxiv and Exod. xxiv are really very closely related.

There also seems to be a connection in cultic history corresponding to this close connection of the two traditions. The story related in Joshua iii. f. is good evidence, insofar as it is of an aetiological cast,[103] that there were twelve stones 'according to the number of the tribes of Israel' (iv. 8) in the shrine at Gilgal. Although the name Gilgal means 'stone-circle' it can hardly be assumed that there were precisely *twelve* stones on this spot in the pre-Israelite period.[104] The number twelve is not accidental; the stones are permanent representatives of the nation's twelve tribes. Gilgal appears to have been the cultic centre of the tribal confederacy for a short time immediately prior to the formation of the Israelite state.[105] It probably belongs, therefore, to the cult-places which replaced Shechem as the central shrine of the amphictyony.[106] It was in the course of this

[100] Cf. N. Noth, *History of Israel*, p. 133.

[101] Cf. B.H.—cf. also Gen. xxxiii. 20.

[102] See also Gen. xxxi. 43–55. Cf. for instance J. Pedersen, *Israel. Its Life and Culture, I–II*, pp. 307 f. The understanding of the sacred stone as a covenant-witness is doubtless the result of a change of meaning in older ideas. On this cf. G. van der Leeuw, *Religion in Essence and Manifestation*, pp. 53 ff.

[103] Cf. Joshua iv. 6, 9, 21.

[104] Cf. H-J. Kraus, 'Gilgal. Ein Beitrag zur Kultusgeschichte Israels', *VT* 1, 1951, pp. 185, 193.

[105] Cf. A. Alt, 'Josua', *Kleine Schriften*, I, p. 184.

[106] Cf. also H-J. Kraus, *op. cit.*, pp. 193 f. (with reference to Deut. xi. 25 f.). On the probable sequence of amphictyonic centres, cf. A. Alt, *op. cit.*, pp. 191 f.; and 'Die Wallfahrt von Sichem nach Bethel,' *Kleine Schriften I*, especially p. 85; M. Noth, *History of Israel*, pp. 94 f.

movement, which can no longer be fully reconstructed, of the amphictyonic cult-centre from Shechem to Gilgal that the extension of the single stone of Joshua xxiv. 26 f. (which witnessed the making of the covenant) to the twelve pillars of Exod. xxiv. 4. (which symbolised the Israelite tribes) took place. Quite obviously the Sinai tradition at this point reflects the results of developments in the history of the cult.[107] It becomes clear, moreover, that the twelve pillars of Exod. xxiv. 4 do not represent the cultic usage of a particular *local* shrine, any more than the proclamation and writing of the law and the promise of obedience in Exod. xxiv. 3–8 do. Thus, although various local cult-places undoubtedly possessed their own particular pillars,[108] it is certain that the tradition of Exod. xxiv. 4 reflects those pillars which the amphictyonic cult of Yahweh had attached to itself, and had subordinated to its own aims and had transmitted along with other objects and traditions[109] when it moved to new places. Once again this makes it apparent how closely the history of the Sinai tradition is interwoven with the history of the amphictyonic cult: the tradition of Exod. xxiv. 3–8, to judge by the twelve stones which symbolised the amphictyony, clearly maintained its links with the Israelite tribal confederacy even beyond Shechem. Thus the tradition reflects the conclusion of the process which aimed at a more complete interpretation of the pillars in the sense of the covenant made with Yahweh.

Summary. The tradition preserved in Exod. xxiv. 3–8, like the tradition of Exod. xxiv. 1a, 9–11, has been given shape by referring to a cultic-ritual practice in the early history of the people of Yahweh. In that Exod. xxiv. 3–8 referred to the twofold sprinkling of blood (v. 6, 8), instead of to the rite of eating and drinking together, the tradition of the covenant made at Sinai became more

[107] If it is assumed that Gilgal replaced Shechem as the amphictyonic shrine, the possibility that the Sinai-tradition played an important rôle at Gilgal must also be reckoned with (cf. H-J. Kraus, *op. cit.*, p. 193 f., especially his theory, based on Deut. xi. 25 f., that the celebrations at Ebal-Gerizim were moved to Gilgal). If there is evidence for twelve stones 'according to the number of the tribes of Israel' at Gilgal, then, in view of the almost literal agreement of this tradition with that of Exod. xxiv. 4, which is undoubtedly concerned with what happened on Sinai, it is more probable that the twelve stones at Gilgal were related to the making of the covenant on Sinai *from the first*. The mere fact that the Gilgal-stones are located in different, irreconcilable places makes it impossible to be sure that they were originally related to the crossing of the Jordan and the conquest of Canaan, as the aetiological story in Joshua iv now seeks to show. Whether at some later date the erection of the twelve stones became part of a festival at Gilgal celebrating the occupation of Canaan is a question that need not be gone into here. Cf. H-J. Kraus, *op. cit.*, pp. 194 f., and M. Noth, *Das Buch Josua, HAT* 1/7, 2nd ed., p. 33.

[108] Cf. for instance Judges ix. 6 (B.H.); Gen. xxxiii. 20; xxviii. 18.

[109] Incidentally the Ark of the covenant also appears in Gilgal according to Joshua iv. 5, 9 f.

complex and varied. The development of the tradition of vv. 3–8, which in form and diction presupposes the ideas and terminology of Israel's sacrificial cult (v. 6, 8), also took place within the context of the history of the pre-exilic tribal confederacy: the unique participation of the young men of Israel in the sacrificial acts (v. 5) is to be explained in terms of an early stage of the confederacy's cultic history. The proclamation of the law and the promise of obedience by the people (v. 3, 7) does not reflect the individual practice of a particular local shrine, but is a specifically amphictyonic ritual practice which is attested both at Shechem and in the state-cult at Jerusalem. Likewise, the tradition about the law being written down (v. 4) does not reflect circumstances peculiar to Shechem but conditions belonging to the cult-centre of the tribal confederacy, which the Sinai story here refers to aetiologically. Finally, in the reference to the twelve pillars (v. 4) there are traces of a development which must have taken place in the history of the amphictyonic cult. Thus the tradition embodied in Exod. xxiv. 3–8 not only indicates that it arose and was developed within the pre-exilic tribal union of Israel; it also reveals to what extent ancient rites, cultic practices, circumstances and technical terms contributed to its formation.

4. Exodus xxiv. 13a, 14

In connection with the discussion of the tradition about the twelve pillars (Exod. xxiv. 4) there is one final fragment of tradition to be considered, namely the words of Exodus xxiv. 13a, 14,[110] which also belong to E probably: 'So Moses rose *with his servant Joshua*'.[111] How has it come about that Joshua is mentioned here in the centre of the Sinai-tradition?[112] It is clear that Joshua had no place here originally. It is practically certain in view of the trustworthy tradition of his inheritance and grave at Timnath-serah in the hill-country of Ephraim (Joshua xxiv. 30) that he was an Ephraimite.[113] There is good evidence that the tradition of Joshua xxiv. is also right from a historical viewpoint in ascribing the leading rôle in the all-Israelite assembly at Shechem to Joshua and (insofar as it is interested from an aetiological viewpoint) in tracing back the Shechemite covenant-

110 *Vide supra*, section I. 6.

111 Cf. v. 13a; cf. also Exod. xxxiii. 11 (Num. xi. 28) and section II. 10.

112 On this question cf. also K. Möhlenbrink, 'Josua im Pentateuch', *ZAW* 59, 1942/3, p. 26. M. Noth, *Überlieferungsgeschichte des Pentateuch*, pp. 192 f.

113 Cf. A. Alt, 'Josua', *Kleine Schriften*, I, p. 186.

cult to him.[114] It was, in fact, in this very cult that the Sinai tradition had its *Sitz im Leben* in the very early period.[115] This is also attested by the numerous agreements between the passages of the Sinai tradition we have already discussed and the cult at Shechem disclosed by Joshua xxiv; Deut. xxvii.; xi. 29 f.; and Joshua viii. 30 f. This close connection is the first indication of the way in which the figure of Joshua made its way into the Sinai tradition and found a place next to Moses.[116]

But it was not as the central figure of a local, Shechemite tradition but as the figure connected with the Israelite amphictyony from its inception and hence linked with it even beyond Shechem probably that Joshua secured such a place. In favour of this is the following traditio–historical consideration: the Ephraimite Joshua probably had nothing to do with the Benjaminite stories in Joshua i–xi, which were partly connected[117]—aetiologically at any rate—with Gilgal.[118] His name was probably inserted at a later date into the stories which crystallised round Gilgal; from here it seems to have spread into all Israel.[119] This suggests that development of Benjaminite stories in an amphictyonic sense went hand in hand with the introduction of Joshua and that both processes alike were the result of the gradual movement of the amphictyony's centre from Shechem to Gilgal for a time: in view of the key position of Joshua in the Shechem tradition his transference to Gilgal is only to be expected. If this hypothesis is correct, it would prove that the figure of Joshua, freed from connections with tribal history and local cult, finally came to belong to the wider context of the tribal confederacy of all Israel. His appearance in Exod. xxiv. 13a could be a fresh indication, therefore, that the Sinai tradition was transmitted and given shape in close connection with the institutions and history of the amphictyony.

5. Exodus xx. 2–17

The *Sitz im Leben* of the Decalogue, Exod. xx. 2–17 (Deut. v. 6 f.), in a cultic festival has, through the investigations of S. Mowinckel[120]

[114] Cf. M. Noth, *Das System der zwölf Stämme Israels*, *BWANT*, IV, 1, pp. 69 f.; *The History of Israel*, p. 93; A. Alt, *op. cit.*, p. 191 f. For a discussion of the views of E. Auerbach, *VTS* 1, 1953, p. 3 and H. H. Rowley, *From Joseph to Joshua*, p. 126 see O. Kaiser, 'Stammesgeschichtliche Hintergründe der Josephsgeschichte', *VT* 10, 1960, pp. 12 f.

[115] Cf. G. von Rad, *Das formgeschichtliche Problem des Hexateuch* (=*Gesammelte Studien*, pp. 44 f.). See also the previous section above, II. 3.

[116] Cf. also H-J. Kraus, *Gottesdienst in Israel*, p. 59.

[117] Cf. A. Alt, *op. cit.*. pp. 183 f.

[118] Cf. *ibid.*, pp. 186 f.

[119] Cf. also R. Bach, 'Josua', *RGG*, 3, 3rd ed., col. 872.

[120] *Le Décalogue*, 1927, pp. 114 f.

and G. von Rad[121]—especially through their use of Psalms 50 and 81—been practically certain for a long time and there is no need to repeat the proof of this here. The fact that the Decalogue in its final form contains so many explanatory clauses is to be ascribed to its cultic origin and use:[122] they grew up in the course of its long and active use in the recital of rights and duties in the cult for the renewal of the covenant.[123] The fact that the Decalogue was finally taken up again in Deuteronomy can hardly be understood apart from this continuing cultic activity.[124]

If the cultic *Sitz im Leben* of the Decalogue is, according to all the evidence, certain, the question of its *origin* also points to the sphere of the Israelite cult: form-criticism has shown that the apodeictic legal clauses, which, linked together, form the basis of the Decalogue, had their *Sitz im Leben* 'not in the various places where lay judgement was given'[125] but, as the form and content of this type of justice demonstrate, in a sacral act involving all Israel.[126] But if the separate commandments of the Decalogue are derived from the cult of ancient Israel, there is still the question of where the form which lies at the basis of the Decalogue *as a whole* originated: were there any documents in the world surrounding Israel parallel, in form at least, to the Decalogue, or was the Decalogue a unique creation of Israel? Is there any evidence among the neighbours of ancient Israel of a well-established pattern of words to which the Decalogue could have been related in its formal structure and upon which it could have been modelled? To answer this we shall consider particularly the Hittite state-treaties from the archives at Boghazköy.[127] The 'vassal-treaties'[128] (covenants) which have been

[121] *Das formgeschichtliche Problem des Hexateuch* (=*Gesammelte Studien*, pp. 29 f.).

[122] With A. Alt, *Die Ursprünge des israelitischen Rechts* (=*Kleine Schriften*, I, pp. 329 f.).

[123] On the formal expansion in Exod. xx. 5b, 6 cf. J. Scharbert ('Formgeschichte und Exegese von Exod. xxxiv. 6 f. und seiner Parallelen', *Bibl.* 38, 1957, p. 134), who shows that it is derived from the cultic tradition and has been woven into the framework of the festival-proclamation of the covenant-clauses.

[124] Cf. A. Alt, *op. cit.*

[125] *Ibid.*, p. 323.

[126] Cf. *Ibid.*, pp. 324 f.

[127] Cf. G. E. Mendenhall's article, 'Covenant Forms in Israelite Tradition', *BA*, 17, no. 3 (Sept. 1954), pp. 50 f.; and K. Baltzer, 'Das Bundesformular. Sein Ursprung und seine Verwendung im Alten Testament', *ThLZ*, 83, 1958, col. 585 f. (Baltzer's dissertation, referred to in his article, only became available to the author of the present work in January 1961, when it was published in the series *Wissenschaftliche Monographien zum Alten und Neuen Testament* ed. by G. Bornkamm and G. von Rad. The German version of the present study was already in process of being printed, however, so that Baltzer's work, which does not deal with the Decalogue in detail—see p. 37, n. 1 of his book—could not be given proper consideration.) In the following pages the editions of the texts used are: E. F. Weidner, *Politische Dokumente aus Kleinasien. Die Staatsverträge in akkadischer Sprache aus dem Archiv von Boghazköi*, 1923 (henceforth abbreviated to *W*); J. Friedrich, *Staatsverträge*

recovered all possess a common outline.[129] Before examining in detail, however, whether this outline can be considered a formal model of the Israelite Decalogue, it must first be decided whether the Hittite covenant-treaties which have been discovered were within reach of ancient Israel from a chronological and geographical point of view and could thus have been known. The first point to establish is that the treaties in question come from the fourteenth and thirteenth centuries B.C.[130] Many of them are signed by princes of Syrian peoples, for example Kings Aziru (Hittite; Aziraš), Duppi-Tešup and Bentešina of Amurru,[131] which lies north of the Lebanon; other signatories are Rimišarma, King of Ḫalap (corresponding to Aleppo),[132] and Tette, King of Nuḫašši,[133] an area south of the line Hamath–Höms and south of Aleppo.[134] Moreover it is significant that everything points to Pharaoh Ramses II having regarded the Hittite treaty-forms as valid; he made a covenant with Ḫattušil III on their basis.[135] It may be taken as certain, therefore, that this covenant-form was generally well-known in the region of Syria and was even used as far as Egypt. There are indications that the Hittites, for their part, were not the first to create this form but could have borrowed it from Mesopotamia,[136] so that we may be dealing with what was basically an international covenant-form in the Near East of the second millenium B.C., which simply by chance happens to have become well-known through Hittite documents. Whatever the exact truth, everything points to this covenant-outline having been well-known in ancient Israel also. We are justified, therefore, in examining in detail whether the number and nature of concurrences

[129] V. Korošec has proved this in his work *Hethitische Staatsverträge. Ein Beitrag zu ihre juristischen Wertung, Leipziger rechtswissenschaftliche Studien*, Vol. 60, 1931; cf. especially pp. 12 f. On the term 'vassal-treaty' cf. *op. cit.*, pp. 5 f., 19 f.

[130] On the dating cf. V. Korošec, *op. cit.*, pp. 1 f. The Aramaic vassal-treaties of the stele of Sefire I–III, however, show that this same covenant-form was still in use in N. Syria, which was an area of Hittite influence, in the eighth century B.C. On this cf. J. A. Fitzmyer, 'The Aramaic Treaty from Sefire in the Museum of Beirut', *CBQ*, 20, 1958, pp. 444–476.

[131] Cf. W, pp. 70–75 and 76–79; F1, pp. 4–25 and W, pp. 124–135.

[132] Cf. W, pp. 80–89.

[133] Cf. W, pp. 58–69.

[134] For details, cf. W, pp. 12 f., n. 3.

[135] Cf. W, pp. 112–123.

[136] Cf. V. Korošec, *op. cit.*, pp. 23 f.; G. E. Mendenhall, *op. cit.*, pp. 53 f.

---

des Ḫatti-Reiches in *hethitischer Sprache, I Teil, MVÄG*, 1926 (henceforth abbreviated to: F1); *II Teil, MVÄG*, 1930 (abbreviated to: F2).

[128] For a description of this method of regulating relations with subject peoples, cf. A. Moortgat in: *Ägypten und Vorderasien im Altertum*, p. 353, and A. Alt, 'Hethitische und ägyptische Herrschaftsordnung in unterworfenen Gebieten', *Kleine Schriften*, III, p. 99 f.

permit the view that Israel's Decalogue was modelled on this outline.

In the preamble of the Hittite vassal-treaties the author and lord of the covenant which is to guarantee the safety of the vassal is named: 'Thus (says) the Sun Šuppiluliuma, the Great King, King of the land of Ḫatti, the Prince . . .'.[137] 'Thus (says) the Sun Muršiliš, the Great King, King of the land of Ḫatti, the Prince, the son of Šuppiluliuma, the Great King . . .'.[138] 'Thus (says) His Majesty Muwatalliš, the Great King, King of the land of Ḫatti . . .'.[139] Likewise the Decalogue begins with the author of it giving his name: 'I am Yahweh, your God . . .' (Exod. xx. 2a).[140]

This introduction of himself* on the part of the founder of the covenant is usually followed in the outline of the Hittite treaties by a *historical prologue* in which the lord and author of the covenant relates the great deeds which he has kindly performed for the benefit and welfare of the vassal concerned and in return for which the vassal is obliged to render permanent gratitude and constant obedience:[141] '. . . although you were sick I, the Sun, have put you in your father's place and have sworn (your) sisters(?), your brothers and the land of Amurru to you'. After I did this, 'Behold I took you in oath for the King of the land of Ḫatti, for the land of Ḫatti and for my sons (and) my descendants'.[142] 'Behold, Ḫuḳḳanāš, I have protected thee and honoured(?) thee as a simple(?) but good (man) and have given thee a friendly introduction in Ḫattušaš in the midst of the people of Ḫajaša. . . . Recognise, then, Ḫuḳḳanāš, only the lordship of the Sun . . .'.[143] Likewise in the Decalogue the introduction of the founder of the covenant is immediately followed by the historical prologue with its consequent obligations of gratitude and obedience, '. . . who brought you out of the land of Egypt, out of the house of bondage; you shall . . .' (xx. 2b).

The most important passages of the historical prologue in the

[137] See W, p. 58 f., l. 1. Cf. also A. Moortgat, *op. cit.*, p. 356.
[138] See F1, p. 106 f., l. 1.
[139] See W, p. 80 f., l. 1. Cf. further W, p. 76 f., l. 1; F1, p. 4 f., l. 1; W, p. 80 f., l. 9; W, p. 124 f., l. 1; F2, p. 50 f., l. 1.
[140] On the distinctiveness of this formula, cf. for instance K. Elliger, 'Ich bin der Herr—euer Gott', *Heim-Festschrift*, pp. 9–34; W. Zimmerli, 'Die Weisung des Alten Testaments zum Geschäft der Sprache', in *Das Problem der Sprache in Theologie und Kirche*, p. 13.
[141] On the other hand, see below, pp. 88 f. See also A. Moortgat, *op. cit.*, pp. 361, 363.
[142] See F1, p. 10 f., ll. 16 f.
[143] See F2, p. 106 f., l. 1. Further examples in W, p. 16 f., ll. 50 f.; p. 58 f., l. 2 f.; p. 76 f., 2 f.; p. 82 f., l. 11 f.; p. 130 f., l. 37; F1, p. 118 f., ll. 32 f.

* Tr. note: the German word is 'Selbstvorstellung', occasionally translated 'manifestation of himself' with reference to Yahweh, cf. III. 3.

Hittite outline are written in the *I-Thou* style. To take just one example: 'Now have I, the Sun, done (this) for thee, Bentešina, I have made thee king over the land of Amurru'.[144] Corresponding to this in the Decalogue are the words: 'I am Yahweh, thy God, who brought thee out . . .'.

The historical prologue finds its natural, direct continuation in the separate clauses of the covenant, with the most basic and comprehensive demand usually heading the list: '. . . as I, the Sun, did not trouble thee formerly(?), Kupanta-KAL, do thou protect the Sun in future, Kupanta-KAL'.[145] Or, turning to Hukkanaš, Šuppiluliuma, after enumerating his good deeds, continues: 'Now, Ḫuḳḳanāš, recognise only the rule of the Sun . . .'[146] In the Decalogue the words recalling the deliverance from Egypt are immediately followed by the basic demand of Yahweh's covenant: 'thou shalt have no other gods before me (*'al pānay*)'.

That dependence on the founder of the covenant excludes any concurrent dependence on others is clearly expressed in the words to Ḫuḳḳanāš quoted above: 'Now, Ḫuḳḳanāš, recognise only the rule o the Sun . . . Further, recognise no other lord, whoever may be behind the back of the Sun; only recognise the Sun . . . .'[147] The vassal Kupanta-KAL is enjoined: '. . . do not revolt from the Sun—and have nothing to do with this man and do not worry about him! As thou hast (previously) supported the Sun, do so later(?) also'.[148] It is clear that Yahweh addresses his people Israel equally *exclusively* in the first commandment.

Finally, in the Hittite vassal-treaties, what the king stipulates as clauses of the covenant are called his 'words'. The vassal is warned to observe 'the words of this treaty'.[149] Any alteration in 'the words that are inscribed on the tablet' is forbidden.[150] 'The word of His Majesty, the Great King, is not to be repudiated (and) not to be broken. Whoever alters (it) shall die.'[151] The commands of the Decalogue are also called 'words': 'And God spoke all these words' (Exod. xx. 1).

Finally, the possibility that the covenant might be broken is countered in the Hittite vassal-treaties with express *sanctions*. It is said

[144] See W, p. 130 f., l. 37.
[145] Cf. F1, p. 118 f., ll. 32 f.
[146] Cf. F2, p. 106 f., l. 1; cf. further W, p. 18f., l. 60 f.; p. 60 f.; p. 130 f., ll. 37f.
[147] Cf. F2, p. 106 f., ll. 8, 14 f.
[148] See F1, p. 122 f., l. 5 f., Cf. also F1, p. 130 f.; W, p. 18 f., l. 60 f.; W, p. 130 f., ll. 41 f.
[149] Cf. W, p. 32 f., l. 59.
[150] Cf. W, p. 28 f., l. 38.
[151] Cf. W, p. 80 f., l. 5 f.

for instance: 'If you, Mattiwaza . . . and (you) the sons of the Ḫurri country do not fulfil the words of this treaty, may the gods, the lords of the oath, blot you out, (you) Mattiwaza and (you) the Ḫurri men together with your country, your wives and all that you have . . .'.[152] Elsewhere it is said: 'If Tette does not observe these words of the treaty and oath . . . , by these gods, may they destroy Tette together with his person, his wives, his sons, his descendants, his house, his city, his land and his possessions.'[153] On the surface, the main body of the Israelite Decalogue does not seem to contain any corresponding sanctions in the case of the covenant being broken by disobedience. It should be remembered, however, that the apodeictic legal clauses which belong to the oldest constituent parts of the Decalogue are essentially categorical prohibitions, which as such are absolute and represent the most powerful sanctions.[154] The categorical and unconditional nature of the Ten Commandments really contains within itself the same judgement of death or curse on disobedience that is expressed in other apodeictic sequences by a *môṯ yûmāṯ* or *'ārûr*.[155] That this does not misinterpret the character of the Ten Commandments is clear from the fact that they were not understood in any other way in the oldest circles of tradition:[156] the gloss, Exod. xx. 7b, according to which Yahweh does not fail to punish the man who disobeys him, is instructive in this connection. Similarly also the gloss in Exod. xx. 5b about *'ēl ḳannā'*, who visits the iniquity of the fathers upon the children to the third and fourth generation of those who hate him.[157] All the evidence goes to show that the sanctions which belong to this renowned covenant-form in the event of the treaty being broken most probably found a correspondence, formally at any rate, in the categorical and unconditional nature of the apodeictic clauses of the Decalogue.

Summing up, then, we may say that the parallels between the above Hittite covenant-treaties and the Israelite Decalogue are so numerous and so striking that one can hardly avoid the view that the Ten Commandments are—formally—modelled on the covenant-form that is revealed in the vassal-treaties of the Hittites and was

[152] Cf. W, p. 32 f., l. 59 f.; cf. also p. 50 f., l. 25.

[153] See W, p. 68 f., l. 59 f.; cf. further W, p. 74 f., l. 13 f.; F1, p. 24 f., l. 21 f.

[154] Cf. A. Alt, *Die Ursprünge des israelitischen Rechts* (=*Kleine Schriften*, I, p. 321).

[155] Cf. for instance Exod. xxi. 12, 15–17 in comparison with Deut. xxvii. 15–26. Cf. A. Alt, *op. cit.*, p. 315.

[156] Cf. B. Gemser, 'The importance of the Motive Clause in O.T. Law', *VTS*, 1, 1953, pp. 50, 63 f.

[157] Cf. also Exod. xxxiv. 14 and Joshua xxiv. 19 f. Cf. further H. J. Stoebe, 'Die Bedeutung des Wortes *ḥäsäd* im Alten Testament', *VT*, 2, 1952, p. 250.

probably in general use in the Near East of the second millenium B.C.[158] Now that it has been shown how far the most important elements in the structure of the Decalogue are paralleled by elements within the Hittite covenant-form, a number of other elements in this treaty form, relating not so much to the inner structure of the treaty as to the cultic framework in which they are set, will be pointed out. This will raise the question whether these elements also, which are equally part of the covenant-outline, have any correspondence in the case of the Decalogue.

Reference may be made, firstly, to the fact that according to all the evidence an essential feature of the covenant-form which occurs in the Hittite state-treaties was the fact that they were *drawn up in writing*. The treaty was not fully valid until it was written down. Otherwise it would be difficult to understand why the loss of the written document should be clearly so unbearable. The Hittite king, Muršiliš II (Muwatalliš), says in his treaty with Rimišarma: 'A tablet of the treaty for Rimišarma, the king of the land of Ḫalap—, my father Muršiliš made (it) for him; but the tablet was stolen. I, the Great King, have written him a second tablet, sealed it with my seal and given (it) to him. Henceforth(?) no one is to alter the words of this tablet'.[159] And according to the treaty of Šuppiluliuma and Mattiwaza whoever breaks or alters the written terms of the treaty is to be cursed.[159a]

Was the writing down of Israel's Decalogue given a meaning corresponding to that attached to the Hittite documents? It has been established in an earlier connection[160] that there must have been written copies of the law in active use in close connection with the proclamation of God's justice both in the covenant-cult at Shechem and in the Temple at Jerusalem in the last few decades before the exile. If tradition linked the written record of Yahweh's words in Exod. xxiv. 4 with the Decalogue by means of Exod. xx. 1, then in view of the value generally attached to a written document throughout the ancient Orient and its importance in the fulfilment of a treaty[161] and in view of the evidence that a similar state of affairs existed in Israel there can be no good grounds for interpreting such a document in the case of the Decalogue as improbable. There is even less reason for doing this with regard to the Decalogue since it is expressly

[158] Cf. also G. E. Mendenhall, *op. cit.*, p. 54, n. 12.
[159] See W, p. 80 f., l. 3 f.
[159a] Cf. W, p. 28 f., l. 37 f.
[160] *Vide supra*, section II. 3, pp. 52 f.
[161] Cf. on this V. Korošec, *op. cit.*, pp. 15 f.

stated in the old Yahwistic tradition of Exod. xxxiv. 27 f.,[162] which is repeated in Deut. x. 1–5—clearly because it was regarded as a reliable reference[163]—that the 'ten words' were written down. Besides, what else in fact could have been written on the two stone tables, which both the Elohistic and the Yahwistic accounts refer to on more than one occasion,[164] but a text of extreme brevity such as exists for instance in a legal summary like the Decalogue? To this extent it may be allowed that H. Gressmann was right in saying that the necessary equivalent of the Tables of the Law was the Ten Commandments.[165] All in all there are good grounds for the view that the covenant-form followed by the Hittite treaties acted as a formative influence in the case of the Decalogue and the motives which led to it being written down.

On more than one occasion the treaties referred to make it clear that there were at least two parts to this making of a written record: the Hittite king as the founder of the covenant is responsible for the written record of the treaty, a copy of which is given to the vassal. Ḫattušil III, for example, in his treaty with an Amorite king says: 'I, the Great King, wrote (it, i.e. the tablet) to Bentešina, the King of the land of Amurru . . . and gave it to him'.[166] In view of this it might at least be asked whether the Elohistic account of Exod. xxiv. 12b; xxxi. 18b; xxxii. 16, according to which God himself inscribed the tables of stone and then delivered them to the covenant-people through Moses, could not have been influenced by this already existing form—a form which, as already stated, was part of the covenant-outline. (The description in the Elohistic tradition of Exod. xxiv. 4, which is linked with the Decalogue by means of Exod. xx. 1, and in the Yahwistic tradition of Exod. xxxiv. 1a, 4, 27 f., according to which Moses, and not Yahweh, writes the document, is not substantially different from this other version, since Moses acts here on Yahweh's orders and in Yahweh's place.)

Now that it is quite clear from the treaty between Muršiliš II and Rimišarma what real importance the existence of a written copy of

[162] *Vide supra* section I. 10. The verses referred to are older, at any rate, than the gloss (probably influenced by E) in Exod. xxxiv. 1b, according to which Yahweh himself is responsible for the writing, whereas in Exod. xxxiv. 27 f. Moses does the writing. The words 'ten words' (xxxiv. 28) certainly belong to the oldest part of these verses. Cf. H. Holzinger, *KHC*, 2, p. 119.

[163] Cf. v. 4. Some of the exact words in the above section of Deuteronomy are taken from Exod. xxxiv.

[164] Cf. Exod. xxiv. 12b; xxxi. 18b; xxxii. 15 f., 19–E; Exod. xxxiv. 1a, 4, 27 f.–J.

[165] *Mose und seine Zeit, FLRANT*, 18, p. 190. 'Das notwendige Äquivalent zu den Gesetzestafeln sind die Zehn Gebote . . .'.

[166] See W. p. 128 f., l. 29 f.; cf. further W, p. 80 f., l. 4 f.; 124 f., l. 6.

the treaty had for the realisation of the covenant (*vide supra*), it is easy to understand that the question of its *deposition* must also have been important. It is expressly stipulated in the treaty between the Hittite king, Šuppiluliuma, and Mattiwaza, the king of Mitanni: 'a duplicate of this tablet has been deposited before Šamas of Arinna, since Šamas of Arinna directs the rule of the king and queen. (A copy) has also been deposited before Teššub in the land of Mitanni.'[167]

Was there any element in the Decalogue corresponding to this aspect of the Hittite covenant-outline? Here again the not unfounded view that the Ten Commandments were written down leads almost necessarily to the further view that the Decalogue which was fixed in writing was deposited in a holy place. What else, in fact, could have been done with the document? Where but in the shrine of the covenant-God was the covenant-document, such as the Decalogue clearly was, judging by its structure, to be appropriately guarded? How could the covenant-treaty, whose embodiment in a document was considered of such real importance for the realisation of the treaty in the world of the ancient Orient, better be protected from destruction and loss than by being deposited in a shrine? But the assumption that the Decalogue was deposited in this way does not depend simply on such general reflections.[168] There is other evidence also: for instance, in the passage containing cultic ordinances in Deut. xxxi. 9–13, which provides for the periodic proclamation of the law, there is reference to this law being written down and deposited in a shrine—both in the same context. In v. 9 it says: 'And Moses wrote this law, and gave it to the priests the sons of Levi, who carried the Ark of the covenant of the Lord . . . '. According to Deut. xxxi. 26 Moses says, 'Take this book of the law, and put it by the side of the Ark of the covenant of the Lord your God (that it may be there for a witness against you . . .).'[169] These verses (clearly a secondary addition) obviously presuppose not only the cultic practice of a periodic recital of the law, which we shall return to later, but also the fact of a document and, linked with this, the custom of depositing the law in the shrine. Everything points to a close connection between the two. If it is assumed from the ordinance about a regular, periodic proclamation of the law that it was connected with 'an already

[167] See W, p. 26 f., l. 35 f. Cf. also G. Ricciotti, *The History of Israel*, I, p. 213, par. 253.

[168] Cf. for a fuller treatment the investigation of A. H. J. Gunneweg (which has been published meanwhile): *Mündliche und schriftliche Tradition der vorexilischen Prophetenbücher*, *FRLANT*, 73, pp. 78 f.

[169] Cf. On these verses O. Eissfeldt,' Die Umrahmung des Mose-Liedes', Deut. xxxii. 1–43 und des Mose-Gesetzes Deut. i–xxx in Deut. xxxi. 9–xxxii, 47', pp. 413 f.; cf. *BSAW*, vol. 104, part 5, pp. 48 f.

existing or at least still remembered older ordinance',[170] it may likewise be suspected that the written record of the law and its deposition in the shrine presuppose a corresponding older usage. If this indicates that the practice of depositing the text of a covenant-law in the shrine was well-known and well-attested in Israel also, then the tradition of Deut. x. 1–5, which (with clear reference to Exod. xxxiv.) expressly relates this cultic practice to the tables of the Decalogue, need not be considered inconceivable, at any rate. However one imagines this deposition in the cultic centre to have been transacted in detail,[171] the fact that documentary records which were important for the realisation of the covenant with Yahweh, as the Decalogue was, *were* deposited in the covenant-shrine is beyond dispute. It may be said, therefore, that the covenant-outline attested in the Hittite state-treaties was paralleled also in this respect in the Decalogue.

When these Hittite documents had been deposited in some holy place, however, this fact alone, although very important, was not sufficient. The documents deposited in the cultic centre were also to be used in the regular *recital of the treaty*. In the treaty of Šuppiluliuma and Mattiwaza the deposition of the document and its recital are spoken of in *one* breath: 'A duplicate of this tablet has been deposited before Šamaš of Arinna . . . In the Mitanni land also (a duplicate) has been deposited before Teššub. At regular intervals(?) they shall read it in the presence of the king of the Mitanni land and in the presence of the people of the Ḫurri country.'[172] But although the connection between the deposition of the treaty and its public recital emerges clearly, the stipulations quoted throw no light upon the time-sequence involved.[173] In this respect, however, the treaty between Muwatalliš and Alakšanduš is quite clear; 'moreover, this tablet which I have dispatched to you, Alakšanduš, is to be recited in your presence three times each year, and you, Alakšanduš, shall become familiar with it'.[174] Something similar should probably be read at the end of the treaty imposed on Kupanta-KAL.[175]

Once again the question arises as to whether the Decalogue, which has been shown to be a covenant-treaty in its structure, was also publicly read out in a similar way at regular intervals. It is true there

[170] A. Alt, *op. cit.*, *Kleine Schriften*, I, p. 326.
[171] Cf. for instance the reflections of H. Gressmann, *op. cit.*, pp. 188 f.
[172] See W, p. 26 f., l. 35 f.; cf. also W, p. 48 f., l. 7 f.
[173] On the linguistic difficulties of the passage, cf. W, p. 29, n. 3.
[174] See F2, p. 76 f., l. 73 f.
[175] Cf. F1, p. 150 f., l. 1 f.

is no regulation about this in the text of the Ten Commandments. Yet there can be no doubt that the Decalogue was proclaimed at more or less regular intervals in Israel's cult in some form or other.[176] The apodeictic clauses alone, which form the basis of the Decalogue, can only be understood both in respect of form and content against such a background of regular public proclamation: the I-thou style of these clauses corresponds to such a situation. The number ten, the uniformity of the separate commands, the marked brevity—all this shows consideration for the powers of comprehension and memory on the part of someone listening. Only a continuing cultic vitality, moreover, as already stated, can explain the plethora of interpretative clauses in the Decalogue and the reappearance of the Decalogue in Deuteronomy. In an earlier context the conclusion was reached[177] that there must have been a (more or less) regular proclamation of the law connected with the institution of the Israelite tribal confederacy, at least from the time of the covenant-cult at Shechem, similar to that practised in the cult of the Temple at Jerusalem later. This practice reveals the point in the worshipping life of the Israelite tribal confederacy at which, even apart from this, there would have been need felt for such a precise and definite summary of the law, well fitted for public proclamation in the cult, as in the case of the Decalogue. It may be affirmed, therefore, that the element of the covenant-form which related to the regular, public recital of the covenant-treaty also had a parallel in the Decalogue.

The Hittite vassal-treaties usually contained a list—very extensive, on the whole—of *witnesses to the covenant*. The nature of such a list may be illustrated by brief examples: '. . . because of this treaty we wish to invoke the gods of what is secret and the gods who (are) lords of the oath. They can enter, they can listen and (be) witnesses. Šamaš of Arinna, who directs the rule of the king and queen in the land of Ḫatti, Šamaš, lord of heaven, Teššub, lord of Ḫatti . . .' etc. etc.[178] In another treaty we read: '. . . for this oath we have summoned the thousand gods to the judgement-hall, and they are to hear and be witnesses . . .'.[179] Then there follows the roll-call of the gods who are acting as witnesses. It is noticeable how 'heaven and earth'

[176] Cf. the works of S. Mowinckel, G. von Rad, A. Alt, and J. Scharbert referred to above. Cf. also Psalms l, lxxxi.

[177] *Vide supra*, p. 40 f.

[178] Cf. W, p. 28 f., l. 38 f.; likewise p. 48 f., l. 10; further W, p. 66 f., ll. 9 f., 74 f., l. 1 f.; F2, p. 14 f., l. 1 f.; p. 76 f., l. 80 f.; p. 110 f., ll. 41 f.

[179] See F1, p. 68 f., ll. 55 f.

are always named as witnesses towards the end of the enumeration.[180] The formulae which introduce the lists of the gods make it abundantly clear that corresponding to this part of the Hittite treaty was a cultic act in which these gods were invoked in order that they might hear and witness the covenant-oath.[181]

Is there any evidence that there were covenant-witnesses for the Israelite Decalogue also, safeguarding its observance? It can be stated straightaway that the fundamental clause of the Yahwistic covenant, as it is formulated in the First Commandment (Exod. xx. 3), 'you shall have no other gods before me', utterly excludes the possibility of 'other gods' being invoked as witnesses to the ratification of a covenant like the Decalogue. No exact parallel, therefore to the lists of gods in the Hittite treaties can be expected in the Israelite Decalogue.[182] Nevertheless, this feature of witnesses ratifying the covenant is not absent in the relevant tradition of Israel. The existence of a written record was in itself a witness—in Israel as elsewhere (cf. for instance Deut. xxxi. 26b). But this formal characteristic had assumed an even more clear and definite shape in Israelite tradition: in the words of judgement found in the Prophets and Psalms,[183] which are even directed against Israel itself, heaven and earth are frequently invoked[184] as witnesses and judges.[185] All these words of judgement, like the judgement against Israel, are fundamentally connected with the ideas of the covenant.[186] Judgement and words of judgement against Israel are, in fact, only possible on the assumption of the covenant-relation, within which Israel receives Yahweh's gifts and accepts the obligation to obey his commands. Heaven and earth are invoked because they are witnesses of the covenant on both sides. In this respect Ps. 50 is particularly significant. Whether it is a direct or indirect reflection of a cultic ceremony

[180] Cf. for instance W, p. 30 f., l. 53; p. 50 f., l. 24; p. 68 f., l. 44; p. 74 f., l. 10; F2 p. 16 f., l. 27; p. 80 f., l. 26; p. 112 f., l. 58 f.

[181] Cf. the picture in the journal of the *Deutsche Orient-Gesellschaft*, 61, plate 15, 2 of a drawing of a procession of gods which surrounded a cultic centre (Yazilikaya) near the capital of the Hittite empire (Boghazköy) and which is perhaps to be understood in terms of this cultic act. This picture is also reproduced in G. E. Mendenhall, 'Covenant Forms in Israelite Tradition', BA 17/3, 1954, p. 61.

[182] Cf. also G. E. Mendenhall, *op. cit.*, p. 66.

[183] Cf. E. Würthwein, 'Der Ursprung der prophetischen Gerichtsrede', *ZThK*, 49, 1952, pp. 1 f.

[184] Cf. E. Würthwein, *op. cit.*, pp. 4, 10, 15, n. 2. Cf. apart from this Deut. xxxi. 28 also.

[185] Cf. L. Köhler, 'Die hebräische Rechtsgemeinde', in: *Der hebräische Mensch*, p. 152: 'Richter und Zeuge sind . . . nicht von einander geschieden. Derselbe Mann kann in derselben Sache und an derselben Gerichtstagung als Zeuge und als Richter angerufen werden'.

[186] Cf. A. Weiser, *The Psalms*, p. 36; E. Würthwein, *op. cit.*, p. 12.

in its present form,[187] the outlines of some sort of cultic action can be recognised in its structure. What is important from our present point of view is that the act of judgement relating to the covenant-people clearly reveals the close connection between the recapitulation of the Decalogue (vv. 7b, 18–21) and the invocation of the covenant-witnesses (especially v. 4): 'He calls to the heavens above and to the earth, that he may judge his people'. In this cultic act which seems to have had the character of a Judgement-scene it becomes apparent that heaven and earth are witnesses, as in the covenant with Yahweh and the clauses of the Decalogue. In the Hittite vassal-treaties, too, as stated, 'heaven and earth' were always invoked as covenant-witnesses. This indicates afresh the extent to which the covenant-form underlying the Hittite vassal treaties was paralleled in the Decalogue. Finally, in this connection, it remains to notice that this feature (the covenant-witness) also reappears in a different shape in the Israelite tradition: in the cult of the covenant at Shechem according to Joshua xxiv. 26 f.[188] a large stone acted as witness that the covenant had been made—a stone which Joshua erected in explicit connection with a written record of the law and which he is supposed to have presented to the covenant-people with the words: 'Behold, this stone shall be a witness against us; for it has heard all the words of Yahweh which he spoke to us. . . .' (Joshua xxiv. 27). On the understanding that the Sinai tradition must once have formed the content of the ancient covenant-festival at Shechem,[189] this stone serving as a witness reaches back into the immediate environment of the covenant made at Sinai. (A further consideration is the fact that such a stone was probably thought of as Yahweh's dwelling in popular piety[190]—a view suggested by Gen. xxxi. 45 f. (JE) also—so that, lying suppressed behind the stone of witness in the authorised tradition there may well be concealed the idea of popular piety that Yahweh himself was the covenant-witness.) The close connection between the stone at Shechem and the pillars mentioned in Exod. xxiv. 4 has already been established in an earlier chapter.[191] Although there is no doubt that in this passage of the Sinai tradition the twelve stones have been

[187] Cf. G. von Rad, *op. cit.*, *Gesammelte Studien*, p. 30. On the other hand, see for instance E. Würthwein, *op. cit.*, p. 12, Cf. moreover W. Caspari, 'Kultpsalm 50', *ZAW*, 45, 1927, pp. 254–66.

[188] Cf. above, p. 54 f. (In Joshua xxiv. 1, 25 the *MT* 'Shechem' is to be preferred to the *LXX* 'Shilo.' So also J. Muilenburg. *VT* 9, 1959, p. 357.)

[189] Cf. G. von Rad, *op. cit.*, *Gesammelte Studien*, p. 47.

[190] Cf. for instance G. Beer, *Steinverehrung bei den Israeliten*, pp. 10 f.; A. Jirku, *Die Ausgrabungen in Palästina und Syrien*, p. 91.

[191] Cf. above, p. 54 f.

interpreted as representatives of the twelve tribes of Israel, not as covenant-witnesses, it is not improbable that this explanation of the Elohist in Exod. xxiv. 4 has suppressed and replaced a version corresponding to Joshua xxiv. 26 f.: at an earlier date this passage of the Sinai tradition also probably mentioned a stone of witness. In the course of the attempt to rob the pillars more and more of their independent importance,[192] however, and to subordinate them more securely to the aims of the cult of Yahweh, the witness-stone of Shechem was transformed into the symbolic stone of the tribal confederacy.[193] It is probable, therefore, that the unit of tradition dealing with the making of the covenant on Sinai (Exod. xxiv. 3–8) also contained a reference to the covenant-witness, which was a characteristic element of the ancient treaty-form.

At the beginning or the end of the list of witnesses mentioned in the Hittite treaties there may occur these words: those named 'are to be witnesses to this treaty and to the oath'.[194] Or: 'We have summoned a thousand gods to the hall of judgement for this oath, and they are to listen and be witnesses'.[195] It will turn out well, 'if you, Mattiwaza, and (you), the Ḫurrians, observe this treaty and oath'.[196] The vassal himself is called 'a man of oath and treaty'.[197] The conclusion to be drawn from all this is that, linked with the cultic invocation of the gods, the 'lords of the oath',[198] the vassal also bound himself to the oath and treaty with a ceremonial oath. The signing of the covenant was obviously accompanied by a cultic *affirmation of obligation.** There are no texts which prove that when the treaty was periodically recited, as shown above, in the presence of the vassal prince (and his people) they responded in some way confirming their oath. One can only assume that the vassal and his people could not let the proclamation of the law take place in silent passivity without them making any response. At this point they could have appealed in some way to the oath of obedience they had once taken.

Was there a similar affirmation of obligation associated with the proclamation of the Decalogue? We shall begin by recalling the

[192] On the older forms of stone-worship, cf. for instance G. Beer, *op. cit.*, pp. 8 f.; G. van der Leeuw, *Religion in Essence and Manifestation*, pp. 53 ff. See also R. Brinker, *The Influence of Sanctuaries in Early Israel*, p. 52.

[193] Cf. above, p. 46.

[194] See W, p. 68 f., l. 45 f.

[195] See F1, p. 68 f., l. 55 f.

[196] See W, p. 52 f., l. 35.

[197] Cf. W, p. 62 f., l. 26 f.

[198] Cf. W, p. 28 f., l. 39.

* Tr. note: the German word is 'Verpflichtungsakt'; cf. III. 3 below. Another translation would be 'act of commitment'.

result of an earlier discussion,[199] according to which (cf. Joshua xxiv. 24; Deut. xxvii. 15 f.) the amphictyonic cult at Shechem, like the cult at Jerusalem sometimes under the monarchy (cf. 2 Kings xxiii. 3; xi. 17; 2 Chron. xv. 12, 14) and like the worship of the post-exilic community (cf. Neh. viii. 6), issued in an affirmation of obligation by the people of Israel, such as they repeatedly made afresh in response to the proclamation of God's commands (in 2 Kings xxiii. 3 the people's response is joined with that of the king). The formal nature of the three versions of Israel's oath of covenant-obligation on Sinai in Exod. xxiv. 3, 7; xix. 7 f. also tells in favour of the affirmation of obligation to the published commands of God being a cultic, recurrent act. In the composition of the Sinai tradition the formalised precepts of Exod. xxiv. 3, 7 have been related to the Decalogue by means of Exod. xx. 1. The existence of a recurrent, cultic affirmation of obligation in relation to this particular summary of the commandments is very probable in the light of all the evidence, especially if the list of apodeictic legal clauses in Deut. xxvii. 15 f., for instance, was also part of the response of the cultic community binding them to obedience. Everything suggests, therefore, that there are good grounds for the view that the Decalogue was followed, each time it was proclaimed, by an affirmation of obligation on the part of the community, so that this feature of the covenant-outline (cultic affirmation of obligation) was also paralleled in the cultic context of the Decalogue.

Summary. From the point of view of form not only does the inner structure of the Decalogue correspond in a number of striking ways to the covenant-outline familiar from the Hittite vassal-treaties, but the manner and style of the cultic use of the Israelite Decalogue obviously correspond to that cultic framework of the Hittite state-treaties which accompanied the covenant-outline. The following correspondences have been demonstrated: the covenant author's introduction of himself at the beginning of the treaty, the historical prologue, the I-thou style of the most important parts of this prologue, the fact that the prologue is followed immediately by the covenant-clauses (with the most fundamental and comprehensive demand heading the list), the exclusive claims of the initiator of the treaty, the description of the clauses as 'words' of the author of the covenant, the sanctions to be applied in the case of the covenant being broken, the written record of the treaty, the two actions connected with its record in writing—namely its deposition and its

[199] *Vide supra*, pp. 40 f.

periodic recital—the presence of covenant-witnesses and finally the affirmation of covenant-obligation. Now that the reasons have been given for the view that the covenant-form underlying the Hittite vassal-treaties was also familiar to ancient Israel it may be considered proven that the formal structure of the Decalogue should not be considered as Israel's creation but as modelled on this existing, well-established treaty-form.

Looking back at the passages of the Sinai tradition discussed earlier, it is noticeable that in the unit of tradition Exod. xxiv. 3–8 there are several of the formal elements which have been shown to belong to this covenant-outline and to which parallels have also been established in the Decalogue and its cultic framework. In its account of the making of the covenant on Sinai Exod. xxiv. 3–8 includes the following elements which are characteristic of this covenant-outline: 1. the public recital of the covenant-treaty (v. 7; cf. v. 3), 2. the ceremonial affirmation of obligation by the covenant-people (*ibid.*), 3. the written record (v. 4a) and 4. witnesses to the making of the covenant (in the shape of pillars—v. 4b). If the conjecture of G. E. Mendenhall[200] is correct, namely that this outline implied there was a ceremonial rite associated with the affirmation of covenant-obligation, the sacrifice of Exod. xxiv. 5 and above all the rite of the twofold sprinkling of blood in Exod. xxiv. 6, 8 could be regarded as a fifth structural element of the covenant-form to be found in what is a comparatively small unit of tradition, Exod. xxiv. 3–8. There is no need to assume that this striking accumulation of four or five elements characteristic of the covenant-outline is purely accidental. Rather, the tradition of Exod. xxiv. 3–8 obviously reflects something of the covenant-form—the same form which provided the formal model for the Decalogue. Both units of tradition have been equally subject to its formative influence. Both find their common denominator in it. Both, when considered from the point of view of this covenant-outline, reveal their similarity of internal structure. The fact that they were combined in the course of the tradition's history and that they stood directly next to each other prior to the insertion of the Book of the Covenant[201] is not altogether irrelevant. What has here been joined together in the history of tradition originally belonged together. The Decalogue is essentially the *sēp̄er habbᵉrîṯ*.[202]

[200] Cf. *ibid.* pp. 60 f.
[201] *Vide supra*, section I. 2.
[202] Cf. Exod. xxiv. 7.

It is true, of course, that we are not indebted to the skill of a 'source-author' or the insight of a tradent for the combination of these traditions in accordance with their related character. If both the Decalogue and Exod. xxiv. 3–8 received their present shape under the influence of a covenant-outline already in existence, so also the *further* development, in the course of which these two traditions were combined, is most naturally explained as having taken place under the influence of the same covenant-outline: the parts modelled on it, the historical tradition of the covenant made on Sinai and the written record of this, were combined in a way corresponding to their internal structural links. In this structure both traditions are set in the proper light to illumine their real nature.[203]

The suggestion that this covenant-form not only impressed itself on the basic material of the two sets of tradition but continued to be vital and active carries great weight, especially when the results of the examination of the traditions in Exod. xxiv. 3–8 are recalled. According to these results the account of the making of the covenant on Sinai was paralleled in all important points in cultic practice. The public recital of Yahweh's commands (Exod. xxiv. 3, 7) corresponded to a more or less regular, periodic recital of God's law in the covenant-cult. The ceremonial affirmation of obligation by Israel on Sinai (*ibid.*) corresponded to the cultic community's repeated promises of obedience in the cult.[204] Parallel to the account of Yahweh's commands being written down in Exod. xxiv. 4a is the cultic act of recording the law in writing, or in other words the fact of a written draft of the law.[205] The pillars of Exod. xxiv. 4b, which witness the making of the covenant on Sinai (*vide supra*), evidently corresponded to the pillars which accompanied the cult of Yahweh when it was transferred from one place to another.[206] (The description of the sacrifice which ratified the covenant and the sprinkling of blood in Exod. xxiv. 5, 6, 8 has been handed down, judging by the evidence, under the influence of a corresponding priestly ter-

[203] It may be observed here that the distinctive union of legal and historical tradition in the OT. goes back to this structure which was conditioned by the covenant-form which already existed (cf. G. E. Mendenhall, *op. cit.*, pp. 70 f.). It is, moreover, foreshadowed in a distinctive characteristic of the internal structure of this covenant-form: the introduction of the Hittite vassal-treaty prepares the way for the following clauses of the covenant and confirms them by means of a historical prologue. Similarly the clauses of the covenant in the Israelite Decalogue are based on a historical prologue which refers to Yahweh's saving-history. Thus, from the very beginning law and salvation-history were linked at this point.

[204] *Vide supra*, pp. 40 f.

[205] *Vide supra*, pp. 44 f.

[206] *Vide supra*, pp. 45 f.

minology).[207] If, then, these four different elements (the reading of the law, the oath of obedience, the written document and the act of witnessing the making of the covenant) in Exod. xxiv. 3–8 obviously took shape under the influence of this covenant-form and find their unity within the framework of this covenant-outline, the cultic practices which correspond to them ought also to be understood as a unity rather than disparate elements. For instance, apart from the fact that the reading of the law and the written document, on the one hand, and the reading of the law and the oath of obedience, on the other, require each other and must be related, the tradition also contains other specific indications that these cultic practices did not exist in isolation from each other but all belonged to *one* context. It has been repeatedly demonstrated in considering the traditions of Exod. xxiv. 3–8 that the corresponding cultic practices were not, on the whole, attached to different local shrines at any given time, but rather found their way from the covenant-cult at Shechem to the cult of the Jerusalem Temple under the monarchy in connection with the sacral tribal confederacy of Israel.[208] Their connection with each other is also rooted in this common link they have with one and the same institution.[209] Everything favours the view, therefore, that this covenant-form not only shaped the kernel of the traditions in Exod. xxiv. 3–8 and Exod. xx. 1–17, as stated, but that it also continued to be alive and active in the cultic practices corresponding to these traditions, keeping them within the framework of its outline and thus at length combining these two parts of the Sinai tradition. All the cultic practices, therefore, which have been examined in discussing the above traditions, evidently took their unity from this covenant-outline. The cult in which they had their place can be called, in view of this, the *covenant-cult*. Any influence of contemporary cultic practice that made its mark on these passages of the Sinai tradition and thus contributed to their eventual shape is, from all the evidence, best considered as a retroactive influence of that cult in which the same covenant-form that had previously determined the basic structure of these units of tradition was still at work.

The covenant-form active in Israel's cult, however, not only united the Decalogue, Exod. xx. 1–17, and the tradition of the covenant made on Sinai, Exod. xxiv. 3–8; it should also probably be under-

[207] For the influences on the diction of this verse cf. above, p. 38, n. 73.

[208] *Vide supra*, pp. 41 f.

[209] This connection is also apparent, for instance, in Joshua xxiv; Deut. xxvii, 15 f.; 2 Kings xxiii. 1–3; Deut. xxxi 9–13; Neh. viii; Ps. l, which refer to clusters of themes associated with these cultic practices.

stood as one of the driving forces in the whole process of the composition of the Sinai traditions. It probably included in its structure the ceremonial rite which accompanied the oath of covenant-obligation[210] and thus may have brought about the insertion of the ancient piece of tradition regarding the covenant-meal in Exod. xxiv. 1a, 9–11, thereby linking it with the tradition of the covenant-sacrifice and the sprinkling of blood (Exod. xxiv. 5, 6, 8).

6. Exodus xix. 3b–8

The Elohistic tradition of Exod. xix. 3b–8 also mentions the Sinaitic covenant.[211] Yahweh's word is conveyed to Israel by the mediation of Moses: 'Now, therefore, if you will obey my voice and keep my covenant, you shall be my own possession (*s^egullâh*)[212] among all peoples; for all the earth is mine' (xix. 5). The relation of Israel to Yahweh, it is well-known, is described three times in Deuteronomy by the same term *s^egullâh* (vii. 6; xiv. 2; xxvi. 18), and twice by the same phrase *mikkol hā'ammîm* (vii. 6; xiv. 2). In all three cases this particular relationship is undoubtedly referred to with a view to basing the aims and requirements of Deuteronomy on it and getting them established in Israel.[213] The very fact that this idea of the chosen people could be appealed to and was in fact appealed to more than once presupposes, however, that it was already very well-known and widely established. This raises the question once more whether it was not perhaps in Israel's cult that its relationship to Yahweh was described in this way and made known to the cultic community. Deut. xxvi. 17–19 points to this: 'You have made Yahweh declare (*he'^emartā*)[214] this day that he is your God . . . (v. 17), and Yahweh has declared this day (*he'^emīreka*) that you are a people for his own possession (*'am s^egullâh*) . . .' (v. 18).[215] There

[210] Cf. G. E. Mendenhall, *op. cit.*, pp. 60 f.

[211] On the limits of this section and its inclusion in the E-source cf. above, I. 3.

[212] The basic meaning of the word is probably 'what has been spared, savings, treasure', corresponding to the Akkadian *sikiltu*. So M. Greenberg, 'Hebrew *s^egullā*: Accadian *sikiltu*', *JAOS* 71, 1951, pp. 172–4. For other explanations of the word cf. also M. Buber, *Königtum Gottes*, 3rd ed., p. 206, n. 69.

[213] Even if C. Steuernagel (*Das Deuteronomium, HK* 3/1, p. 146) is right in thinking that xxvi 17–19 depends on xxviii. 69–xxix. 28 and was added to xxvi. 16 later, this would not disprove our view; it would only illustrate how men tried to base the warning to obey the Deuteronomic clauses and laws on this *s^egullâh mikkol hā'ammîm*.

[214] The *haireisthai* of the LXX in vv. 17–18 can hardly have preserved the original meaning of the passage.

[215] The various changes proposed in Deut. xxvi. 17–19 find no support in the tradition of the Greek text, at any rate. Cf. also the Papyrus Greek 458 from the second century. B.C. according to the *Catalogue of the Greek and Latin Papyri in the John Rylands Library Manchester*, vol. iii, ed. by C. H. Roberts, p. 5.

can be no doubt that these words refer to a cultic act corresponding to the affirmation of covenant-obligation.[216] Yahweh has promised to make his covenant 'today', and Israel has promised to obey it 'today'. This can only be the 'today' of worship, the day on which the covenant with Yahweh is realised anew,[217] the day on which Yahweh makes himself known as Israel's God through the declaration of a cultic official and formally binds the cultic community to himself as his *'am s^egullâh*. It is because this clearly involves a very familiar, formal promise, undertaken in a cultic act, that at three different points in Deuteronomy the discussion revolves round such a formula, the same formula on each occasion.

The cultic act of affirming covenant-obligations, in which this formal phrase was rooted, must then be understood, however, as one of the circumstances *presupposed* by the Deuteronomic reform, otherwise it could hardly have served as a point of contact for the Deuteronomic exhortation by reason of its formality. The same conclusion is also strongly suggested by the fact that in his preaching the prophet Jeremiah tried to go back to the 'covenant-formula' which had evidently been handed down in the cult at Jerusalem: 'I will be your God, and you shall be my people'.[218] Both in content and style this formula is obviously very closely related to the formula disclosed by Deuteronomy. Everything suggests, therefore, that even *before* Jeremiah and the Deuteronomic reform there must have been an affirmation of covenant-obligations in the cult at Jerusalem at which Yahweh formally declared himself Israel's God and Israel acknowledged itself as the people belonging to Yahweh.[219]

With regard to Exod. xix. 5 the following comments must be made: the fact that this verse, like Deuteronomy, describes Israel as Yahweh's *s^egullâh mikkol hā'ammîm*, is not to be taken as involving the literary dependence of either passage on the other;[219a] rather Exod. xix. 5 is to be understood in connection with the same cultic affirmation of obligation and the same covenant-formula as the Deuterono-

[216] According to G. Fohrer 'Der Vertrag zwischen König und Volk in Israel', *ZAW* 71, 1959, p. 21, this was related to the treaty with the king. Cf. below, pp. 74 f.

[217] Cf. G. von Rad, *Das formgeschichtliche Problem des Hexateuch* (=*Gesammelte Studien*, pp. 35 f.)

[218] Cf. for instance Jer. vii. 23; xi. 4; xxiv. 7; xxx. 22; xxxi. 1, 33; xxxii. 38. Cf. A. Weiser, *Der Prophet Jeremia*, *ATD* 21, 3rd. ed., pp. 470 f.

[219] According to A. Weiser ('Das Deboralied, eine form-und traditionsgeschichtliche Studie', *ZAW* 71, 1959, p. 73) this song from the early history of Israel, which seems to have been a liturgical composition for the celebration of the cult of Yahweh, contains a brief, formal confession of faith in Yahweh (the words of Judges v. 3—'I belong to Yahweh'—which are to be understood as an independent clause), which had its *Sitz im Leben* in the cultic ceremony for the renewal of the covenant.

[219a] Cf. also G. von Rad, *op. cit.*, *Gesammelte Studien*, p. 47, n. 47.

mic preaching also refers to. Both in form and content this verse undoubtedly refers to such a cultic formula and scene.

If Exod. xix. 5 is compared with Deut. xxvi. 17 f., however, the result is that in Deuteronomy Israel's *s^e^gullâh*-profession of faith is nearer to the original interpretation of the unconditional promise than the text of the passage in Exodus. In Exod. xix. 5 the covenant-formula is subordinate to the exhortation: '*If*, then, you will obey my voice and keep my covenant, you shall be my own possession among all peoples . . .'. This hortatory modification and application of the covenant-formula is not without parallel in the cultic tradition, as is shown by Ps. l. 7; lxxxi. 9–12; xxxiii. 12 and cxliv. 15 and especially by Ps. xcv. 7, and as is indirectly implied by Jer. vii. 23 and xi. 4, which clearly embody a cultic-hortatory style. Exod. xix. 5, therefore, is not only related to the cultic affirmation of covenant-obligation in content, insofar as there is an element of this covenant-formula present, but may in fact, judging by its cultic-hortatory language, have grown out of the liturgy of the covenant-cult.

What can be said particularly of Exod. xix. 5, however, applies also to the *whole* of Exod. xix. 3b–8. It is closely connected with the same covenant that is embodied in contractual form in the Decalogue and the ratification and cultic observance of which is attested especially in Exod. xxiv. 3–8. This connection is apparent from the fact that within this unit of tradition several of the elements which are characteristic of the Decalogue and its formal model,[220] the covenant-form[221] well-known from the Hittite vassal-treaties, recur. It is significant, for instance, that the exhortation in Exod. xix. 4[222] to obey Yahweh's voice and keep his covenant (v. 5) is preceded and confirmed by an emphatic reference to what has previously taken place between the parties to the covenant: by his gracious act of deliverance at the Exodus, Yahweh, the author of the covenant, has bound Israel to gratitude and obedience. Moreover, this historical prologue is in the I-thou style, just like the Decalogue and the covenant-form on which it was based. There is, of course, only a summary reference to the separate clauses of the covenant (v. 5a). But the basic clause which was characteristic of the covenant-form and of the Decalogue that was modelled on it, namely that the author of the covenant makes exclusive claims on his 'partner', is very clearly marked (Exod. xix. 5b: 'you shall be my own possession'

[220] Cf. above section II. 5.

[221] Cf. also the essay of J. Muilenburg, 'The form and structure of the covenantal formulations', *VT*. 9, 1959, pp. 354 f.

[222] On the age of this passage cf. M. Buber, *op. cit.*, p. 64.

—*sᵉgullâh*). Finally in v. 8, again corresponding to the covenant-outline, the people 'reply' with a formal promise of obedience to the proclaimed will of God.[223] It may be taken as probable, therefore, that the whole structure of Exod. xix. 3b–8 is based on that of the Decalogue (Exod. xx. 2–17), as the *sēḇer habbᵉrîṯ*, and on the act of making a covenant, as reflected particularly in Exod. xxiv. 3–8. All the evidence suggests that Exod. xix. 3b–8, like these two other pieces of tradition, took shape in the context of the covenant-cult and under the formative influence of the covenant-form which found expression in the cult.

In addition, the style and language of Exod. xix. 3b–8, which shows signs of a definite rhythm in its central section, reveal that the present form of the passage stems from Israel's worship.[224] Verses 3 and 4, for example, clearly bear a liturgical-hortatory stamp just as much as v. 5: the commissioning formula. *kō tō'mar lᵉḇēyṯ ya'ᵃkōḇ wᵉṯagged libnê yiśrā'ēl* (v. 3), is invested with special solemnity as a result of its unusual *parallelismus membrorum*,[225] which is exactly what one would expect in the context of a religious ceremony of worship. The fact that the synonymous parallelism Jacob/Israel occurs chiefly in the Psalms[226] apart from here confirms the suspicion that this formula goes back to the linguistic usage of the cult. The historical prologue, one of the elements of the covenant-outline, found in Exod. xix. 4, which emphasises the deliverance of the Exodus, certainly possesses a cultic-hortatory character in view of its striking link with a verse in the Song of Moses (Deut. xxxii. 11), where the same metaphor (eagle, *nešer*) as is used in the Sinai-pericope is used in a liturgical-hortatory context.[227] The introductory words, 'you have seen . . .', which appeal to the personal experience of the hearers and which frequently occur in this form in religious exhortations,[228] indicate that they, too, had their *Sitz im Leben* in the exhortation of worship.[229]

[223] Cf. above on Exod. xxiv. 3, 7.

[224] Cf. also J. Muilenburg, *op. cit.*, pp. 352 f.

[225] Cf. S. Mandelkern, *Veteris Testamenti Concordantiae*, 2nd ed., p. 118.

[226] Cf. for instance Ps. xiv. 7 (liii. 7); cv. 23; cxiv. 1; cxxxv. 4; and especially cxlvii. 19.

[227] On the pre-monarchic dating of the Song (eleventh century) cf. O. Eissfeldt, 'Das Lied Moses Deuteronomium xxxii. 1–43 . . . ', *BSAW* Vol. 104, part 5, pp. 15–24; W. F. Albright, 'Some remarks on the Song of Moses in Deuteronomy xxxii', *VT* 9, 1959, pp. 339 f.

[228] Cf. Deut. xxix. 1 for the most extensive parallel; also Deut. i. 19, 31; iv. 9; x. 21; Josh. xxiii. 3. Moreover, the hortatory mode of speech delights in referring to Yahweh's saving act in bringing the Israelites out of Egypt; on this cf. also Deut. vii. 18; xi. 3, 4. See also the survey of J. Muilenburg, *op. cit.*, p. 354.

[229] The numerous points of contact between Exod. xix. 3b–8 and the language and style of Deuteronomy (cf. for instance the list in B. Baentsch *HK* 2/1 p. 171; see also M.

The following conclusions seem quite certain, therefore: Exod. xix. 3b–8 is structurally related to the written covenant of the Decalogue and the act of making a covenant; its form and development were conditioned by the covenant-cult and the covenant-form to which the cult gave expression; it emphasised an act of covenant-obligation and its formula; and lastly, but not least, it played an active part in the cult in the form of liturgical exhortation.

Exod. xix. 5 promised Israel that if she were obedient and loyal to the covenant she would then really be Yahweh's 'own possession among all peoples' in accordance with her cultic declaration; in Exod. xix. 6a, a further definition of the chosen people is set alongside, *we'attem tihyu-lî mamleket kōhanîm wegôy kādôš.*[230] *We'attem* ('and you') is used adversatively here and the general train of thought could be paraphrased as follows: 'You above all shall belong to me. The right to choose you is based on the fact (*kî*) that the whole earth and therefore all peoples belong to me. *You*, however, belong to me by an act of choice and especially because you are allied to me by a special internal organisation and structure not shared by other nations. The whole earth is mine;[231] *but you* shall be mine as *mamleket kōhanîm wegôy kādôš*.' W. Caspari has shown that these concepts, which seek to indicate how Israel belonged to its god in a different manner from other nations, also refer to the internal structure and institutions of the chosen people.[232] In estimating the significance possessed by the term *mmlkt* in this passage it is useful to consider its use in

[230] Cf. on this passage and its varied interpretation in the history of OT. textual transmission and criticism R. B. Y. Scott, 'A kingdom of priests (Exod. xix. 6)', *OTS* 8, 1950. pp. 213 f. Scott himself (like J. B. Bauer, 'Könige und Priester, ein heiliges Volk (Exod, xix. 6)', *Biblische Zeitschrift*, N.F. 2, 1958, pp. 283 f.) understands the passage as follows: ' " a kingdom set apart like a priesthood", and possessing collectively the priestly status of a "holy nation" ' (p. 218).

[231] Cf. below pp. 75 f.

[232] 'Das priesterliche Königreich', *ThBl.* viii, 1929, col. 105 f.

Haelvoet, *La Théophanie du Sinai*, *ALBO* II. 39, pp. 376 f.) do not necessarily imply dependence on Deuteronomy (M. Noth, *Exodus*, p. 157 obviously takes a different view). S. Mowinckel offered a different interpretation in *Le Décalogue*, p. 7: 'The Deuteronomic character of an expression does not necessarily prove that it is of recent origin. It only proves that the expression has become part of the language of the cult; for D was published by personnel of the Jerusalem Temple'. The fact that the liturgical-hortatory style of Deuteronomy does not belong exclusively to Deuteronomy has been proved by G. von Rad in his form-critical studies of the Holiness Code (cf. *Studies in Deuteronomy*, pp. 25–9). A Weiser, *Der Prophet Jeremia*, *ATD* 21, 4th ed., p. xxxvii, n. 1 observes that the liturgical-hortatory preaching form shows signs of having been in existence before Deuteronomy. Cf. also J. Bright, 'The date of the prose sermons of Jeremiah', *JBL* 70, 1951, pp. 25 f.

Phoenician inscriptions of the 5–4th cent. B.C.[233] One's first impression is that *mlk* and *mmlkt* both mean 'king'.[234] That there is a distinction is suggested by the fact that for a title directly connected with the name of its bearer 'king' (*mlk*) is always used, not 'kingdom' (*mmlkt*) (cf. the inscription from Byblus dealing with Jeḥomelek,[235] ll. 1, 7–9, and the Sidonian inscription of Ešmun'azar, ll. 1, 2, 13–15), whereas, if a specific holder of the office of king is not intended so much as the office itself or all its possible holders collectively, then 'kingdom' is used instead of 'king' (cf. the Jeḥomelek-inscription, l. 2: *mmlkt 'l gbl*, cf. *ibid.* l. 11, and the Ešmun'azar-inscription, ll. 4, 6, 20: *kl mmlkt wkl 'dm*). The abstract *mmlkt*, therefore, refers to the king's sphere of activity and his office as a permanent institution rather than any particular representative or holder of this office (cf. also 1 Sam. x. 18). The formula *kl mmlkt wkl 'dm*, which is used on several occasions in Phoenician inscriptions to describe or address the *whole* public *en bloc*, makes it clear that *mmlkt* is understood here as an organic component of a whole that is greater than the ruling body to which the inhabitants of the state concerned are subject and ally. Since king and people are frequently mentioned together in this way in the O.T. also,[236] and since there are other examples of a whole being described in two parts without its own name (world=heaven and earth),[237] this suggests that the phrase *mmlkt khnim wgoy kdoš* in Exod. xix. 6 is also to be understood as a similar synthesis of two allied powers, especially since considerable difficulties would arise if the copula here were interpreted epexegetically and the two ideas joined by it had to be understood independently and in opposite senses.[238] Thus, in Exod. xix. 6, by all the evidence Israel, the peculiar people of God, is described in two ways: a holy nation[239] (i.e. separated for Yahweh) with the kingly office and authority of priests at its head. This description of the people of God, which suits the pre-monarchic sacral tribal confederacy of Israel very well, stems from the time when the institution of the monarchy in Israel was not yet established. The *mmlkt khnim*, however, is not an inde-

[233] A different view is taken by M. Buber, *op. cit.*, p. 104 and 206. Since, however, in 1 Kings x. 20 and Amos vii. 13 the word *mmlkt* is most probably to be understood from the Phoenician (with W. F. Albright, *JAOS* 60, 1940, p. 422), the quotation of Phoenician inscriptions seems justified.

[234] Cf. M. Lidzbarski, *Handbuch der nordsemitischen Epigraphik*, I. Text, p. 310.

[235] According to M. Lidzbarski, *op. cit.*, pp. 416 f.

[236] For details cf. W. Caspari, *op. cit.*, col. 106 f.

[237] Cf. for instance Gen. i. 1; xiv. 19; Ps. lxxiii. 25; lxxxix. 12; Jer. xxiii. 24.

[238] Further details in W. Caspari, *op. cit.*, col. 107 f.

[239] This expression is un-Deuteronomic. Cf. G. von Rad, *Das formgeschichtliche Problem des Hexateuch* (=*Gesammelte Studien*, p. 47, n. 47).

pendent authority; rather, it is subject to the will of Yahweh. This finds clear expression in the formula *thiu li mmlkt khnim* also. This *mmlkh* belongs to Yahweh and obeys him; he is its head. Israel, Yahweh's *s^e^gullâh mikkol hā'ammîm*, is related to Yahweh in its two-fold structure of holy nation and priestly *mmlkh* and therefore belongs to him in a special way.

When it is seen how deeply the Elohistic tradition of Exod. xix. 3b–8 is rooted—in fundamentals—in the ancient Israelite institution of the sacral tribal union[240] another impression also strikes one: everything points to it having been easy at that time to think of Yahweh in connection with a 'kingdom' and to regard him as the highest authority to which it was subject. Although Yahweh is not expressly called 'king' here, it is clear that this category was not considered incompatible with his nature.[241] Yahweh himself meets this separate, peculiar people and reveals his will in the kingly office and rule of the priests. Would not Yahweh also, therefore, have been understood in a manner corresponding to the way he had manifested himself?[242]

An affirmative answer to this question commends itself from another direction. As stated, the written covenant of the Decalogue (Exod. xx. 2–17) and the unit of tradition at present under discussion (Exod. xix. 3b–8) are both based upon a covenant-form similar to that found in the Hittite vassal-treaties. This covenant-form, also to be found in the covenant with Yahweh and its cult, was in turn based on *state-treaties*, which at least among the Hittites, were made and concluded by the ruling Hittite *king*. The King always begins to speak in the first words of the treaty: 'Thus (says) the Sun, Šuppiluliuma, the Great King, King of the land of Ḫatti . . .'.[243] 'Thus (says) the Sun, Muršiliš, the Great King, King of the land of Ḫatti . . .'.[244] 'Thus (says) his Majesty, Muwatalliš, the Great King, King of the land of Ḫatti . . .'.[245] It is inconceivable that when the covenant-form underlying these state-treaties was used in connexion with the covenant with Yahweh this important feature of these treaties could be completely disregarded. Since the form of the Decalogue

[240] Cf. also G. von Rad, *op. cit.*, p. 48.
[241] Cf. also W. Caspari, *op. cit.*, col. 109.
[242] Cf. H. Gross, *Weltherrschaft als religiöse Idee im Alten Testament*, *BBB* 6, pp. 23 f.
[243] Cf. E. F. Weidner, *Politische Dokumente aus Kleinasien*, pp. 58 f.
[244] Cf. *ibid.*, pp. 76 f., and J. Friedrich, *Staatsverträge des Ḫatti-Reiches in hethitischer Sprache, I Teil*, pp. 4 f.
[245] Cf. E. F. Weidner, *op. cit.*, pp. 80 f; cf. also *ibid.* pp. 88 f.; J. Friedrich, *op. cit.*, pp. 106 f.; *II Teil*, pp. 4 f.; 50 f.; 106 f.

was modelled on this existing outline and since Israel's covenant-cult made use of this covenant-form, it would have been difficult to omit all reference to the fact that up till then it had always been the *king* who conducted political action on behalf of the state in this way and whose will was made law. In fact, one could draw the conclusion that in Israel the need for such an omission was never felt, because it seemed thoroughly compatible with Yahweh's nature that he should reveal his will in the same form that the kings elsewhere were accustomed to use. It follows from this that Yahweh was not thought of as king for the first time during Israel's monarchy or through the assumption of pre-Davidic cult-traditions in Jerusalem.[246] Even if this applies only to the content and not to the name, Yahweh could have been placed in the category of king at the latest by the time this covenant form was taken over and made use of.[247] At any rate, the covenant which was made with Israel and was modelled on this form, could be justly described as a royal covenant in this sense.[248] It seems, therefore, that the ideas of covenant and king were closely linked from the beginning; they did not present themselves as two sharply separate expressions when ancient Israel was seeking to describe the distinctiveness of its relationship to God.[249] This does not mean, of course, that *one* set of ideas may not have been more prominent than another.

Exod. xix. 3b–8, the kernel of which goes back to Israel's early history, as stated, thus provides very early evidence of Yahweh's

[246] Cf. H. Schmid, 'Jahwe und die Kulttraditionen von Jerusalem', *ZAW* 67, 1955, pp. 168 f. (This study puts forward the theory that after the capture of Jerusalem the pre-Israelite deity *'El 'elyôn*, who was enthroned on Zion as creator and king, became fused with Yahweh in the cult there, as a result of which the royal titles of this deity were transferred to Yahweh.)

[247] Cf. now also G. Fohrer, 'Der Vertrag zwischen König und Volk in Israel', *ZAW* 71, 1959, p. 21. See also above p. 68. The idea of Yahweh's kingship would only take definite shape, of course, when the emergent institution of the *earthly* kingship in Israel was defined as dependent on and subject to Yahweh. Cf. for instance 1 Sam. viii (esp. v. 7 f.) and Ps. ii (esp. v. 6 f.).

[248] It was a royal-covenant by which the people of God were constituted as 'Israel'. Its name, which seems to mean 'may God prevail' (cf. M. Noth, *Die israelitischen Personennamen im Rahmen der gemeinsemitischen Namengebung*, *BWANT* iii. 10, pp. 207 f., 191 f.), could, especially if it were to be understood primarily as the name of a fellowship and only secondarily as *nomen personae*, be harmonised with this: 'Israel' is the sacral tribal confederacy which exists to fulfil the wish, 'may God prevail'. (Cf. also Ps. cxiii. 1 where Israel is apostrophised as Yahweh's 'servants'—a description which stems from serving at court. On the 'servant Israel' see also O. Kaiser, *Der Königliche Knecht*, *FRLANT* 70, pp. 45 f. etc.) On the description of the covenant announced in Exod. xix. 3b-8 as a 'royal covenant' cf. moreover M. Buber, *Königtum Gottes*, pp. xli, 99 f., and now also J. Muilenburg, *op. cit.*, pp. 352, 354.

[249] *Contra* the interpretation of A. Alt, 'Gedanken über das Königtum Jahwes', *Kleine Schriften*, I, p. 345.

kingship: 1. the covenant-form which finds expression in this piece of tradition in referring to Yahweh's revelation of his will depicts Yahweh in the rôle of royal covenant-author. 2. the phrase *thyu li mmlkt khnim* which occurs in this same passage (v. 6a) suggests that the category of king must have been considered compatible with Yahweh's character. Since, judging by style and vocabulary, the tradition of Exod. xix. 3b–8 had its *Sitz im Leben* in the exhortations of worship, it follows that Yahweh's covenant with his people was interpreted as a royal covenant in this cultic context. In this connection reference may be made once again to the fragment of tradition contained in Exod. xxiv. 1a, 9–11,[250] which suggested that the Sinaitic covenant was sealed by a common sacrificial meal in the presence of Yahweh who was enthroned on the *Ark*. Since, however, the Ark was regarded in ancient Israel as a throne-seat[251]—this was also its original meaning—and since even before Isaiah Yahweh's royal title was connected with it,[252] it may be accepted that in Exod. xxiv. 1a, 9–11 the covenant made on Sinai was in practice considered a royal covenant.

The contents of Exod. xix. 3b–8 not only presuppose Yahweh's kingship but also his lordship and ownership of the whole earth (v. 5b). These two views of God are combined not only here but also in Israel's cultic tradition: in the account of the call of Isaiah the seraphim praise King Yahweh Ṣeba'oth, who has appeared in the temple,[253] as the one whose glory fills the whole earth (cf. vi. 3, 5).[254] In Ps. xxiv Yahweh, the king of glory, (cf. v. 7–10), is praised as the lord of the earth (v. 1). In Ps. xlvii and xcvii also Yahweh is worshipped as king[255] and regarded as lord of the whole earth (cf. xlvii. 3, 8, 9; xcvii. 1, 5). This is another clear sign of the close relationship between this piece of Elohistic tradition and the Israelite cult and its forms of tradition. Exod. xix. 5bβ which attests Yahweh's lordship over the world probably originated in connection with this cultic tradition. Moreover, the cultic parallels just quoted all point to the

[250] Cf. above section II. 1.

[251] Cf. especially the Ark-sayings in Num. x. 35 f. and the account of Isaiah's call in Isa. vi. 1 f. Cf. in addition A. Alt, *op. cit.*, *Kleine Schriften* I, pp. 350 f., and M. Dibelius, *Die Lade Jahwes*, pp. 59 f.

[252] Cf. especially Ps. xxiv. and A. Alt, *ibid.*

[253] Cf. I. Engnell, 'The call of Isaiah', *UUÅ* 1949/4, pp. 27 f., 31; M. Schmidt, *Prophet und Tempel*, p. 33.

[254] See also the introduction of Hezekiah's prayer in Isa. xxxvii. 16.

[255] The problem discussed by D. Michel ('Studien zu den Thronbesteigungspsalmen', *VT* 6, 1956, pp. 40 f.), *viz.* how the enthronement-acclamation, *YHWH mlk*, is to be understood, can be left undecided in the present context.

sphere of the Temple at Jerusalem in the pre-exilic period.[256] But, just as the idea of Yahweh's kingship did not originate in the cult at Jerusalem under the monarchy (*vide supra*), so also the possibility that belief in Yahweh's lordship over the world may have arisen in Israel's pre-monarchic period must be taken into account.[257] It is impossible to be quite sure (in spite of the strong similarity of diction—cf. for instance Exod. xix. 5b and Ps. xcvii. 5) whether the Elohistic tradition of Exod. xix. 5 was, in fact, handed down and shaped in the worship of the Temple at Jerusalem in the pre-exilic period. But, at any rate, Exod. xix. 3b–8 contains an element which was related to the cultic tradition of Israel and which, in the context of this tradition, establishes Yahweh's right to choose his own people.

Summary. The following conclusions may be drawn about the tradition of Exod. xix. 3b–8. The kernel of it is rooted in the sacral tribal confederacy of ancient Israel and it is structurally related to the covenant with Yahweh, with regard both to the making and the writing of it (Exod. xx. 2–17). It was given its present form under the influence of the covenant-form which found expression in the cult. In v. 5bα there is a reference to the affirmation of covenant-obligation and the formula used for this. V. 5bβ makes use of a theme which seems to be connected with the cultic tradition that celebrates the kingly rule of Yahweh. Apart from these numerous connections with the worship of Yahweh and its traditions, it can be demonstrated that on grounds of language, style and content it is probable that the unit Exod. xix. 3b–8 is also a product of liturgical exhortation. Finally, with reference to the work of G. von Rad,[258] it may be briefly mentioned that the position of this piece of tradition within the context of the whole Sinai-pericope seems to correspond to the outline of a cultic ceremony, which, it is clear, was normally intro-

[256] On this application of Psalms xlvii and xcvii cf. H. Schmid, *op. cit.*, pp. 185 f., and his discussion with H-J. Kraus, *Die Königsherrschaft Gottes im Alten Testament*, *BHTh* 13; cf. recently also O. Eissfeldt, 'Das Lied Moses Deuteronomium xxxii. 1–43 und das Lehrgedicht Asaphs Psalm lxxviii', *BSAW* vol. 104, pt. 5, p. 20. The psalm of Hannah in 1 Sam. ii, 1–10, which speaks of Yahweh's lordship over the earth (cf. vv. 8, 10) may also stem from the temple-cult at Jerusalem (cf. v. 10).

[257] The Song of Moses (Deut. xxxii) could point to this, insofar as it defends Yahweh's uniqueness and his superiority over his rivals (vv. 17, 21, 37 f.). On the dating of the Song in the pre-monarchical period cf. O. Eissfeldt, *op. cit.*, pp. 15-24; W. F. Albright, 'Some remarks on the Song of Moses in Deuteronomy xxxii', *VT* 9, 1959, pp. 339 f. Deut. xxxii, 8, if understood according to W. F. Albright, *op. cit.*, pp. 343 f. instead of according to O. Eissfeldt, 'El and Yahweh', *JSSt* 1, 1956, pp. 25–37, could also be used as evidence that belief in Yahweh's lordship over the world was already held.

[258] Cf. for details, *Das formgeschichtliche Problem des Hexateuch* (=*Gesammelte Studien*, esp. pp. 35, 47).

duced by an exhortatory passage. All things considered, it is clear that the unit of tradition just referred to corresponds most closely both in form and content to the requirements of an exhortatory (and programmatic) foreword.

7. Exodus xxxiv. 1, 4, 10–28

These particular verses in chap. xxxiv consist of *Yahwistic* elements[259] referring to the making of the covenant on Sinai. Prior to their connection with Exod. xxxii. they made no mention of the broken Sinaitic covenant being restored or of the tables that had been smashed being repaired, but—as in the Elohistic passages we have discussed so far—they simply spoke of the making of the covenant on Sinai and the tables of the commandments which formed the basis of it. Whereas rival variants of tradition are usually interwoven, here the parallel accounts of the Elohistic and Yahwistic traditions, linked together by the theme of restoration, follow each other.[260] The word *kārî'šōnîm* in xxxiv. 4 and similarly all the words from *kārî'šōnîm* to *šibbartā* in xxxiv. 1 only go back to this literary arrangement,[261] which is not the primary interest of this present study.

One of the oldest components of this Yahwistic tradition is to be found in Exod. xxxiv. 10aα; 'And he (sc. Yahweh) said, "Behold, I make a covenant".' The Hebrew expression used here, *kārat̲ berît̲* (as in Exod. xxxiv. 27), which has an exact parallel from pre-Israelite times in the expression *TAR beriti*[262] which is attested in N. Syrian documents from the first third of the 14th century B.C., undoubtedly once described the sacred rite of making a covenant by dissecting a sacrificial animal,[263] a rite which is described in the O.T. in Gen. xv. 9 f., 17 and Jer. xxxiv. 18 f. It is quite probable that in the context of Exod. xxxiv the expression is no longer used to refer to this special rite. It is evident that it not only denotes a cultic ceremony accompanying the making of the covenant but refers generally and comprehensively to the actual making of the covenant in all its aspects.

The expression *kārat̲ berît̲* in xxxiv. 27, which is one of the oldest strands of chap. xxxiv, forms part of a most unusual construction—

[259] Its allocation to J is discussed in section I. 10b. Exod. xxxiv. 2–3, 5–8 is discussed in section II. 12.

[260] Cf. H. Gressmann, *Die Anfänge Israels*, 2nd ed., *SATA* 12, p. 61.

[261] Cf. above, section I. 10a.

[262] Cf. W. F. Albright, 'The Hebrew Expression for "Making a Covenant" in Pre-Israelite Documents', *BASOR* 121, 1951, pp. 21 f.

[263] Cf. M. Noth, 'Das alttestamentliche Bundschliessen im Lichte eines Mari-Textes' *Gesammelte Studien*, pp. 144 f.

kāratī 'itteḵā beriṯ w'eṯ-yiśrā'ēl: Yahweh makes[264] a covenant with Moses and with Israel. It was noticed a long time ago that *w'eṯ yiśrā'ēl* is a clumsy phrase and may therefore be a later addition.[265] A further reason for regarding it as a later addition is that after Moses—in view of the linguistic usage of other Yahwistic passages (cf. for instance Exod. xix. 9 f.)—one would have expected *w'eṯ hā'ām*. Everything suggests, therefore, that the passage once referred to a covenant which Yahweh made with Moses[266] and which the people did not share in except indirectly.[267] This version of the Yahwistic tradition agrees in content also with the description of the Elohistic account of the making of the covenant,[268] according to which Moses mediates the covenant.

The Yahwistic formula *kāraṯtî 'itteḵā beriṯ(w'eṯ yiśrā'ēl)* corresponds, apparently, to a specific form of covenant-making practised in Israel's cult. It can be seen particularly clearly in the account of the renewal of the covenant, which took place in the context of the cult-reform of King Josiah. 2 Kings xxiii. 3 says: 'And the king stood by the pillar and made a covenant (*wayyiḵrōṯ 'eṯ habberiṯ*) before the Lord to walk after the Lord and to keep his commandments and his testimonies and his statutes, with all his heart and all his soul, to perform the words of this covenant that were written in this book; and all the people joined in the covenant (*wayya'amōḏ kol-hā'ām babberiṯ*).' Since it is the *Sinaitic* covenant[269] that is being renewed here, the description of 2 Kings xxiii. 3 may be compared with the wording of Exod. xxxiv. 27bβ: King Josiah takes over the rôle of covenant-mediator and makes a covenant before (and naturally also *with*) Yahweh[270] on his own behalf first of all; only when this has been done does the cultic community of Israel join in the covenant. Similarly, according to Exod. xxxiv. 27 Yahweh makes the covenant firstly with Moses since he is the covenant-mediator; everything points to the people participating only indirectly. In view of the

[264] On the perfect form cf. Beer-Meyer, *Hebräische Grammatik*, § 101, 2b (esp. the reference to Gen. xxiii. 11).

[265] Cf. B. Baentsch, *HK* 2/1, p. 285.

[266] The context makes it impossible to refer *'itteḵa* to Israel. *Contra* R. Kraetzschmar, *Die Bundesvorstellung im Alten Testament in ihrer geschichtlichen Entwicklung*, p. 89.

[267] Even if *w'eṯ yiśrā'ēl* were *not* a later addition, xxxiv. 27β could hardly be understood in any other way in view of the emphatic position of *'itt eḵa* in front of it.

[268] The tradition of Exod. xxiv. 1a, 9–11 is difficult to assess in this respect in view of its fragmentary nature.

[269] Cf. also H-J. Kraus, *Gottesdienst in Israel*, pp. 87-91.

[270] The phrase '*before* Yahweh' is probably meant to discourage (among other things) the idea that Yahweh could be dealt with as if he were simply an equal partner to the treaty. Cf. M. Noth, *ibid.*, *Gesammelte Studien*, pp. 152 f. For a different view cf. G. Fohrer, 'Der Vertrag zwischen König und Volk in Israel', *ZAW* 71, 1959, p. 14.

fact that King Hezekiah also, according to the work of the Chronicler, intended 'to make a covenant with the Lord, the God of Israel' (2 Chron. xxix. 10), which clearly takes for granted that it was the duty of the king of Judaea and Jerusalem to enter into a covenant with Yahweh on his own initiative and on his own behalf,[271] it is reasonable to assume that the method used on the occasion of the Josianic reform in making a covenant was not invented *ad hoc* but (this is *one* possibility, at least) had been used in the worship of the Temple at Jerusalem under the monarchy.[272] The unusual wording of the Yahwistic tradition *kāraṯtî 'iṯtᵉḵā bᵉrîṯ* (*w'ᵉṯ yiśrā'ēl*) clearly presupposes a cultic ceremony for the making of the covenant such as could have been practised in the cult of the royal shrine at Jerusalem.[273]

This act of making a covenant could not be defined, however, as a peculiarity of the temple-cult at Jerusalem under the monarchy. The Song of Deborah from the period of the Judges, a passage whose antiquity is unquestioned and which is to be understood as a cultic liturgy of the tribal confederacy, already presupposes such a ceremony of covenant-renewal in the covenant-oath *'ānōkî layhwh* (Judges v. 3b) which was made by an authorised cultic-official (Deborah?) charged with this task and which was uttered in the name of the whole community gathered together;[274] one person spoke for everyone and the whole tribal confederacy shared in the cultic promise made by the one (cf. esp. Judges v. 2, 9).[275] It is also probable that the tradition of the assembly at Shechem—according to which Joshua bound himself and his family to Yahweh in a solemn promise (Joshua xxiv. 15b), in which he was joined subsequently by all the people (Joshua xxiv. 24 f.)—was based on a recollection of the same *modus procedendi*, which was later used in the state-cult at Jerusalem whenever the covenant was renewed. This suggests that corresponding to the peculiar wording of the Yahwist there was a set method of making (or renewing) a covenant, which was practised

[271] This assumption, which the account starts from, is instructive, in spite of the historical unreliability of the Chronicler's work (cf. W. Rudolph, *Chronikbücher*, *HAT* 1/21, p. 293).

[272] Cf. in this connection also G. Widengren, *Sakrales Königtum im Alten Testament und im Judentum*, pp. 29 f; further pp. 15 f.

[273] It is improbable that in this passage 'the Sinai tradition is only an aetiological legend of the royal cult at Jerusalem'—a point raised by G. Widengren in the form of a question (*ibid.*, pp. 29 f.)—in view of the great variety of ways in which the tradition speaks of Moses as covenant-mediator. See below.

[274] Cf. A. Weiser, 'Das Deboralied. Eine gattungs- und traditionsgeschichtliche Studie', *ZAW* 71, 1959, esp. p. 73. See also above, section II. 6.

[275] Cf. A. Weiser, *ibid.*, on this passage.

not only in the state-cult at Jerusalem but also in the festal cult of ancient Israel. If, then, this way of making a covenant can be traced in Israel's earliest history, it could, in fact, in accordance with the tradition of Exod. xxxiv. 27, have been used even in Mosaic times. It is self-evident that the covenant of Yahweh with Moses or a later covenant-mediator could only have arisen on the *cultic* level. To that extent, therefore, these words of Yahweh are inseparable from their cultic background and, on the whole, cannot be understood apart from it.

The covenant mediated in this way was ratified according to Exod. xxxiv. 27 on the basis of certain *d^e^ḇārîm*, which Yahweh expressly ordered to be written down. According to Exod. xxxiv. 1a, 4, 28b they were written on tables of stone. In view of the importance which was widely attributed to the written record of authoritative texts in the ancient Orient[276] and in view of the fact that the Hittite vassal-treaties of the 14th and 13th century B.C. had to be set down in writing, according to the covenant-outline on which they were based, in order to possess validity,[277] it is quite feasible that there were written statements of covenant-words attached to the Sinaitic covenant[278] also from the earliest period of its existence. According to Deut. x. 1–5 the tables mentioned in Exod. xxxiv. 28 were preserved with the 'ten words' (see below) in the Temple. For the reasons already given it is quite likely that here again in this passage the Jerusalemite procedure—basically, at least—reaches far back into the pre-monarchical period of Israel's history.[279] It may be assumed, therefore, that behind the command of Yahweh in Exod. xxxiv. 27 that Moses should write down the words of the covenant there was the fact, well-known to the cultic community, of a corresponding written document deposited at the covenant-shrine. Yahweh's instruction to Moses to prepare two stone tables and to use them for the written record of the words of the covenant (cf. Exod. xxxiv. 1a, 4, 28b) would have been understood in Israel both at and before the time of Deuteronomy, probably even a long time before, in view of the fact that the tables of the covenant were deposited at a holy place. The record of the tradition was understood as the explanation of a cultic situation.

[276] Cf. the literature cited in Korošec, *op. cit.*, p. 15, n. 6.
[277] Cf. the example quoted above on p. 55.
[278] Cf. also G. E. Mendenhall, *op. cit.*, pp. 64 f.
[279] The custom of depositing important documents of religious, political and private life in holy places was widespread throughout the ancient Orient. Cf. A. Jirku, *Altorientalischer Kommentar zum AT*, pp. 184 f.

Proof that the phrase 'ten words' in Exod. xxxiv. 28 belongs to the oldest stratum of the tradition is to be found in the fact that—apart from other reasons[280]—it is impossible to derive exactly ten commandments from the passage Exod. xxxiv. 10–26, which was obviously added later and is predominantly legal.[281] If there had been no mention of the 'ten words' already present, it would never have occurred to anyone to call them 'ten words' on the basis of vv. 10–26, which are a later addition and not a unity in themselves.[282] There can hardly be any doubt that the phrase 'ten words' in Exod. xxxiv. 28 originally referred to a Decalogue which was systematically constructed and uniform in style. Since Exod. xx. 2–17 contains a similar passage—in the shape it was given later—which is shown by its structure to have been the document linked with the making of a covenant, this strongly suggests that this Decalogue which constitutes the basis of Exod. xx was originally referred to here also in the Yahwist's account of the making of the covenant and was at one time reproduced in front of Exod. xxxiv. 27, 28.[283] For these two verses clearly refer to *dᵉḇārîm* which directly preceded them. It is not easy to imagine that vv. 27, 28, in their present form, look back to a Decalogue included at an earlier point. It is difficult now, of course, to answer the question how it came about that this Decalogue which was originally referred to had to quit its place in the Yahwistic account of the making of the covenant. It is not sufficient explanation to say that in the redaction of the Elohistic and Yahwistic passages of tradition care was taken to avoid a repetition of the Ten Commandments already included in Exod. xx,[284] since it had already

[280] Cf. H. Holzinger, *KHC* 2, p. 119; further C. H. Cornill, 'Zum Segen Jacobs und zum jahwistischen Decalog,' *BZAW* 27, 1914, p. 111.

[281] Cf. W. Rudolph, *Der 'Elohist' von Exodus bis Josua*, *BZAW* 68, p. 59, n. 1.

[282] A. Alt, *Die Ursprünge des israelitischen Rechts* (=*Kleine Schriften* I, p. 317, n. 1) describes them as 'a secondary conflation' from the point of view of form. It is generally recognised today that these verses do not contain a second Decalogue as thought (according to E. Nestle, *ZAW* 24, 1904, pp. 134 f.) by an Alexandrian theologian of the fifth century A.D. and also by J. W. v. Goethe later ('Zwo wichtige bisher unerörterte biblische Fragen, zum ersten Male gründlich beantwortet von einem Landgeistlichen in Schwaben'). Cf. also R. Kittel, *Geschichte des Volkes Israel*, 3rd. ed. I, p. 493, esp. n. 1; W. Rudolph, *op. cit.*, p. 59; M. Buber, *Moses*, pp. 120 f. Nor is there anything to support the view that the basis of Exod. xxxiv, interpreted as a cultic Decalogue, is older than the so-called ethical Decalogue in Exod. xx. 2–17 (so J. Wellhausen, *Die Composition des Hexateuchs*, p. 85, esp. n. 2; further also for instance B. Duhm, *Israels Propheten*, pp. 33, 35 f.; C. H. Cornill, 'Zum Segen Jacobs und zum jahwistischen Dekalog', *BZAW* 27, pp. 109 f.; H. Holzinger, *KHC* 2, p. 120; R. Smend, *Die Erzählung des Hexateuch*, pp. 178 f. G. Beer, *HAT*, 1/3, pp. 162 f. For a different view see H. Holzinger, *op. cit.*, p. 120, and H. Schmidt, 'Mose und der Dekalog' in *Eucharisterion*, *FRLANT* 36, pp. 100 f.). Cf. finally the work of R. Smend on the history of the exegesis, *Das Mosebild von Heinrich Ewald bis Martin Noth*, *BGBE* 3, 1959, pp. 9 f.

[283] Cf. for instance W. Rudolph, *op. cit.*, p. 59; E. Auerbach, *Moses*, p. 164.

[284] So R. Kittel, *op. cit.*, pp. 494, n. 1.

been decided in the account of the making of the covenant on Sinai not to interweave the parallel variants of tradition as elsewhere but to arrange them consecutively, with the theme of 'restoration' to connect them (see above, p. 77). Why, then, should the redactor[285] suddenly grow tired of repetition and give up his self-adopted method? Why should he deny himself a second reproduction of the Decalogue which the narrative led up to, only to find himself with a gap between Exod. xxxiv. 10aα and xxxiv. 27, 28 which he had then to try to fill? And why, finally, should he not have filled this gap—at least this would have been consistent—with the same Decalogue that according to Exod. xx. 2–17 must have been well-known and ready to hand? Why did he burden himself instead with the discrepancy between the contents of the original and the restored tables?[286] There is no evidence, therefore, to suggest that the Jehovistic* editor suppressed or omitted the second record of the Decalogue before Exod. xxxiv. 27, 28. Since there is so little in Exod. xxxiv. 10–26 that clashes with the interpretation of the Yahwistic account of the establishment of the covenant-tables as the story of the *restoration* of the broken tables (cf. Exod. xxxiv. 1, 4) there can hardly be any doubt that the nucleus of vv. 10–26 was *already in existence*. The narrative had to be harmonised with this. The result is obvious in the still independently transmitted Yahwistic tradition: the Decalogue originally referred to was replaced by the kernel of vv. 10–26.[287]

The question of the motive of this insertion and the origin of the nucleus of these verses cannot be answered without consideration being given to the circumstance that there is an extensive parallel[288] to Exod. xxxiv. 14–26 in Exod. xxiii. 12–19, a passage which belongs to the Book of the Covenant. The exact relationship of the two passages to each other is difficult to assess. It is improbable that the stipulations in Exod. xxxiv. 14–26[289], inserted in the Yahwistic tradition of the making of the covenant on Sinai in place of the original Decalogue, were derived from Exod. xxiii. 12–19 and were thus in

[285] On the meaning of this word cf. A. Weiser, *Introduction to the Old Testament*, p. 125.

[286] These questions would apply *mutatis mutandis* to W. Rudolph, *op. cit.*, p. 59 also.

[287] Whether this happened at the literary or pre-literary stage need not be gone into here. Cf. also below p. 88, n. 322.

[288] Cf. on the following the synoptic table III, showing the Book of the Covenant and Exod. xxxiv, in A. Jepsen, *Untersuchungen zum Bundesbuch*, *BWANT* III. 5, p. 108.

[289] Disregarding in the first place the later portions of this section.

* Tr. note: Jehovistic is used to refer to passages in which Yahwistic and Elohistic elements have been harmonised by a later editor.

literary dependence on the Book of the Covenant,[290] since this would not explain the peculiarities of the latter.[291] Nor is the reverse solution, making Exod. xxiii dependent on Exod. xxxiv,[292] satisfactory, since this also would fail to account for the differences between Exod. xxxiv and Exod. xxiii.[293] The fact of extensive agreement in the contents of the stipulations (for an occasional exception, cf. for instance Exod. xxiii. 14), almost complete parallelism in the sequence of clauses, linked with considerable differences in wording is best explained by the view that the two sections both go back to a common source. They represent two distinct expressions of a single legal complex.[294] It is understandable that in the meantime separate attempts at harmonisation were made in the course of the further literary transmission of Exod. xxxiv. and Exod. xxiii.

The variant which has been worked into Exod. xxxiv. contains the following stipulations, which together constitute a 'calendar of the festivals': 'The feast of unleavened bread you shall keep . . . at the time appointed, namely, the new moon Abib,[295] for in the month (see below) Abib you came out from Egypt' (Exod. xxxiv. 18; cf. xxiii. 15a). 'And you shall observe the feast of weeks with(?) the first fruits of the wheat harvest and the feast of ingathering at the year's end' (Exod. xxxiv. 22; cf. xxiii. 16). 'Three times in the year shall all your males appear[296] before the Lord your God (see below),

[290] So A. Klostermann, *Der Pentateuch* II, pp. 527 f.

[291] Cf. A. Jepsen, *op. cit.*, p. 94 At any rate, his theory that Exod xxxiv. 20bβ is dependent on Exod. xxiii. 15b (cf. *op. cit.*, pp. 91 f.) does not seem to be well established, seeing that it is supported by the textual tradition of only one Greek manuscript (k–cf. Brooke-McLean 1/2, p. 273).

[292] Cf. *inter alios* J. Wellhausen, *Die Composition des Hexateuchs*, p. 90 (560); H. Holzinger, *KHC* 2, pp. 96 f; B. Baentsch, *HK* 2/1, pp. 185, 208; cf. however the interpretation of O. Eissfeldt, *Einleitung in das Alte Testament*, 2nd ed., pp. 255 f., according to which *those* stipulations in Exod. xxxiv. 14–26 which had no parallel in Exod. xx. 22–xxiii. 12 were appended to the Book of the Covenant in Exod. xxiii. 13–19 by the Jehovistic redactor with the intention of making Exod. xxxiv. 14–26 intelligible as a repetition of the words revealed before the first making of the covenant in Exod. xxiv. But, from this point of view, it remains inexplicable why a parallel to Exod. xxxiv. 14a had to be added in Exod. xxiii. 13b, since a classical one already existed in the Decalogue in Exod. xx. 3. On the other hand, it is not clear how far Exod. xxiii. 14 could have served to make this section in Exod. xxxiv. appear as a repetition, since it is not followed by anything analogous. Finally, it is remarkable that Exod. xxiii. 13–19, although it is supposed to owe its existence simply to the literary measures of a redactor, nevertheless often uses its own distinctive vocabulary, as opposed to Exod. xxxiv. (cf. for instance Exod. xxiii. 16 with Exod. xxxiv. 22; Exod. xxiii. 13b with Exod. xxxiv. 14a).

[293] Cf. further A. Jepsen, *op. cit.*, pp. 93 f.

[294] This is also the conclusion of A. Jepsen, *op. cit.*, p. 94.

[295] Cf. E. Auerbach, 'Die Feste im alten Israel', *VT* 8, 1958, p. 1; further S. Mowinckel, *Religion und Kultus*, p. 58.

[296] The discussion about *qal* or *niphal* in W. Baudissin, '"Gotteschauen" in der alttestamentlichen Religion', *ARW* 18, 1915, pp. 181 f. can be disregarded in the present context.

the God of Israel' (Exod. xxxiv. 23; cf. xxiii. 17). It is further stipulated: 'You shall worship no other god' (Exod. xxxiv. 14a; cf. xxiii. 13b). 'You shall make for yourself no molten gods' (Exod. xxxiv. 17). 'All that opens the womb is mine' (Exod. xxxiv. 19a). 'And none shall appear[296] before me empty' (Exod. xxxiv. 20b; cf. xxiii. 15b). 'Six days you shall work, but on the seventh day you shall rest' (Exod. xxxiv. 21a; cf. xxiii. 12a). 'The best of the first fruits of your ground you shall bring to the house of the Lord your God. You shall not boil a kid in its mother's milk.' (Exod. xxxiv. 26; cf. xxiii. 19). All these stipulations are of a cultic-ritual nature. They were unquestionably used by the priesthood of a shrine of Yahweh to direct the laity associated with the shrine.[297] It is from *their* point of view that Yahweh's demands are set forth: None shall appear before me empty; the best of the first fruits of your ground you shall bring to the house of the Lord your God; all that opens the womb is mine; three times in the year shall all your males appear before the Lord your God, the God of Israel! If a shrine of Yahweh is accepted as the original *Sitz im Leben* of *one* of these series of cultic stipulations this naturally suggests the same for the parallel series in the Book of the Covenant. These two variants of a common original (see above) certainly did not acquire their own particular form through development in 'popular oral tradition',[298] but probably in their different shrines.[299] In view of the importance which was attributed in the ancient Orient to the written record of authoritative texts and their deposition in holy places (see above) and considering that the centres of the art of writing and the upholders of *written* tradition (especially in the case of cultic laws)[300] were to be found chiefly in shrines, it is very probable that these cultic laws were set down and transmitted *in writing* at some shrine or other; hence Exod. xxxiv. 14–26 and Exod. xxiii. 12–19 can be understood as two different recensions of the one cultic law.[301]

What, then, was the *historical* setting of such a law? Since the variants in Exod. xxiii. 12–19 were able to find a place in the Book of

[297] Cf. B. Duhm, *Israels Propheten*, p. 37 f. (with reference, it is true, to the supposed cultic Decalogue); A. Jepsen, *op. cit.*, p. 94; M. Buber, *Moses*, p. 121.

[298] *Contra* A. Jepsen, *ibid.* How could 'popular oral tradition' deal with material of this nature?

[299] Similarly R. Kittel, *Geschichte des Volkes Israel*, 3rd ed., I, p. 493.

[300] Cf. S. Mowinckel, *Jesaja-Disiplene, Profetien fra Jesaja til Jeremia*, p. 127; A. Jirku, *op. cit.*, pp. 184 f., and especially A. H. J. Gunneweg, *Mündliche und schriftliche Tradition der vorexilischen Prophetenbücher . . .*, *FRLANT* 73, pp. 78 f.

[301] R. Kittel, *op. cit.*, p. 493, n. 2 points to the fact that in Greece also 'copies of old documents' were made for other shrines, 'an indispensable precaution in case of the original being destroyed by fire or act of aggression'.

the Covenant, the formation of the Book of the Covenant, probably in the pre-monarchical period, may be accepted as the *terminus ante quem*.[302] There is a strong case for making the entry of the Israelites into Palestine the *terminus post quem*.[303] Contact with Canaanite festivals and sacrificial customs first makes itself felt in the cultic stipulations of this law.[304] The agricultural festivals of Canaan are given a place (cf. Exod. xxxiv. 18a, 22). Only the first beginnings of Israelite modification are observable: thus, one clear example of this is the explanation in terms of salvation-history that is given for the purely astronomical date (up till then) of the feast of unleavened bread, 'for in the month Abib you came out from Egypt'. Since the same reason (given emphasis by its connection with the fundamental date of Israelite tradition—cf. Exod. xx. 2b) occurs in the parallel passage Exod. xxiii. 15a with only slightly different wording, it may well belong to the older stratum of these cultic stipulations. The fact that the word *ḥōḏeš* is used in the sense of 'month', and not 'new moon' as in the first half of the verse, is not conclusive for a post-exilic origin, since *ḥōḏeš* in the sense of 'month', but closely connected with and having overtones of 'new moon' (= the days from one new moon to another),[305] occurs in ancient Yahwistic traditions of the Pentateuch (cf. Gen. xxix. 14; Num. xi. 20).[306] The use of *ḥōḏeš* instead of *yeraḥ* arises from the fact that the closer this explanatory clause could approximate even in vocabulary to what was to be explained the more authentic it was bound to seem.[307] The ancient stipulation that every male Israelite was to make three pilgrimages every year to the place where Yahweh, the God of Israel (see below), was present (Exod. xxxiv. 23), also probably helped to maintain and advance the cult of Yahweh in the midst of its Canaanite environment. Later criticism of such pilgrimages by the prophets (cf. for instance Amos iv. 4; v. 5) should not mislead us as to their positive function in the self-preservation of the people of Yahweh after the entry into Palestine.[308] In short, the cultic stipulations of Exod. xxxiv[309] (and xxiii) grew out of the desire to take account of Israel's new position after the conquest and to subject it to the criticism of the

[302] Cf. A. Jepsen, *op. cit.*, pp. 95, 98 f.
[303] Cf. *ibid.* p. 95.
[304] Cf. also H-J. Kraus, *Gottesdienst in Israel*, pp. 9, 18 f.
[305] Cf. also R. de Vaux, *Ancient Israel*, p. 183.
[306] See also R. de Vaux, *ibid.*
[307] *Contra* E. Auerbach, 'Die Feste im alten Israel', *VT* 8, 1958, pp. 1 f., 8.
[308] Cf. also W. Eichrodt, *Theology of the Old Testament*, I, p. 365.
[309] Exod. xxxiv. 11–13, 15 f., 24 were obviously added later; they follow up the debate with Canaanite *mores* in the sense of Deuteronomy. Cf. Deut. xii (esp. xii. 3) and xvi. 21.

covenant made with Yahweh. It is clear that this activity proceeded from those shrines of Yahweh where these stipulations were accepted and applied.

Perhaps one of the first places that comes to mind in this connection is the temple at Shiloh, although there is no certainty in the matter.[310] Insofar as Shiloh sheltered the Ark during the period of the Judges (cf. 1 Sam. iii. 3; iv. 4)[311] this would satisfactorily account for stipulations which use the formula 'to appear before Yahweh' (cf. Exod. xxxiv. 20b*β*, 23) and which thus probably presuppose Yahweh's cultic presence. Express reference to the then existing shrine of the Ark would be found in Exod. xxxiv. 23 (xxiii. 17) if the reading of the Samaritan Pentateuch *hā'ārōn yhwh*[312] could be accepted instead of the unparalleled *hā'āḏōn yhwh*.[313] The description of Yahweh as *'ᵉlōhê yiśrā'ēl* (Exod. xxxiv. 23), associated with the tribal sanctuary at Shechem (Ebal) according to Gen. xxxiii. 20; Joshua xxiv. 2 and Joshua viii. 30 and later found in use at Shiloh according to 1 Sam. i. 17, having made its way there in connection with the Ark perhaps,[314] also points to Shiloh as the source of this cultic law.[315] Since the name *yhwh 'ᵉlōhê yiśrā'ēl* refers to the God who chose the tribal confederacy of Israel for his own possession[316] in contrast to the native Canaanite deities, the wording of this pilgrimage-law provides further evidence of the tendency to maintain the covenant with Yahweh in spite of Canaanite influences. Finally, the fact that Exod. xxxiv. 23 (xxiii. 17, 24) required *three* pilgrimages each year, whereas according to 1 Sam. i there was in fact only one pilgrimage in the year to Shiloh,[317] would not be an

[310] There is a list of Palestinian shrines to which pilgrimages were made in E. Auerbach, *op. cit.*, p. 17.

[311] Cf. A. von Gall, *Altisraelitische Kultstätten*, *BZAW* 3, pp. 105 f.; K. Galling, *BRL* col. 490 f.; also H. Kjaer, 'The excavation of Shilo', *JPOS* 1930, pp. 87 f.

[312] Cf. E. Auerbach, *op. cit.*, p. 16, n. 1.

[313] Cf. S. Mandelkern, *op. cit.*, p. 14.

[314] Cf. section II. 1 above: further C. Steuernagel, 'Jahwe, der Gott Israels', *BZAW* 27, pp. 342-9; M. Noth, *Das System der zwölf Stämme Israels*, pp. 94 f.; and A. von Gall, *op. cit.*, p. 105.

[315] The words *'ᵉlōhê yiśrā'ēl* which occur in xxxiv. 23 but not in xxiii. 17 need not be a later addition: the assumption of C. Steuernagel's literary-critical argument (*op. cit.*, p. 340) that Exod. xxiii is dependent on Exod. xxxiv cannot be accepted in view of what we have said earlier. Thus, a reference back from xxiii. 17 to the earlier form of xxxiv. 23 is not possible. It is quite inconceivable that *'ᵉlōhê yiśrā'ēl* was meant to affirm that one had to appear before Yahweh at Jerusalem and at no other cultic centre. This Deuteronomic aim would have been worded differently, judging by Deut. xvi. 16. In fact, Steuernagel himself remarks elsewhere that this name for God was not invented 'in order to express the opposition of Yahweh worshipped in Jerusalem and Yahweh worshipped at the high places' (*op. cit.*, p. 342).

[316] Cf. C. Steuernagel, *op. cit.*, pp. 345 f.

[317] See also A. Lods, 'Eléments anciens et éléments modernes dans le rituel du sacrifice israélite', *RHPhR* 1928, p. 403.

intolerable difference, insofar as this cultic law may have urged the trebling of the pilgrimages and hence the reception of these three agricultural festivals into the cult of Yahweh[318] in the very course of the debate with existing practice; this would fit in quite well with the whole character of this cultic law. If there is a great deal to be said for the temple at Shiloh being the source and guardian of these cultic stipulations, it would not be difficult to understand how, in the case of Shiloh, which after Shechem and Bethel became the cultic centre of the Israelite tribal confederacy,[319] it was felt necessary and opportune to come to terms with the new position in Canaan. The amphictyonic traditions had made their way here through their link with the Ark of the covenant; with the Ark to rely upon, the debate could be ventured. The cultic stipulations in Exod. xxxiv. 14–26 (xxiii. 12–19) are to be understood in connection with this.

If this elucidates the question of the origin of the stipulations which were worked into the Yahwistic account of the making of the covenant, it also suggests the answer to the question of the *motive* for the dislocation, which has caused the Decalogue originally referred to in Exod. xxxiv. 28 ('ten words') to lose its place in the J-account. Like the Book of the Covenant as a whole[320] and its cultic law (Exod. xxiii. 12–19) in particular, the cultic stipulations of Exod. xxxiv, which are closely connected with the latter, represent a law which in spite of every adaptation to the new conditions of life following the entry into Palestine resolutely resisted the danger of complete Canaanisation by upholding and promoting the indispensable aims and principles of the covenant and cult of Yahweh. Corresponding to the importance of such a law for the tribes of Israel when they settled in Canaan, not only the Book of the Covenant with its cultic regulations but also the stipulations of Exod. xxxiv. 14–26 were set in contexts which could give them a special degree of authority and emphasis. Hence, the Book of the Covenant (Exod. xx. 22–xxiii. 19) displaced the Decalogue (Exod. xx. 2–17) in its rôle of *sēp̱er habbᵉrîṯ*, on the basis of which the Sinaitic covenant was made (cf. Exod. xxiv. 3–8)[321]; similarly, everything

[318] E. Auerbach's literary-critical argument (cf. *op. cit.*, pp. 14 f.), which separates Exod. xxiii. 14 from the cultic stipulations of Exod. xxiii and xxxiv. and rejects any connection between the required pilgrimages and these agricultural festivals, is not convincing, since it argues from the 'cultic Decalogue' of Exod. xxiii. 10–19; xxxiv. 17–26, which is certainly not recognised 'on all sides' as stated. See above.

[319] Cf. M. Noth, *The History of Israel*, pp. 94 f.

[320] Further details in A. Jepsen, *op. cit.*, pp. 100 f.

[321] Cf. above, section I. 2, above.

suggests that the cultic stipulations of Exod. xxxiv supplanted the 'ten words' which were the basis of the covenant according to J (Exod. xxxiv. 27). The maintenance of the Sinaitic covenant in the changed situation after Israel settled in Canaan depended on this new law being upheld.[322] It was this conviction and not any rather clumsy, literary editing in the Jehovistic compilation or redaction[323] that was responsible for the insertion of the bulk of these stipulations between Exod. xxxiv. 10aα and Exod. xxxiv. 27, 28, to replace the original Decalogue in the Yahwistic account of the making of the covenant.

By their insertion, however, these cultic stipulations obviously came under the formative influence of the covenant-outline which underlay the Hittite vassal-treaties and which also served, as stated earlier, as the formal model of the Israelite Decalogue.[324] The context of xxxiv. 1a, 4 f., 10aα, 27 f., which formerly contained the covenant-document setting out the 'ten words', was influenced by this covenant-form in several places.[325] The covenant was made on the basis of certain 'words' (xxxiv. 27 f.). Stress is laid on the fact that they were written down (xxxiv. 1a, 4, 27 f.). Consequently, this must also have been true of the deposition of the written document. Immediately before the actual clauses of the covenant are made known the author of the covenant reveals his name (xxxiv. 6.). It may be inferred from xxxiv. 10aα that this was in the I-thou style. It was into such a context then, that the cultic stipulations of vv. 14–26 were inserted. They approximate to the structure outlined above, at least insofar as they both place the most fundamental and comprehensive stipulation at their head (xxxiv. 14a). Here, too, the exclusiveness with which the covenant-people are addressed is un-

[322] The question, when and under what historical circumstances this new law was inserted in the tradition of covenant making, which was subsequently given literary form by the Yahwist, must remain open—whether it was in the literary or pre-literary stage of tradition that it was worked into G, the common source underlying J and E, as assumed by M. Noth (*Überlieferungsgeschichte des Pentateuch*, p. 41 f.), or only into J. These cultic stipulations (later used by the Yahwist) could have found their way into the tradition at Shiloh (rather than Shechem) in connection with the *first* confrontation with the Canaanite world. The insertion of this cultic law may have been undertaken and carried through in the early period of Israel's monarchy—perhaps to counteract the revival of Canaanite influence, which had become a national problem in Israel's domestic politics with the incorporation of the remaining Canaanite regions into the kingdoms of Judah and Israel under David (cf. A. Alt, 'Die Staatenbildung der Israeliten in Palästina', *Kleine Schriften* II, pp. 49–53). The possibility of a return to the Shiloh-tradition at this time is not to be excluded, if even David was acquainted with an institution of the temple at Shiloh in connexion with the Ark. Cf. also O. Eissfeldt (*BSAW* vol. 104, part 5, p. 42.) on Ps. lxxviii.

[323] Cf. for instance G. von Rad, *Theology of the Old Testament* I, p. 189, n. 4.

[324] See above, sections II. 5 and II. 6.

[325] Cf. on what follows, pp. 51 f. above.

equivocally confirmed. Emphasis is added later by the characterisation of Yahweh as *'el ḳanna'* thus linking the event with and assimilating it to the Decalogue (cf. Exod. xx. 5). A formal element which was missing from these cultic stipulations has now been added —obviously under the influence of the covenant-form referred to in xxxiv. 10.—namely, *the historical prologue.* In the prologue of the Hittite vassal treaties, as stated above, not only the great deeds performed by the author of the covenant on behalf of the vassal, as a result of which the vassal was bound to render lasting gratitude and constant obedience, were enumerated. The preface to the covenant-treaty always contained a vigorous reference to the fact that the originator and lord of the covenant could prove terrible and mighty against enemies and rebels.[326] Thus, in the prologue of the treaty between the Hittite king Šuppiluliuma and Mattiwaza, the king of Mitanni, we read: '(I), the Great King, the hero, the King of the land of Ḫatti, made myself feared by Tušratta, the king of the land of Mitanni. I plundered the lands this side of the river . . . .' A few lines later we read: 'The Great King, King of the land of Ḫatti, showed his might before him'. And a little later in connection with the enemies of the Hittite king we read: 'But the Sun Šuppiluliuma, the Great King, the hero, the King of the land of Ḫatti, the beloved of Teššub, defeated them'.[327] Whole sections in the prologues of such treaties are devoted to demonstrating the power of the author of the covenant to prove himself terrible and mighty. Thus it may be taken as a characteristic of this covenant-form that in the historical prologues modelled on it the following two points may be coupled together: the reminder of help given and obligations incurred thereby is linked with the warning reference to the formidable power of the author of the covenant. There is a parallel to this ambivalent element in the covenant form in Exod. xxxiv. 10, which contains a preface proclaiming Yahweh's terrible and mighty acts and which also seems to contain a promise for his covenant-people: 'Before all your people I will do marvels, such as have not been wrought in all the earth or in any nation; and all the people among whom you are shall see the work of the Lord; for it is a terrible thing that I will do with you'.[328] Thus the covenant-clauses, which the cultic stipulations

[326] Cf. for instance in W, pp. 2 f., 58 f., 82 f.

[327] See W, pp. 2 f., ll. 3 f.; pp. 4 f., l. 10, 14.

[328] The fact that the historical prologue in this case does not refer to the saving act which has already taken place in the deliverance from Egypt but is given a future reference, promising Yahweh's future activity, may spring from the fact that those who are referred to here did not share in the Exodus but only became covenant-members of the tribal union in Canaan; they had still to prove their obedience to the new law, which conflicted with the Canaanite situation.

in Exod. xxxiv. 14–26 now have to do duty for, are introduced in a manner corresponding to this covenant-outline. The accretion of Exod. xxxiv. 10 could be a further indication that the covenant-form known from the Hittite state-treaties may not only have served as a formal model of the Decalogue but may also have had a real influence on the shape of the tradition we are dealing with here. Since it has been established in a previous context[329] that this covenant-form must have played an active part in Israel's cult, it is reasonable to assume that the tradition of the making of the covenant in Exod. xxxiv was handed down in connection with Israel's covenant-cult.

8. Exodus xxxiv. 9

The Yahwistic account[330] of God's appearance on Sinai breaks off at Exod. xxxiv. 8. Just as the account (Exod. xxxiv. 1, 4, 27 f) describing the stone tables of the Commandments did not originally refer to the renewal of these tables after the breach of faith recorded in Exod. xxxii (see above), so here the theophany on Sinai was not described in the first place with reference to a previous breach of the covenant. The fact that Moses hastens to throw himself down, according to Exod. xxxiv. 8, was not originally intended to accompany the prayer which occurs in xxxiv. 9 and which assumes that Israel has sinned; it simply described the unavoidable human reaction to the overwhelming epiphany of Yahweh:[331] Moses throws himself to the ground and worships.[332] The references in Exod. xxxiv. 9 to the stiff-necked people and the forgiveness of sin indicates that the contents of this verse are a later addition, which presupposes that the story of the 'Golden Calf' has been worked into the narrative. Judged also by diction, verse 9 depends on the Jehovistic complex Exod. xxxii–xxxiv. The words 'if now I have found favour in thy sight', which are not peculiar to the Yahwist[333] but which clearly constituted an expression he was fond of using,[334] are undoubtedly derived from the Yahwistic passage Exod. xxxiii. 12–17. This passage

[329] See above section II. 5, pp. 66 f.

[330] Cf. above, I. 10b.

[331] Cf. for instance Exod. xxiv. 1; xxxiii. 10; 1 Sam. i. 3, 19; Ps. xcix. 5; cxxxii. 7. Cf. also below p. 141.

[332] In addition, F. Hesse, *Die Fürbitte im Alten Testament*, p. 96 should be consulted.

[333] Cf. for instance Judges vi. 17; 1 Sam. xxvii. 5; Esther v. 8; vii. 3. It is clear from 2 Sam. xvi. 4; Esther v. 8; vii. 3; viii. 5 that we are dealing with a formula used to address the king. (Cf. also 1 Sam. xvi. 22, where Saul refers the expression to himself. Cf. further Gen. l. 4, where the court of Pharaoh is addressed in these words). The fact that in the Sinai tradition (of J) this formula is used of Yahweh indicates that he is regarded and honoured as *king* here also. Cf. section II. 6.

[334] Cf. Gen. l. 4; Num. xi. 11, 15.

provides the first expression of this theme—bearing in mind the underlying stratum of tradition—which reflection modifies in the course of the conversation (cf. vv. 12, 13, 16, 17). The view that xxxiv. 9a is a fragment of the original source continuing xxxiii. 12–17[335] should not be accepted, since Moses' conversation with Yahweh, from the point of view of both form and content, is terminated in xxxiii. 17. Rather, Exod. xxxiv. 9a is the product of a later hand, connected by its wording with Exod. xxxiii. 12 f. The invitation in xxxiv. 9aβ to God to go with Israel when it leaves Sinai may certainly have been made with reference to the same conversation, xxxiii. 12–17. At all events, the fact that in xxxiv. 9 the expression *hālak 'im* which is used in xxxiii. 16 (J) was only partly utilised and the preposition *'im* was replaced by *b*^e^*ḳereḇ*, which occurs twice in the Elohistic parallel Exod. xxxiii. 3b–6, indicates that Exod. xxxiv. 9 in the JE complex has been influenced by Exod. xxxiii and presupposes it. Definite proof that there really is such a reference to the E stratum is to be found in the fact that in Exod. xxxiv. 9bα, an exact parallel to xxxiii. 3b (cf. xxxiii. 5), the reason 'for it is a stiff-necked people' follows *b*^e^*ḳereḇ* (+ suffix). It is striking that this same expression, which in Exod. xxxiii. 3b explains why Yahweh *cannot* go with Israel, in Exod. xxxiv. 9 is supposed to explain the request for Yahweh to go with them: 'let the Lord, I pray thee, go in the midst of us, for it is a stiff-necked people'. It is true that the use of this argument in its opposite sense is made easier by the fact that the Lord who is addressed here is no longer primarily the God who exterminates his disobedient people (cf. xxxiii. 3bβ) but 'a God merciful and gracious, slow to anger and abounding in steadfast love and faithfulness' (xxxiv. 6).[336] Although God was described in this way, however, the thought that Yahweh should remain in the midst of his people in spite of their disobedience was felt to be so disquieting that from the very beginning the prayer for forgiveness was needed to counterbalance it. Exod. xxxiv. 9aα and 9bβ, therefore, were probably connected from the beginning. The origin of Exod. xxxiv. 9b will be examined later, but one thing is clear: it is not derived like the rest of the verse from the complex of tradition represented by Exod. xxxiii.

Leaving aside, therefore, the question of the origin of the separate component parts of v. 9 and taking its secondary character as

[335] Similarly E. Auerbach, *Moses*, pp. 123 f.

[336] Cf. H. J. Stoebe, 'Die Bedeutung des Wortes *ḥäsäd*', *VT* 2, 1952, pp. 249 f. See also pp. 137 f. below.

proven, it is necessary to consider the motives which led to its insertion between the Yahwistic sections Exod. xxxiv. 1–8 and 10–28. Since the Elohistic passages of tradition in Exod. xxiv had already mentioned the making of the covenant on Sinai, the Yahwistic parallels, as stated, were reinterpreted as descriptions of the *restoration* of the smashed tables and the broken covenant and brought within the framework of Exod. xxxiv. (In the course of this reinterpretation the words from *kārīʾšōnîm* to *šibbartā* in xxxiv. 1 and the word *kārīʾšōnîm* in xxxiv. 4 were inserted; see above.) Can, then, the insertion of Exod. xxxiv. 9 in this context also be explained? The reference to the people being stiff-necked and the prayer for forgiveness in the second half of the verse can, in fact, be understood from its context in this revised and re-edited passage: the reproach of obstinacy in the complex of tradition which has survived refers to the breach of the covenant described in Exod. xxxii and explains in its own way why Exod. xxxiv. 10 f. describes the making of a new covenant. The prayer for forgiveness springs from the disturbance of the covenant relationship and enables Yahweh's words in xxxiv. 10a to be understood as the gracious response to this prayer.

On the other hand, the first half of the verse with its request that Yahweh should go in the midst of his people cannot be understood from the context and aims of this revision. To what extent could Moses' words 'let the Lord, I pray thee, go in the midst of us', have the purpose of making the covenant of J appear as the second covenant, following the breach of the covenant in Exod. xxxii? Exod. xxxiv. 9a requires another explanation. Why, according to the account of the theophany on Sinai, is the theme of Yahweh's going with his people taken up again? Was it not discussed more than once in Exod. xxxiii and finally concluded according to Moses' wishes in two conversations recorded in vv. 12–15 and 16–17? Or has this theme been resumed in the context of the tradition of Exod. xxxiv because it could be illuminated from a new angle? It can hardly be maintained, in view of the fact that Moses' request remains unanswered on this occasion,[337] that the Yahwistic account of the making of the covenant was considered to provide an answer. It is very improbable that this particular account would have appeared so instructive and important to a redactor on the question of Yahweh's going with his people that he would have considered it

[337] E. Auerbach's explanation, according to which Moses enforced the fulfilment of his prayer by cunning and magic after it had been rejected, is unlikely. It is only possible if the tradition of Exod. xxxiv. 1–8, 10a, 27–28 is completely excised (cf. *op. cit.*, pp. 123–4). See section II. 12.

worthwhile repeating it. There is only one explanation left, therefore: this question is not raised afresh in Exod. xxxiv. 9 in order to make an advance on Exod. xxxiii. 14, 17. In fact the question is no longer being discussed for its own sake. Rather, the context of Exod. xxxiv in itself obviously demands that Moses' prayer be repeated at this point. In what sense is it demanded? Presumably, in the following respect: Exod. xxxiv. 10aα makes it clear that in the Yahwistic account of the making of the covenant Yahweh's words are reported in the first person, 'Behold, I make a covenant. (Before all your people I will do marvels . . .)'. This use of the first person presupposes a theophany. There is a conclusive account of it in Exod. xxxiv. 5–8. Now, however, the original 'ten words', as shown earlier,[338] have been replaced by the cultic stipulations of Exod. xxxiv. 14–26, which presuppose the situation after the conquest in that they check the danger of Canaanisation and describe the new law which the Israelites had to observe after their settlement in Canaan if the Sinaitic covenant was to continue in Canaan also. Yahweh speaks in the first person in these new stipulations also, 'You shall worship no other god . . . And none shall appear before me empty' etc. This too, presupposes a theophany. Not only the form but also the content suggests this. This new law is not simply given the form of a word from God; it is addressed to Israel by the God who is not limited to appearances on Sinai but who still reveals himself even in Canaan as the living and present God. It raises the question of Yahweh's presence in Canaan. It demands an answer. Exod. xxxiv. 9a gives it with reference to the JE complex of Exod. xxxiii; Israel owes Yahweh's presence to the prayer of Moses. He witnessed the original theophany on Sinai. But Moses did not regard it as a gift solely to himself made solely for the purpose of distinguishing, exalting and encouraging him before others. In his prayer for Israel he implores God to let this gift of his presence prove real in the midst of his people even in the future. Moses, the mediator of the covenant, reveals the miracle of the theophany to the whole nation in his prayer: 'If now I have found favour in thy sight, O Lord, let the Lord, I pray thee, go in the midst of us'. The Jehovistic redaction would certainly not have attached this prayer to the description of the theophany, if the appearance of God which is attested here had been considered simply a fact of past history, never to be repeated. It only made sense to attach the prayer to Exod. xxxiv. 5–8 because at that time the theophany described here was regarded as realising what it repre-

[338] *Vide supra*, section II. 7.

sented. Exod. xxxiv. 9a makes it clear that the theophany on Sinai, described at this point by the tradition, was in Israel's own eyes its most fundamental experience; moreover, it had the power to become real again by God's grace even in the present situation of the nation which was now settled in Canaan (*bᵉḳirbēnû*). Verse 9 reveals that Israel handed down the tradition of the theophany on Sinai not simply because of its interest in past history but far more because it was stirred and impelled by the desire to realise what is described here. The fact that such an expectation was possible is also to be ascribed to the prayer of Moses. For Israel this prayer was the prime cause and explanation of Yahweh's revelation of himself in the land Canaan.[339]

The prayer of v. 9 also sheds an illuminating light on the account of the making of the covenant in Exod. xxxiv. 10 f. By inserting Moses' prayer for God's presence during the journey into Canaan immediately before Yahweh's words, 'Behold, I make a covenant' (Exod. xxxiv. 10aα), the Jehovistic redaction emphasises these words as the answer by which Yahweh implicitly promises to go with the Israelites into Canaan. The making of the covenant is announced not by the God who formerly appeared on Sinai but rather by the merciful and gracious God who was asked by Moses to go with his people to Canaan and to manifest his presence to them there also. Judging by the prayer of Moses which now precedes the announcement of the covenant, asking Yahweh to reveal himself in the midst of the people after the settlement in Canaan and, as stated, assuming it, the Yahwistic account of the making of the covenant was also understood and used in the sense of a Palestinian ceremony of covenant-renewal. From this point of view it would be perfectly natural that after entering Canaan the former 'ten words' were replaced by the new law which counteracted the danger of Canaanisation. These new cultic stipulations of Exod. xxxiv. 14–26, like the prayer of Exod. xxxiv. 9a, could, in fact, be taken as evidence that there was a ceremony of covenant-renewal after Israel settled in Canaan corresponding to the Yahwistic account of the making of the covenant: Moses' prayer presupposes such a ceremony and the cultic stipulations are to be understood as the embodiment of the covenant-law required by such a ceremony. Moreover, if it was demonstrated at an earlier point[340] that the wording of Exod. xxxiv. 27bβ in the Yahwistic account reflects the making (or renewal) of a covenant,

[339] Cf. also below, section II. 12.
[340] Cf. on the following, section II. 7.

such as was to be found both in the pre-monarchic period and in the state-cult of Jerusalem, this confirms the view that the account in Exod. xxxiv. 10 f. was linked with a ceremony of covenant-renewal. A further observation pointing in the same direction is this: behind the command of Yahweh in Exod. xxxiv. 27a to make a record of the words of the covenant is the cultic situation presupposed by the deposition of such a written record at the shrine of the covenant. Finally this view is confirmed by the way in which the new covenant words of Exod. xxxiv. 10 f. have been given their shape under the influence of a covenant-form (cf. v. 10) which was apparently still used in Israel's cult. All this adds up to *one* coherent picture: the Yahwistic account of the making of the covenant has been constructed in accordance with certain cultic facts and modes of procedure (v. 27 f.); it has been reflected upon and revised with a view to the cultic realisation of what is described (v. 9a); it has found expression within the cult for the renewal of the covenant in connection with a changed historical situation (v. 14–26) and its shape has been influenced by the covenant-form which was still a living force in Israel's cult (v. 10). Everything suggests that it was very closely connected with the cultic ceremony of covenant-renewal practised in Canaan.

If the Jehovistic redaction interrupts the Yahwistic tradition by the insertion of Moses' prayer in Exod. xxxiv. 9 in order to link and co-ordinate the tradition with the cultic realisation of the tradition relating to the theophany and the making of the covenant, then in inserting Moses' prayer[341] at this particular point it corresponds to a definite cultic pattern. There is no doubt that intercessory prayer had a place in the cult from a very early period in Israel's history.[342] Moreover, it seems to follow from Joshua vii. 6–9; Deut. ix. 18 f., 25 f.; Num. xvi. 19–22 (P); Ezek. ix (esp. v. 8) and xi (esp. v. 13) that the intercessor prostrated himself before the place where Yahweh appeared and lodged his plea for Israel in this way. It was in accord with this custom that the connection of Moses' prayer with Exod. xxxiv. 8, which describes how Moses prostrated himself before Yahweh when he revealed himself, commended itself. On the other hand, if this intercessory prayer, which is also concerned with the forgiveness

[341] Insofar as Moses includes himself with those for whom he prays in Exod. xxxiv. 9 it is hardly possible to separate his intercessory prayer from petitionary prayer; this proves it to be a relatively late construction. Cf. F. Hesse, *op. cit.*, pp. 95, 51.

[342] Cf. G. von Rad, 'Die falschen Propheten', *ZAW* 51, 1933, p. 115; P. A. H. de Boer, 'De voorbede in het Oude Testament', *OTS* 3, 1943; F. Hesse, *op. cit.*, pp. 5 f., 109; W. Eichrodt, *Theology of the Old Testament* I, p. 167.

of sins (Exod. xxxiv. 9bβ), had been inserted before the account of the making of a covenant in Exod. xxxiv. 10 f. which is obviously used in the sense of a ceremony of covenant-renewal, it could still have corresponded to a definite liturgical sequence. In fact, it may be perceived from Neh. ix that the post-exilic community made a confession of sin (v. 2) before the renewal of the covenant (v. 38).[343] In the rule of the Qumran community, which undoubtedly reflects Old Testament cultic tradition,[344] the annual renewal of the covenant was preceded by an express confession of sin.[345] Thus there may have been a definite liturgical connection between the renewal of the covenant and the confession of sin, especially since the content in both cases requires it. In principle this connection need not have been post-exilic; it is observable really in the renewal of the covenant by the assembly at Shechem, in that Joshua, before specifically accepting the duties of the covenant (Josh. xxiv. 24 f.), refers to the sins of Israel (v. 19 f.) and requires that they be solemnly renounced (v. 23). If, then, the Jehovistic redaction inserts the prayer for the forgiveness of sins, which really is an implicit confession of sin, prior to Exod. xxxiv. 10 f., it must have been arranged according to an already existing liturgical pattern. If the first half of v. 9 serves cultic interests, the latter half of this verse also has an obvious liturgical appeal. If Exod. xxxiv. 9a deals with the cultic realisation of the traditions relating to theophany and the making of the covenant, Exod. xxxiv. 9bβ completes the tradition from a liturgical point of view. There is all the more reason, therefore, for the view that the the tradition of Exod. xxxiv has been associated with a cultic act embodying this.

Finally we must consider the question of the origin of Exod. xxxiv. 9bβ—*wᵉsālaḥtā laʿᵃwônēnû ûlᵉḥaṭāʾṯēnû ûnᵉḥaltānû*. It has not been derived from Exod. xxxiii. like the rest of v. 9. Solomon's prayer consecrating the Temple (1 Kings viii. 22–61)—liturgically very interesting[346]—seems to offer information about its derivation. The crucial verses are vv. 27–30. King Solomon, in his authoritative position as builder and owner of the Temple, High Priest and leader

[343] It is striking that Neh. ix corresponds to Exod. xxxiv. not only in this respect, but also in the designation of God as 'gracious and merciful, slow to anger and abounding in steadfast love' (cf. Neh. ix. 17, 31, 19, 27, 28 with Exod. xxxiv. 6). These striking parallels permit the view that there was a connection of liturgical history between Exod. xxxiv. and the covenant-renewal of Neh. ix. On this latter point cf. also G. E. Wright, *The OT. Against its Environment*. pp. 55 f.

[344] Cf. F. Baumgärtel, *ZAW* 65, 1953, pp. 263 f.

[345] Cf. I QS, col. 1, line 21 f.

[346] Cf. H. Gressmann, *SATA* II. 1, 2nd ed., p. 211.

of the state-cult, asks Yahweh,[347] the God of Israel,[348] to grant the prayers which the covenant-people[349] will shortly offer in the Temple. In vv. 31–53 specific prayers which Yahweh is asked to grant are mentioned. In their present form some of them are undoubtedly exilic or post-exilic,[350] as, for instance, the sixth and seventh cases of prayer in vv. 44–51, which run parallel to the prayer in 1 Kings viii. 33 f. There is no doubt, however, that Solomon's prayer consecrating the Temple contained such specific cases of prayer in its pre-exilic form;[351] they are probably to be found in vv. 31–43. They normally define the case in a complex protasis and implore Yahweh's favour in the apodosis. On several occasions it is said *w^esālaḥtā l^eḥaṭṭa't* or something similar (cf. 1 Kings viii. 34, 36, 30, 39; cf. also 2 Chron. vi.). It cannot be maintained that this expression is an absolutely exilic or post-exilic addition since it appears to form an integral part of these prayers. At the same time it should be accepted that just as Solomon's prayer as a whole was certainly not simply a literary composition, but a cultic reality,[352] so too this obviously formal expression, *w^esālaḥtā l^eḥaṭṭa't* may have been a well-established element of cultic vocabulary.[353] Moreover, in 1 Kings viii. 34, 36 the prayer for the forgiveness of sins is linked with the indication that this concerns Yahweh's own people: 'and forgive the sin of thy people Israel . . . '. Yahweh, the God of Israel, is given other frequent reminders also in Solomon's prayer of consecration that this concerns *his* people. It is in keeping with the general tenor of the whole prayer that in the concluding passages which were added later (vv. 44–51, 52–53) Israel is expressly described as the *naḥ^alāh* (v. 51, 53) which Yahweh separated for himself (v. 53). It is quite likely that older elements which may be of pre-exilic origin have been worked into this later addition.[354] Thus, the confession of sin which is quoted in v. 47 after *lē'mōr* may be a formula which was already

[347] Cf. G. Widengren *Sakrales Königtum im Alten Testament und im Judentum*, pp. 14 f.
[348] On this description *vide supra*, pp. 28 f., 86 f.
[349] Cf. the repeated and emphatic 'thy people Israel'— 1 Kings viii. 30, 33, 34, 36, 41, 43 etc.
[350] For details cf. I. Benzinger *KHC* 9, pp. 61 f.; R. Kittel, *HK* 1/5, pp. 76 f.; cf. also M. Noth, *Überlieferungsgeschichtliche Studien*, esp. pp. 102–109.
[351] Cf. I. Benzinger, *op. cit.*, p. 61.
[352] Cf. H. Gressmann, *op. cit.*, p. 212. The problem of determining the *Sitz im Leben* of 1 Kings viii. more closely (whether it is an Enthronement—festival, cf. S. Mowinckel, *Psalmenstudien*, II, pp. 42; or a Festival for the consecration of the Temple, cf. W. Staerk, *SATA* III. 1, 2nd ed., p. 14; or a royal Zion-festival, cf. H-J. Kraus, *Die Königsherrschaft Gottes im Alten Testament*, pp. 43 f, or something else) may be left open at this point.
[353] A confession of sin is really required at the beginning of the Song of Moses (Deut. xxxii. 3 f.). On the origin of the song in the pre-monarchic period cf. W. F. Albright, 'Some remarks on the Song of Moses in Deuteronomy xxxii', *VT* 9, 1959, pp. 339–346.
[354] Cf. H. Gressmann, *ibid.*

in existence. The prayer for the forgiveness of sins in v. 50a, *wesālaḥtā le'ammeḵa ašer ḥaṭe'u laḵ*, undoubtedly follows an established pattern (see above—cf. vv. 34, 36, 30, 39). The same is probably true of the reason given in v. 51a, 'for they are thy people and thy heritage' (cf. v. 53a). Not least because in a pre-Deuteronomic, cultic ceremony affirming covenant-obligations (inferred from Deut. xxvi. 17–19 *inter alia*) the relation between Yahweh and Israel was formally described by the idea of possession.[355] Everything suggests, therefore, that there are very good grounds for accepting that the prayer, *wesālaḥtā la'awônēnû ûleḥā a'ṭēnû ûneḥaltānû*, in Exod. xxxiv. 9b is not a free literary product of the Jehovistic redactor but was derived from the language used in the prayers of the covenant-cult. It is the act of covenant-obligation, which we have just mentioned and which is referred to by Deut. xxvi. 17, 18a ('You have made Yahweh declare this day that he is your God . . . and Yahweh has made you declare this day that you are a people for his own possession . . . '), that provides the background for a correct understanding of why the prayer for forgiveness when the covenant was broken is linked with the prayer, 'and take us for thine inheritance', in Exod. xxxiv. 9. 'Take us for thine inheritance' refers to a definite act of making a covenant and in this sense is a suitable transition to Yahweh's words, 'Behold, I make a covenant' (Exod. xxxiv. 10a).[356]

Summary. The first half of v. 9 clearly serves to give cultic expression to the tradition of the theophany and the making of the covenant; the second half of the verse completes the unit of tradition in accordance with a liturgical pattern. In addition, the language of Exod. xxxiv. 9b is based on liturgical practice and has reference to a definite cultic act of covenant-making with its associated formulas. Judging by v. 9, Exod. xxxiv was associated with a cultic act in which the traditions embraced by Exod. xxxiv. were embodied.

9. Exodus xxxiii. 1–6, 12–17

The close literary connection between Exod. xxxiv. 9 and Exod. xxxiii. 1–6, 12–17 makes it appear advisable to trace this cross-connection first of all and to discuss Exod. xxxiii (together with Exod. xxxii) before the remaining verses of Chap. xxxiv.[357] As shown earlier,[358] Exod. xxxiii. 1–6 includes the Yahwistic passage xxxiii.

[355] Cf. section II. 6, pp. 67 f., where the word *segullâh* is used.

[356] It is not necessary to emend the MT (by altering *ûneḥaltānû* to *ûneḥiṯānû* = 'and lead us') as is often recommended. Cf. H. Ewald, A. Dillmann, B. Baentsch, and G. Beer.

[357] On Exod. xxxiv. 2–3, 5–8 see section II. 12 below.

[358] See section I. 9 above.

1–3a and the two Elohistic parallel variants xxxiii. 3b–4 and xxxiii. 5–6. The fragment of tradition contained in Exod. xxxiii. 1–3a is continued in the equally Yahwistic verses 12–17. Since xxxiii. 2 is not presupposed by xxxiii. 12, however, verse 2 is to be regarded as a later insertion.[358a] Thematically the tradition of vv. 1, 3a, 12–17 is clearly separate from Exod. xxxiii. 18–23 (J) which is a sort of commentary on Exod. xxxiv. 5 f.[359] On the other hand, since the Yahwistic tradition of Exod. xxxiv. regarding the theophany and the making of the covenant belongs to the combined tradition of Exod. xix, xx and xxiv in respect of content and was only introduced after xxxii. 33 at a later date (see above), the J-account of xxxiii. 1, 3a, 12–17 is not continued till after the P-complex Exod. xxxiv. 29—Num. x. 28.[360] But this should not prevent us from seeing that the ancient Yahwistic tradition in Exod. xxxiii. 1, 3a, 12–17 and in Num. x. 29 f. originally formed a unity. This connection should be borne in mind in examining this passage of Exodus.

According to Exod. xxxiii. 1, 3a Yahweh tells Moses that he and the people should leave Sinai and go to Canaan. To this command Moses replies in xxxiii. 12a: 'See, thou sayest to me, "Bring up this people"; but thou has not let me know whom thou wilt send with me.' Directly following this conversation is[361] the passage Num. x. 29—33a, according to which Moses repeats what he has said and urgently begs the Midianite, Ḥobab ben Re'uel,[362] as one who knows the desert and the places it offers for encampment, to go with them on their journey to Canaan. Since this Midianite 'appears out of the blue as someone well-known . . . this strongly suggests that Yahweh originally referred Moses to this Ḥobab'.[363] A corresponding word of Yahweh has clearly been lost between Exod. xxxiii. 12a (J) and Num. x. 29 f. (J). At any rate, the request of Moses to be informed whom Yahweh is sending with him on the journey to Canaan is to be understood from this context. Moses asks Yahweh in Exod. xxxiii. 12a for an experienced guide through the desert. The importance of the question of a guide for the groups of the future Israel on their way to

[358a] On Exod. xxxiii. 2, see p. 110, n. 423 below.

[359] So B. D. Eerdmans, *Alttestamentliche Studien 3, Das Buch Exodus*, p. 76; W. Rudolph, *Der 'Elohist' von Exodus bis Josua*, *BZAW* 68, p. 57. On vv. 18–23 see section II. 12.

[360] So J. Wellhausen, *Die Composition des Hexateuchs*, pp. 83 f., and G. Westphal, *Jahwes Wohnstätten*, *BZAW* 15, p. 29. On the above P-passage see section I. 1c above.

[361] On this break see what follows. Cf. meanwhile also R. Smend, *Die Erzählung des Hexateuch*, p. 189, and O. Eissfeldt. *Hexateuch-Synopse*, p. 160. On the unity of the fragment cf. W. Rudolph, *op. cit.*, pp. 63 f.

[362] Further details in W. Rudolph, *op. cit.*, p. 63.

[363] G. Westphal, *op. cit.*, p. 29.

Palestine could not have been ignored even if the tradition had not preserved any recollection of it (see also Deut. i, 19).[364]

It is clear that Exod. xxxiii. 12b–17 alters the original meaning of Moses' words in Exod. xxxiii. 12a, if it depicts Yahweh giving instructions that his *pānîm* (v. 14 f.), i.e. himself (v. 16 f.), will accompany them. The question of a human guide through the desert is replaced by the cardinal question, whether, and if so how, Yahweh himself can go with his people to Canaan. Nevertheless, it would be foolish to assign vv. 12a and 12b–17 to different literary sources because of this change of meaning. It is more a matter of two overlapping strata of tradition within *one* source.[365]

Similarly, it should be asked whether it is correct to allocate Num. x. 29–33a and x. 33b to different sources.[366] The first passage, it is true, concerns the selection of Ḥobab ben Re'uel as pilot through the desert, whereas in v. 33b the *Ark* suddenly becomes the leader through the desert and traces out camping-places. In view of the dual character of the Yahwistic tradition in Exod. xxxiii. 12-17, however, this conflict of content should not be immediately resolved by the methods of literary criticism. There is obviously no positive proof that with x. 33b an E-element was attached to the Yahwistic passage Num. x. 29–33a.[367] It is at least equally likely that this half-verse also belongs to the Yahwistic tradition.[368] The possibility that the Yahwist also may have spoken about the Ark should not be rejected in view of Num. xiv. 44 which is probably Yahwistic.[369] Moreover, there is a link, at least linguistically, between Num. x. 33b and Exod. xxxiii. 14, a later stratum within the J-source: in the former the Ark has the task of pointing out *lāhem m^enûḥâh*; in the latter Yahweh says, *wah^aniḥōṯî lāk*, with regard to his *panim* (presence).[370]

[364] Cf. on this for instance E. Auerbach, *Moses*, p. 123; M. Noth, *Die Welt des Alten Testaments*, 3rd ed., p. 150.

[365] See below. Cf. also for instance H. Holzinger, *KHC* 2, p. 110.

[366] Cf. for example B. Baentsch, *HK* 2/2, p. 501 (J. & E.); R. Smend, *op. cit.*, p. 189 (J[1] and J[2] or J[1] and E); O. Eissfeldt, *op. cit.*, pp. 160 f. (L. & J.).

[367] Cf. the arguments of B. Baentsch, *op. cit.*; H. Holtzinger, *KHC* 4, p. 38; R. Smend, *ibid.*

[368] Cf. (apart from W. Rudolph, *op. cit.*, pp. 62 f.) O. Eissfeldt, *op. cit.*, p. 160; R. Smend, *op. cit.*, p. 189; esp. W. Eichrodt. *Theology of the Old Testament* I, p. 111, n. 2.

[369] Cf. R. Smend, *op. cit.*, p. 198; O. Eissfeldt, *op. cit.*, pp. 173, 277.

[370] Num. x. 33b has been worked over at a later date perhaps. At least, the verb *tur* occurs chiefly in later literature (cf. S. Mandelkern, *op. cit.*, p. 1242) and particularly frequently in P (cf. Num. xiii. 2, 16 f., 21, 25, 32; xiv. 6 f., 34, 36, 38). Num. x. 34 was probably added by the P-redactor. The view that it is a later insertion is based on its different position in the LXX, namely after the words of signal in xxxv. 36; there is also some doubt about the correctness of its position in the MT., as the inverted *nun* was intended to show (cf. on this M. Dibelius, *Die Lade Jahwes*, pp. 8 f.; G. von Rad, 'Zelt und Lade', *Gesammelte Studien*, p. 120). Everything suggests that the ending of Num. x. 29–33 was expanded differently.

At any rate it is difficult to assign Num. x. 33b to the E-source. The suggestion that we are dealing here with a younger element in the J-source seems more likely. In this case the two passages Exod. xxxiii. 12–17 and Num. x, 29–33, which were originally next to each other, had a similar form; the older parts, Exod. xxxiii. 12a and Num. x. 29-33a, describe how Moses sought a (human) guide through the desert. These older elements were overlaid by a stratum of tradition which spoke of Yahweh himself (Exod. xxxiii. 16 f.) or his *panim* (Exod. xxxiii. 14 f.) or his Ark (Num. x. 33b) going with Israel to Canaan. There is no doubt that these older passages formed a unity. It is also quite probable that the younger elements were related to one another and belonged together in some way. We shall come back to this later.

What is the explanation of the dual character of the tradition contained in Exod. xxxiii. 12–17? It is certainly not the work of a collator who put together thematically related pieces and abbreviated them to his needs. It would be truer to say the ideas and arguments of Exod. xxxiii. 12b–17 seem to have been sparked off by Moses' word in Exod. xxxiii. 12a: 'See, thou sayest to me, "Bring up this people"; but thou hast not let me know whom thou wilt send with me'. Insofar as this assumes that Yahweh himself does not go with them it gives rise to an argument which is concerned to urge Yahweh himself or his *panim* to go with them to Canaan. And such a concern does not allow the account which begins in Exod. xxxiii. 12a to be quietly brought to an end by Moses' request for a guide through the desert. The tradition points in another direction. On Moses' lips this request becomes an urgent demand for God's presence in Canaan. Everything stands or falls by whether it is fulfilled or not: 'If thy presence will not go with me, do not carry us up from here' (Exod. xxxiii. 15b). God's grace is called in question if Yahweh does not go with them (Exod. xxxiii. 16a). Israel's election is frustrated if Yahweh stays behind (Exod. xxxiii. 16b). He cannot abandon Israel because of his covenant: 'Consider too that this nation is *thy* people' (Exod. xxxiii. 13b).

The passion with which this argument is conducted and with which the narrative of the Midianite Ḥobab ben Re'uel is abruptly set aside is only intelligible against the background of a burning, existing problem. Obviously this consisted in establishing and getting recognition for the conviction that the God who once revealed himself fully and for the first time on *Sinai* was now present with his people in *Canaan* also. Obviously, too, the *first* thrust in this direction is not to be ascribed to the later Yahwistic tradition in Exod. xxxiii. 12b–17. Even in Mosaic times Yahweh is clearly no longer thought of as absolutely tied to Sinai and limited to it. Otherwise, how could ancient Israel have believed that Yahweh showed his might in *Egypt* through the Exodus?[371] According to the two Elohistic variants in Exod. xxxiii. 3b–6, also, Yahweh was not confined to the mount of God; if he stays behind on this mountain it is simply because he has freely chosen to do so. All the evidence goes to suggest that from an early date Yahweh's attachment to Sinai was only relative, although it should not be underestimated. Even the Yahweh worshipped in the state-cult at Jerusalem, who had taken up residence in the Temple (Ps. lxviii. 6, 25, 30, 36) and had chosen Zion for his eternal residence (Ps. lxviii. 17), was still *zeh sīnay*, i.e. Lord of Sinai[372] (Ps. lxviii. 9.), whose epiphany can be described as if the mountain itself were present in the Temple (Ps. lxviii. 18).[373] This makes it extremely clear how even at a later date Yahweh and Sinai belonged inseparably together. If, with M. Noth,[374] the story of Elijah's journey to the mount of God in 1 Kings xix. 3 f. and the nucleus of the list of stations in Num. xxxiii. 3–49 may be taken as evidence of a pilgrimage to Sinai in the pre-exilic period, it follows that there must have been circles in Israel for a long time for whom Yahweh dwelt primarily on distant Sinai and was therefore to be sought there.[375] In contrast to this it may be inferred from the Elohistic and Yahwistic accounts of Israel's ancestors that soon after the conquest there were numerous attempts made to worship Yahweh (instead of the various local *numina*) at the former Canaanite shrines.[376] These attempts have already been given systematic shape in the Yahwist and the Elohist.[377] The younger Yahwistic tradition in Exod. xxxiii. 12b–17 is an example of such a systematic effort

[371] Cf. on this and what follows G. Westphal, *op. cit.*, pp. 29 f., 46 f.

[372] On the translation, corresponding to the Akkadian determinative pronoun *šu* W. V. Soden, *GAG* §46b) and the Arabic *ḏū*, cf. W. F. Albright, *BASOR* 62, 1936, pp. 29 f.; A. R. Johnson, *Sacral Kingship in Ancient Israel*, p. 71, n. 1; J. M. Allegro, 'Uses of the Semitic Demonstrative Element z in Hebrew', *VT* 5, 1955, pp. 309 f.; and C. Brockelmann, *Hebräische Syntax*, §75, p. 69 (details of further literature there). On the other hand cf. H. Birkeland, 'Hebrew *zae* and Arabic *ḏū*', *StTh.* 2, 1950, pp. 201 f.

[373] On the concept of space implied here cf. H. and H. A. Frankfort, *Before Philosophy* (= *The Intellectual Adventure of Ancient Man*), pp. 30 f.

[374] 'Der Wallfahrtsweg zum Sinai (Num. xxxiii.)', *PJ* 36, 1940, pp. 5–28.

[375] Pilgrims of this belief also protested against the nature-worship of Yahweh in Canaan by their journey to Sinai, as M. Schmidt (*Prophet und Tempel*, pp. 16 f.) correctly observes.

[376] Cf. for instance A. Alt, *Der Gott der Väter* (= *Kleine Schriften* I, pp. 6 f.); M. Schmidt, *op. cit.*, p. 16.

[377] Cf. M. Schmidt, *op. cit.*, p. 230, n. 9.

to establish and promote the conviction that Yahweh was attached to his people and present with them in Canaan also.

As in Exod. xxxiv. 9 this aim is embodied in a prayer of Moses.[378] The powerful authority of the man who can say to Yahweh, '... yet thou has said, "I know you by name, and you have also found favour in my sight"' (Exod. xxxiii. 12b), is thrown into the balance. The later Yahwistic tradition is obviously linked at this point with a word of Yahweh addressed to Moses, which the tradition has not preserved for us. Moses' prayer of intercession has been built up of material from this word of mercy which has now disappeared (cf. Exod. xxxiii. 12b, 13a, 16a, 17b). Through the appeal to the special grace attached to the covenant-mediator the God of Sinai is being entreated for his presence in Canaan. Through the reference to the covenant by which Yahweh has bound himself to his people he is being adjured to go with them (cf. Exod. xxxiii. 13b, 16). In all this it is evident that it is not so much the prayer of the mighty man of God in itself which is intended to prevail upon Yahweh as the objective argument, which depends on the covenant-relationship and the covenant-mediation of Moses and which seeks to argue from them.[379] To that extent we are dealing here with a *systematic* attempt to answer the question of the presence of the God of Sinai in Canaan.

Of what nature is the presence of God which is referred to? The question[380] with which Yahweh meets Moses' request, 'Shall my presence go with you ... ?' (Exod. xxxiii. 14), gives a clue. Moses replies to Yahweh's question: 'If thy presence will not go with me, do not carry us up from here' (Exod. xxxiii. 15). What is meant here by *pānîm*? The root of the noun is the verb *pānāh*, which means 'to turn to one side, to turn away from or towards'.[381] *Pānîm*, accordingly, is 'the side which has been turned', 'the front' and in the case of a man, therefore, 'the face'.[382] In Exod. xxxiii. 14 f. *Yahweh's* face is spoken of anthropomorphically: his face is to go with them to Canaan.[383] It should be noticed that 'Yahweh's face' is generally

[378] Cf. F. Hesse, *Die Fürbitte im Alten Testament*, pp. 95 f.

[379] With F. Hesse, *op. cit.*, p. 27 (cf. pp. 19 f.) Exod. xxxiii. 13 is to be regarded as a relatively late piece of intercession; this agrees with the findings of literary criticism and tradition history noted above.

[380] With O. Eissfeldt, *op. cit.*, p. 157; W. Rudolph, *op. cit.*, p. 56; G. Beer, *HAT* 1/3, p. 158 and others, Exod. xxxiii. 14b is to be understood as a question. Cf. Gesenius-Kautzsch, *HG* § 150a; Beer-Meyer, *HG* II, § 111, 1c.

[381] Cf. Koehler-Baumgartner, *LVTL*, p. 765.

[382] Cf. J. Boehmer, *Gottes Angesicht*, *BFChTh* 12, 1908, p. 324; E. Lohse, *prosopon*, *ThWBNT VI*, pp. 771 f.

[383] Cf. also Deut. iv. 37.

spoken of in a cultic context.[384] Thus in Exod. xxxiv. 23 (cf. xxiii. 17) and xxxiv. 20b (cf. xxiii. 15b) the priest of a Palestinian shrine of Yahweh turns to the laity associated with it and addresses them in the following, very ancient stipulations: 'Three times in the year shall all your males appear before the Lord your God, the God of Israel', and 'None shall appear before me empty'.[385] Undoubtedly a visit to a cult-place is required in both cases. The prophet Isaiah asks in one of his oracles of judgement, 'When you come to appear before me (= see my face)[386] . . . who requires of you this trampling of my courts?' (i. 12). Here again to see Yahweh's face means to participate in the cult of Yahweh. Similarly Yahweh's *pānîm* are referred to in Jeremiah's temple-speech (vii. 10): ' . . . and then come and stand before me (= before my face) in this house which is called by my name . . . '. In Zeph. i. 7, probably with reference to a liturgical formula,[387] Yahweh's appearance at the time of sacrifice is announced with the cry, 'Be silent before (= before the face of) the Lord God . . . '. Moreover, the Priestly source calls the shewbread in the Temple 'the bread of the Presence' (Exod. xxv. 30; xxxv. 13; xxxix. 36. cf. 1 Sam. xxi. 7; 1 Kings vii. 48). The phrase 'to seek Yahweh's face' in Ps. xxiv. 6; xxvii. 8; cv. 4; and 2 Sam. xxi. 1 also points to the close connection between Yahweh's face and shrine. It is further presupposed by the expression 'to turn away from Yahweh's face'; compare the formulae 'to bless . . . , curse . . . , make a covenant . . . , offer a sacrifice . . . , shout . . . , rejoice . . . , give thanks . . . etc. before Yahweh's face.'[388] The conclusion to be drawn from all this is that Yahweh's face must have played an important rôle in Israel's cult. All these cultic acts involve a clear reference to Yahweh's *pānîm*.

How did this come about? Since the amphictyonic cult of Yahweh was probably imageless from the very beginning (cf. Deut. xxvii. 15; Exod. xx. 4; xxxiv. 17),[389] it is inconceivable that the cultic worship of images of *Yahweh* could once have formed the basis of the phrase

[384] Cf. on the following E. C. Gulin, *Das Antlitz Jahwes im Alten Testament*, *AASF* 16, 1922, pp. 1 f.; see also E. Lohse, *op. cit.*, p. 774.

[385] Cf. above section II, 7.

[386] With W. Baudissin, ' "Gott schauen" in der alttestamentlichen Religion', *ARW* 18, 1915, pp. 181 f.; and others.

[387] So K. Elliger, *Das Buch der zwölf Kleinen Propheten* II, *ATD* 25, pp. 59 f.

[388] Cf. in detail E. G. Gulin, *op. cit.*, pp. 6 f.

[389] See H. Th. Obbink, 'Jahwebilder'. *ZAW* 47, 1929, pp. 264–274, and recently K-H. Bernhardt, *Gott und Bild. Ein Beitrag zur Begründung und Deutung des Bilderverbotes im Alten Testament*, pp. 144 f.; further G. von Rad, *Theology of the Old Testament* I, p. 214 f.; cf. on the other hand S. Mowinckel, 'Wann wurde der Jahwäkultus in Jerusalem offiziell bildlos?', *AcOr.* 8, 1930, pp. 257–279.

'Yahweh's face'. But the Old Testament expression, 'to behold the face of Yahweh', with which the visit to the shrine is described, has an Akkadian parallel in the expression *amāru pān ili*[390] as well as analogies in Egyptian texts.[391] Judging by the latter especially, these analogies in Egypt and Mesopotamia may well have presupposed the cultic worship of images of the gods.[392] Subsequently this expression will have become accessible to the wandering Israelites through Canaanite mediation.[393] This makes it questionable how far phrases about God's face presuppose image-worship at Canaanite shrines.[394] The important rôle which Yahweh's face clearly plays in cultic contexts is no longer rooted in image-worship in the Old Testament, at least.

It seems to have come to occupy a central place in Israel's cult in connection with another cultic institution. It is striking how often in the Psalms Yahweh's face is referred to in direct connection with his appearance in the shrine. Ps. lxviii begins in the style of the ancient cultic liturgy which has been preserved in the sayings about the Ark in Num. x. 35 f.:[395] 'Yahweh[396] arises; his enemies are scattered, those who hate him flee before him (= before his face). As smoke drifts away,[397] so thou drivest (them) away; as wax melts before fire, so the wicked perish before God (= before his face). But the righteous are joyful; they exult before God (= before his face) and are jubilant with joy. Sing to God; sing praises to his name. Make way[398] for him who rides upon the clouds.[399] YAH is his name;[400] exult before him (= before his face). . . . O God, when thou didst go forth before thy people, when thou didst march through the wilderness, the earth quaked, the heavens poured down

[390] It occurs in a hymn to Ištar. Cf. H Zimmern, in E Schrader, *Die Keilinschriften und das Alte Testament*, 3rd ed., p. 442.

[391] Cf. in detail W. Baudissin, *op. cit.*, pp. 189–192; E. G. Gulin, *op. cit.*, pp. 4 f.

[392] On image-worship in Egypt and Asia Minor cf. H. Schrade, *Der verborgene Gott. Gottesbild und Gottesvorstellung in Israel und im Alten Orient*, pp. 13–23.

[393] That the Canaanites could speak of the *pn* of a deity is clear from the Phoenician description of the goddess Tanit as *Tanit pnē ba'al* (cf. W. Baudissin, *op. cit.*, p. 193). There is no proof as yet of a Canaanite expression equivalent to 'behold Yahweh's face'.

[394] Cf. especially K. Galling, *BRL*, col. 201 f. (esp. line 2); A. Jirku, *Die Ausgrabungen in Palästina und Syrien*, pp. 86 f. (and plate 19); B. Gemser, *RGG* 1, 3rd. ed., col. 1272 (line 2).

[395] Cf. A. Weiser, *The Psalms*, p. 481; H-J. Kraus, *Psalmen*, *BK*. 15, 6, p. 472.

[396] So here and elsewhere instead of *'elōhîm* (redactional in the Elohistic Psalter, Ps. xlii–lxxxix). Cf. the various Introductions to the O.T.

[397] Vocalise as *niphal*.

[398] Derived from the Akkadian *sulū*. Cf. H. Zimmern, *Akkadische Fremdwörter*, 2nd ed., p. 43; Koehler-Baumgartner, *LVTL*, p. 659.

[399] Analogous to the epithet of Baal, *rkb 'rpt*, in the Ras Shamra texts. Cf. C. H. Gordon, *Ugaritic Manual*, p. 324/1763.

[400] Cf. lxx.

rain at the presence of God, the Lord of Sinai,[401] at the presence of God, the God of Israel' (vv. 2–5, 8–9). It is easy to see how closely references to Yahweh's face and his cultic theophany are interwoven. The same is true of Judges v. 5[402] and Ps. xcv. 1 f.; xcvi. 9 f.; xcvii. 2 f.; xcviii. 6 f.[403] In Ps. lxxx. the cry addressed to Yahweh, 'Thou who art enthroned upon the cherubim, appear . . . !' (v. 2), is paralleled by the prayer, 'let thy face shine, that we may be saved' (v. 4). The liturgical formula of the Aaronite blessing in Num. vi. 24 f. also makes clear the connection between Yahweh's face and his theophany.[404] In the Decalogue (Exod. xx. 3) the covenant-God, who speaks in the first person and is present in the cult, demands, 'Thou shalt have no other gods before me (= *'al pānay*)'. Once again *pānîm* and cultic theophany belong together. Finally, the imperatives of Zeph. i. 7 and Hab. ii. 20, which have been influenced by formal, liturgical expressions, reflect this same situation.[405] It is clear from all the evidence, therefore, that Yahweh's face and his cultic epiphany belonged together. This connection is the basis of the particular importance which Yahweh's *pānîm* possessed in Israel's cult.[406]

Incidentally, this connection between Yahweh's face and his epiphany is a distinctive characteristic of the cult of Yahweh: whereas in Egypt and Mesopotamia talk of seeing God's face is dependent on the cultic worship of images of the gods (see above), the corresponding Israelite term is based on the cultic event of the theophany, not on an image of Yahweh. In the former case heavenly beings reveal themselves in the image,[407] in the latter Yahweh meets his people in the dynamic event of the cultic epiphany. No one can or should possess him in an image (Exod. xx. 4).[408] Even in giving himself he remains the sovereign Lord.

In the light of the close connection established between Yahweh's face and his epiphany in Israel's cult the aim of the younger Yahwistic tradition in Exod. xxxiii. 12b–17 may now be determined more precisely: its purpose is not to secure and further the belief that the

401 See n. 368.

402 Cf. A. Weiser, 'Das Deboralied', *ZAW* 71, 1959, p. 74.

403 Cf. A. Weiser, 'Theophanie in den Psalmen und im Festkult', *Bertholet-Festschrift*, pp. 517 f.

404 Cf. A. Weiser, *op. cit.*, p. 519, n. 1.

405 Cf. K. Elliger, *op. cit.*, pp. 45, 59 f.

406 Even more than the conservative nature of sacral language this connection with the cultic theophany explains how, for instance, this terminology which goes back to Yahweh's face was used so widely and persistently to describe a visit to the shrine and participation in the cult of Yahweh.

407 Cf. H. Schrade, *ibid.*

408 Cf. W. Zimmerli, 'Das zweite Gebot', *Bertholet-Festschrift*, esp. pp. 561 f.

God of Sinai, free from all local ties, is also present everywhere in Canaan. It is motivated by a much more special purpose. With the help of the idea of the covenant and the authority of the mediator of the covenant it seeks to establish and gain recognition for the fact that the God of Sinai can also appear and be present in the Palestinian cult of Israel: because Yahweh was moved by entreaties at Sinai to allow his presence to go with his people into the promised land (Exod. xxxiii. 14, 15), therefore Yahweh now causes his face to shine upon the assembled cultic community (cf. Ps. lxxx. 2, 4; Num. vi. 24 f.), therefore Israel is summoned before God's face (cf. for instance Exod. xx. 3), therefore the righteous rejoice and the wicked perish before God's face (cf. Ps. lxviii. 2 f.), therefore the community confesses its faith and sings praises before his *pānîm* (cf. Ps. xcv. 1 f.; xcviii. 6), falls down and intercedes before him (cf. Ps. xcvi. 9). In short, the cultic worship of Yahweh, which presupposes his personal presence,[409] is a practical reality. Israel cannot celebrate the worship of its God on its own initiative or in a place of its own choosing. The cult of Yahweh is only possible where he permits his face to shine.[410] Hence the passionate and emphatic affirmation in Exod. xxxiii. 12 f. that it is Yahweh's will that his presence has accompanied his people to Canaan. This is the way the God who appeared at Sinai reveals himself to the cultic community—by his face.[411] Thus, the later Yahwistic tradition in Exod. xxxiii. 12–17 was determined by an express cultic interest: it is a reflection upon a decisive presupposition of the cult of Yahweh in Canaan.

In this connection we must return once again to the Jehovistic verse Exod. xxxiv. 9.[412] It seemed to serve the cultic realisation of the tradition dealing with the theophany and the making of the covenant in Exod. xxxiv and to give the structure of this chapter a liturgical point of view and to relate it to liturgical vocabulary and form. The suggestion, which ultimately was not derived from *this* verse, that the tradition contained in Exod. xxxiv was given concrete expression in the cult, now seems fully verified in view of Exod. xxxiii. 12–17. There is no doubt that the Jehovistic redaction in Exod. xxxiv. 9 and elsewhere was related to this late Yahwistic tradition (see above).

[409] Cf. S. Mowinckel, *Religion und Kultus*, pp. 52 f., 57; W. Eichrodt, *Theology of the Old Testament* I, pp. 98 f.

[410] Cf. the remarks of W. Baudissin, *op. cit.*, pp. 203 f., on the story of the patriarchs.

[411] In Exod. xxxiii. 16 f. it is clear that for Israel this 'face' was not simply a substitute for God or only a part of him but God himself (*bᵉlektᵉkā ʿimmānu*). On this way of thinking *pars pro toto* in 'myth', cf. H. and H. A. Frankfort, *op. cit.*, p. 20.

[412] Cf. section II, 8.

It is now established, however, that the borrowed elements in Exod. xxxiii. 12–17 do not possess cultic importance simply through their link with the tradition dealing with the theophany and the making of the covenant in Exod. xxxiv. The Jehovistic redaction, it is now clear, moved by the desire to see the realisation of what is described here, went back very relevantly to a tradition which had a cultic orientation from the very beginning. This tradition tackled the fundamental question of the Yahweh-cult in Canaan systematically and affirmed that Yahweh's presence had accompanied Israel to Canaan at Moses' request and according to Yahweh's will. The theophanic God can still give himself to the cultic community in his *pānīm*. Reference to this particular tradition after the account of the primordial theophany at Sinai and before the account of the making of the covenant can hardly have any other intention than that of giving an express reminder that the presupposition for realising what is described now exists in the Palestinian cult also. From the point of view of Exod. xxxiii. 12–17, therefore, the interpretation of Exod. xxxiv suggested earlier is confirmed.

After this digression on Exod. xxxiv we must once more take up the question of what contexts the face of Yahweh, which is spoken of with such emphasis by the younger J-tradition in Exod. xxxiii, belongs to. It has been established that it occurs in connection with the cultic epiphany of Yahweh. Here, in the theophany, the God who first appeared on Sinai, overcomes the spatial barrier[413] separating the distant mount of God (i.e. his heavenly shrine, cf. Ps. xi. 4) and his Palestinian shrine (cf. Ps. lxviii. 18) and reveals himself to the cultic community as the One who is personally present. In the event of the theophany Yahweh's face shines upon the assembled community and encounters it in blessing, challenge and judgement; the community's prayer, confession and praise is addressed to Yahweh's face. The idea of the theophany which transcends the limitations of space has obviously been formed in connection with already existing Syro-Canaanite forms and ideas: in the mythological texts from Ras Shamra, at any rate, Al'iyan Baal is given the epithet *rkb ʿrpt*, 'he who rides on the clouds',[414] a description which is applied to Yahweh in Ps. xviii. 10 f.; lxviii. 5, 34; civ. 3; Deut. xxxiii. 26; Isa. xix. 1. There was a concrete parallel to this term in the Israelite cult—namely, in the *Ark*. The *kappōreṯ* (lid) of the Ark with its winged

[413] Cf. on the mythical understanding of space, H. and H. A. Frankfort, *op. cit.*, pp. 29 f.

[414] See C. H. Gordon, *op. cit.*, p. 324, par. 1763; cf. J. Gray, *The Legacy of Canaan*, *VTS* 5, 1957, pp. 9, 23, n. 8.

cherubim[415] is a copy of the chariot of clouds[416] on which the God of Sinai comes to his people. The copy of the chariot of clouds used by the theophanic God in the shrine of Yahweh will have influenced the portrayal of the theophany in the cult.[417] Since the Ark discharges a function in connection with the cultic theophany it is probable that behind the face of Yahweh in Exod. xxxiii. 14 f. there is not only an epiphany but that Yahweh's *pānîm* are also connected with the Ark. The Old Testament does, in fact, make it clear on several occasions that Yahweh's face, his epiphany, and his Ark are closely connected with each other. In Ps. lxxx. 2, 4 the God of Israel who is enthroned above the Ark is invoked: 'Thou who art enthroned upon the cherubim appear! . . . let thy face shine that we may be saved'. The sayings about the Ark in Num. x. 35 f., which probably stem from the liturgy connected with the oldest cult of the Ark and which clearly belonged originally with the cultic theophany, make it clear[418] that Yahweh's face played a particular part in the theophany above the Ark.[419] In Ps. lxviii, which refers to this same cultic liturgy of the Ark, the same group of ideas recurs—Yahweh's face, cultic theophany, and the Ark (cf. v. 2 f.). Finally, they may also be found in Ps. xxiv. (exp. v. 6 f.) and in the account of the Ark being brought to Jerusalem in 2 Sam. vi. (cf. vv. 2, 5, 14, 17, 18, 21). All in all, it seems justifiable to posit a connection between the face of the God who appears on Sinai (Exod. xxxiii. 14 f.) and the Ark of Yahweh.

The fact that Yahweh's *pānîm* in Exod. xxxiii. 14 have the task of 'procuring resting-places'[420] for Moses and the people is in favour of this view. Although the phrase *wahᵃniḥōṯî lāḵ* may have included the meaning 'to procure rest from one's enemies',[421] which is found in many passages of the Old Testament, the procuring of suitable resting-places on the journey through the desert is certainly included. In Num. x. 33b, however, it is the Ark which has the task of gaining

[415] On the thesis of M. Haran, 'The Ark and the Cherubim', *IEJ* 9, 1959, pp. 32 f. see below, n. 460.

[416] So H. Torczyner, *Die Bundeslade und die Anfänge der Religion Israels*, 2nd ed., p. 45, and A. Weiser, 'Theophanie in den Psalmen und im Festkult', *Bertholet-Festschrift*, pp. 520 f.

[417] The technique of imitative magic which underlies this (cf. for instance S. Mowinckel *Religion und Kultus*, pp. 24 f.) certainly could not exercise a determinative influence in the sphere of the Yahweh-cult (cf. on this G. von Rad, *Theology of the Old Testament* I, p. 34 f.), even if it perhaps contributed to the danger of the Ark being misinterpreted and misused.

[418] Cf. Ps. lxviii. 2, 18. Cf. on this H. Torczyner, *op. cit.*, pp. 7–11. In Num. x. 36 *šᵉḇāh*, 'mount', should be read instead of *šûḇāh*, 'return'.

[419] *Mippāneykā* here does not simply mean 'before you' but 'before your face'. With E. G. Gulin, *op. cit.*, p. 2, n. 4.

[420] Cf. Koehler-Baumgartner, *LVTL*, p. 602.

[421] Cf. Deut. iii, 18 f.; xii. 10; xxv. 19; Joshua xxi. 44; xxiii. 1; 2 Sam. vii. 1, 11; 1 Kings v. 18; 1 Chron. xxii. 9, 18 etc.

information about resting-places for the people on their way to Canaan (*lāṯûr lāhem mᵉnûḥâh*).[422] And according to the battle-cries in Num. x. 35 f. it is also the Ark which puts Israel's enemies to flight.[423] Thus the phrase *wahᵃniḥōṯî lāḵ* in Exod. xxxiii. 14b strongly suggests that the Ark may be in the background of Yahweh's face.[424] If Exod. xxxiii. 12b–17 and Num. x. 33b ought, as suggested at the beginning, to belong to the same stratum within the Yahwistic tradition, this would strengthen the hypothesis further.

Lastly, the *context* also favours it. It is widely and probably rightly assumed that behind the two Elohistic variant traditions of xxxiii. 3b–4 and xxxiii. 5–6 an account of the making of the Ark referring back to the P-passage Exod. xxv. f. has been broken off.[425] These two E-passages both proceed from Yahweh's refusal to go with Israel to Canaan because of its stubborness and his decision to remain behind on the mount of God. Even the Elohistic tradition feels this decision of God's to be a painful problem and seeks a way out. This is obviously prepared for in Exod. xxxiii. 5b: the ornaments that were laid aside were probably used to make an object[426] which would mitigate the punitive effect of Yahweh's decision to remain behind and would accompany Israel to Canaan.[427] Most probably the Ark was emphasised at this point. If the Jehovistic redaction linked vv. 3b–6 (E) with Exod. xxxiii. 1, 3a, 12–17 (J) this may point to the fact that it, too, considered that Yahweh's face (in Exod. xxxiii. 14 f.) and the Ark belonged together.

Summary. At the instigation of an older element (Exod. xxxiii. 12a) the younger Yahwistic tradition of Exod. xxxiii. 12b–17 vigorously defends the conviction that Yahweh was moved by the entreaties of Moses on Sinai to send his presence with his people to Canaan—*that* presence which was revealed to the cultic community in the theo-

[422] How it exercised this task may perhaps be gathered from 1 Sam. vi. 7 f.

[423] According to Exod. xxxiii. 2, which was added to the Yahwistic tradition of Exod. xxxiii. 1, 3a, 12–17 at a later date, *the angel of Yahweh* (cf. LXX on the passage) had the task of expelling Israel's foes. This angel, however, may (as in Exod. xxiii. 20 f.) have been regarded as one of Yahweh's modes of appearing which was connected with the *Ark*. The Ark was probably considered the external *substratum* to which the appearance of the angel of Yahweh was attached. Cf. from this point of view Judges ii. 1–5 particularly. Further details in O. Eissfeldt, 'Lade und Stierbild', *ZAW* 58, 1940/41, pp. 191 f., esp. n. 2; R. Smend, *Die Erzählung des Hexateuch*, p. 274. On the angel of Yahweh cf. G. von Rad, *op. cit.*, pp. 286 f. (further literature given there), and in *ThWBNT* I, pp. 75 f.

[424] Cf. G. Beer, *HAT* 1/3, p. 159; O. Eissfeldt, *op. cit.*, p. 191.

[425] Cf. Among others J. Wellhausen, *Die Composition des Hexateuchs*, p. 93; O. Eissfeldt, *op. cit.*, pp. 191 f.; W. Rudolph, *op. cit.*, pp. 54 f.; G. Beer, *HAT* 1/3, p. 157; G. von Rad, *op. cit.*, p. 237, n. 109.

[426] Cf. the making of cultic objects from the ornaments laid aside in Exod. xxxii. 2 f. (Golden Calf) and Judges viii. 24 f. (ephod).

[427] With W. Rudolph, *ibid.*

phany above the Ark. Without Yahweh's *pānîm* no cult of Yahweh in Canaan would be possible.[428] Hence the passionate argument, which draws upon Moses' place of privilege, his intercession, and the ideas of covenant and election. Exod. xxxiii. 12–17 represents a systematic attempt to set forth the fundamental presupposition of Israel's covenant-cult. Its redactional connection with the E-passage, Exod. xxxiii. 3b–6, should also be understood from this point of view.[429]

Finally, there remains one point to be considered in connection with the E-passages just quoted. It is conspicuous that *two* variants of tradition (Exod. xxxiii. 3b–4 and xxxiii. 5–6) are concerned with the comparatively unimportant theme of putting aside ornaments. Furthermore, Gen. xxxv. 2–4 (E) also describes something similar: the Israelites hand over their ear-rings; they give them to Jacob who buries them under the terebinth at Shechem (v. 4). It is this last passage, perhaps, which explains the unique importance possessed by this theme in the tradition.[430] In Gen. xxxv. 2–4 the act of handing over these ornaments[431] is linked with the renunciation of foreign gods. Since this act of renunciation took place in the assembly at Shechem according to Joshua xxiv. 14, 23 it is quite likely that it was repeated in the shrine at Shechem and that together with the handing over of ornaments it belonged to the wider context of the Shechemite festival of covenant-renewal.[432] Everything suggests that the Elohist had before his eyes the rite of renunciation and the discarding of ornaments, as well as the grave at the terebinth, in which the ear-rings of the Israelites were buried without ceremony, and that he wished to give them an aetiological place in the context of the story of the patriarchs. The aetiological tendency of the narrative in Gen. xxxv. 2–4 becomes perfectly obvious in the final sentence which is attested almost unanimously by the LXX[433] (*kai apolesen auta heos tes semeron hemeras*—v. 4c.). If this cultic custom of renouncing foreign gods and discarding ornaments[434] goes back to the initiative of the patriarch Jacob, it should be asked whether the the Elohistic

[428] Cf. S. Mowinckel, *op. cit.*, pp. 52 f., 57; W. Eichrodt, *op. cit.*, p. 98 f.

[429] On this, however, see H. Torczyner, *op. cit.*, pp. 44 f., dealing with Num. x. 29–36.

[430] Cf. on what follows A. Alt, 'Die Wallfahrt von Sichem nach Bethel', *Kleine Schriften*, I, pp. 79 f.

[431] It was worn as a charm for defence and protection. Cf. for instance P. Volz, *Die biblischen Altertümer*, p. 183.

[432] But this custom of handing over one's ornaments must have arisen elsewhere than at Shechem.

[433] Cf. Brooke-McLean 1/1, p. 98.

[434] It may readily be assumed that statuettes of gods as well as pieces of jewellery could always be smuggled in again. Cf. A. Alt, *op. cit.*, p. 84.

pieces of tradition in Exod. xxxiii. 3b–4, 5–6 were not once aetiological in a similar way, seeking to base the rite of discarding ornaments, as practised in Shechem in the context of the festival of covenant-renewal, on what had happened at Sinai: the members of the Shechemite amphictyony wear no ornaments because of their grief at Yahweh's refusal to go with them to Canaan. They lay aside their ornaments in order to win the favour of their God. The members of the tribal confederacy proceed in this way *mēhar ḥôrēb* (Exod. xxxiii. 6). This expression, which has been objected to for various reasons,[435] would be perfectly intelligible as an aetiological point corresponding to *heos tes semeron hemeras* (Gen. xxxv. 4c). The aetiologies which once belonged to the covenant-cult at Shechem would in this case (following a widespread motif, according to which cultic objects are made from discarded ornaments[436]) not have been placed at the disposal of the account which narrated the making of the Ark until later. Thus Exod. xxxiii. 3b–6 could be an example of how closely the aetiological stories of the Pentateuchal tradition have been interwoven with the history of the amphictyonic cult.

All the evidence, therefore, points to the whole complex of tradition in Exod. xxxiii. 1, 3a, 3b–6, 12–17 having an express cultic orientation. This is true of the tradition of vv. 1, 3a, 12–17, insofar as they grapple with the problem of the presence of the God of Sinai in Canaan and hence with a decisive presupposition of the covenant-cult after the conquest. It is also true of vv. 3b–6, insofar as they seem to have explained a cultic custom of the Shechemite amphictyony on the one hand and the origin of the shrine of the theophany, the Ark, on the other (see below).

10. Exodus xxxiii. 7–11

Quite obviously this passage which belongs to the E-source[437] is not a unity. It is apparent in various places that incompatible elements have been joined together in it: whereas according to xxxiii. 7b the Tent of Meeting can be visited by *every* Israelite, the following verses speak of only Moses having entrance;[438] the people keep back

[435] Cf. for instance M. Noth, *Überlieferungsgeschichtliche Studien*, p. 29, n. 4.

[436] Cf. Judges viii. 24 f. (the construction of an ephod from gold rings taken as booty) and Exod. xxxii. 2 f. (the making of the bull-image with the help of the discarded earrings). The theory of W. R. Arnold (*Ephod and Ark. A Study in the Records and Religion of the Ancient Hebrews*, 1917) that in Judges viii. 27 and elsewhere *'ᵃrôn* should be read instead of *'ēpôd* (pp. 10 f.) and that an Ark-shrine should be assumed for Ophra also, is not convincing.

[437] Cf. above, section I, 9b.

[438] G. von Rad, *Studies in Deuteronomy*, p. 42.

in awe. Whereas according to xxxiii. 11b an official of the cult[439] resided permanently in the Tent, according to xxxiii. 11a 'Yahweh used to speak to Moses face to face, as a man speaks to his friend', which undoubtedly does not permit the presence of a third. Whereas vv. 8 and 10 really assume that the Tent of Meeting is in the *middle* of the *camp*,[440] according to xxxiii. 7 it is distinctly stationed outside and at a distance from it (twice *miḥûṣ lammaḥᵃneh*, once in addition *harḥēḳ min-hammaḥᵃneh*). It is not difficult to bring all these contradictions under one common denominator: an older version of the tradition, according to which the Tent stood in the middle of the camp and could be entered by everyone, has been altered in accordance with the following presuppositions: Israel cannot and should not approach too near to its God; the Tent where God reveals himself is to be removed from the camp; only Moses, who is more than a prophet, not the people, can enter the Tent of Meeting. All these ideas, however, are characteristic of the *Elohist*: it is he who elsewhere also removes the place where God reveals himself from Israel's camp (cf. the pointed repetition of *mērāḥōḳ* in Exod. xx. 18, 21; xxiv. 1b, 2), makes Moses go to God quite on his own (*lᵉḇaddô*, cf. Exod. xxiv. 2, 15a; xx. 19, 21), and constantly uses the category of the prophet (cf. Gen. xx. 7 f.; Exod. iv. 21; Deut. xxxiv. 10 f.; Exod. xxxii. 11, 30 f.; Num. xi. 25 f. and esp. Deut. xxxiv. 10; Num. xii. 5–8).[441] It may be concluded, therefore, that the Elohist has adopted an old tradition about the Tent of Meeting[442] and altered it to suit his leading ideas.[443]

The Elohist is also the source of the two variant traditions in Exod. xxxiii. 3b–4, 5–6 (see above). In both of these it is maintained as

[439] M. Buber, *Moses*, p. 114 explains *nʿr* in this way.

[440] Otherwise it would not have been possible to follow Moses' approach to the Tent of Meeting from every tent in the camp. The way the Israelites prostrate themselves is only intelligible if Yahweh is present *within* the camp. Similarly H. Holzinger, *KHC* 2, p. 109; H. Gressmann, *Mose und seine Zeit*, *FRLANT*, 18, pp. 241 f.; W. Eichrodt, *Theology of the Old Testament* I, p. 110, n. 3; E. Auerbach, *Moses*, p. 160. (Exod. xxxiii. 7–11 is ascribed to P. in Auerbach).

[441] Cf. A. Weiser, *Introduction to the Old Testament*, pp. 113 f.; I. Levy, *VT* 9, 1959, p. 320.

[442] Its kernel may go back to Israel's desert-period. Cf. for instance G. von Rad, *Theology of the Old Testament* I, p. 235.

[443] It goes without saying that it is not always possible to distinguish clearly between the original text and its revision. It should be conceded to A. Kuschke, 'Die Lagervorstellung der priesterlichen Erzählung', *ZAW* 63, 1951, p. 83, n. 53, that the position of the Tent of Meeting outside the camp cannot have come in the first place from a later reviser of the passage. It is embedded too deeply in the text for that. It goes back, as stated, to the source-author himself; it corresponds to his basic purpose. But the view that the tradition taken over by E assumed this Tent to stand in the middle of the camp should not simply be dismissed as untenable and incredible in view of all the evidence. Why cannot P, which often goes back to old traditions in its picture of the camp, have followed an old tradition when it places the Tent in the centre of the camp?

pointedly as in Exod. xxxiii. 7–11 and other E-traditions that Israel does not come too near to its God. The positive statement of xxxiii. 7, 'far off from the camp', is based on the negatively worded statement of God in xxxiii. 3a (similarly xxxiii. 5a), 'I will not go up among you'. God's words to the Israelites, 'If for a single moment I should go up among you, I would consume you' (v. 5a), mean that the Tent of the theophany *necessarily* has to be removed outside the camp. It is most unlikely that the two events are not connected. The Elohist has clearly brought Exod. xxxiii. 3b f. and Exod. xxxiii. 7 f. together in a *single* context and related them to each other.

On the other hand, as already stated,[444] there is everything to be said for the view that originally there was an account of the making of the *Ark* in between these two passages of tradition.[445] The present form, at any rate, of the variant Elohistic traditions in Exod. xxxiii. 3b–4 and 5–6 leads up to such an account. If the Elohist brought together the complex of tradition contained in Exod. xxxiii. 3b f., which would still have been unmutilated in his day, and the tradition underlying Exod. xxxiii. 7–11, he can hardly have felt the Ark and Tent to be incompatible. In fact, he may have thought of them as joined together.

This surmise is favoured by an expression in v. 7: *w*ᵉ*nāṭâh-lô* is well-known as a relic of the Elohist's interpretation[446] which has been smoothed out by the LXX. *Lo* is most naturally explained as referring (cf. the parallel expression in 2 Sam. vi. 17) to the Ark which was once mentioned immediately prior to it: Moses put up the Tent for *it* (sc. the Ark).[447]

Exod. xxxiii. 11 also leads to the assumption that the Ark was situated in the Tent of Meeting of the older tradition. For if this were not the case—if the Tent had been left empty so that Yahweh might appear in it and it might then become the meeting place between God and man from time to time—the constant presence in it of a

[444] See above pp. 110 f.

[445] This older account has been suppressed chiefly because of the P-account (cf. Exod. xxv. 37) dealing with the Ark. G. von Rad ('Zelt und Lade', *Gesammelte Studien*, p. 122) also reckons with a gap in the text at this point. For a different view see M. Haran, 'The nature of the " 'Ōhel Mô'ēdh" in Pentateuchal sources', *JSSt.* 5, 1960, p. 53.

[446] So most recently O. Eissfeldt, 'Lade und Stierbild', *ZAW* 58, 1940/41, p. 191. On the older literature cf. R. Hartmann, 'Zelt und Lade', *ZAW* 37, 1917/18, pp. 212 f.

[447] *Lo* is certainly not to be understood as *dativus commodi* (*ethicus*). The idea that the Tent in which God meets was related to *Moses* would not have been stressed in this way. (Moreover, this use of the pronoun *lo* is common only in later Hebrew and colloquial Hebrew. Cf. Gesenius-Kautzsch, *HG* §119s). The Tent of meeting is not to be thought of as a place of silent contemplation and preparation for prophetic inspiration, since in the older form of the tradition of Exod. xxxiii. 7–11 it was not removed from the camp of the people but stood in the middle of it (see above). *Contra* M. Haran, *op. cit.*, pp. 50–61.

cultic official would not have been necessary or significant.[448] Yet such an official is spoken of more than once in connection with the *Ark*. According to tradition the young Samuel (*hanna'ar*) was permanently on duty before the Ark at Shilo (1 Sam. iii. 3). A similar situation obtained previously at Bethel:[449] Phinehas, the son of Eleazar, discharged the duties connected with the Ark there 'in those days' (Judges xx. 27 f.). This verse[450] implies that this duty was a permanent arrangement, a definite office with a succession of office-holders. When the Ark, returned by the Philistines, was finally deposited in Kiriath-jearim, Eleazar, the son of Abinadab, who had been trained for this work, was appointed to discharge the duties connected with the Ark (1 Sam. vii. 1). If, then, in Exod. xxxiii. 11 Joshua, the son of Nun, resides permanently in the Tent as a cultic official, this is certainly to be understood as service before the Ark. Just as Samuel's youth was distinguished in the tradition by this post of honour, so here the young Joshua is vouchsafed this honour by posterity. If Exod. xxxiii. 7–11 had, as many assume,[450a] really been dealing with an empty Tent-shrine originating in southern Israel (early Judah), it would be difficult to understand how the Ephraimite Joshua[451] should have been connected with it. On the other hand it is easy to understand how the figure of Joshua,[452] which from a traditio-historical standpoint probably belonged primarily to Shechem, became linked with a cultic office which is attested for Bethel and Shiloh, neighbouring amphictyonic centres to Shechem in the course of history. In short, the fact that Joshua did not leave the Tent of Meeting seems to indicate that the Ark, which required constant attendance according to a set rule, stood there. Since Joshua is mentioned in the old stratum of Exod. xxxiii. 7–11 taken over by E

[448] There is nothing in the comparative material drawn by R. Hartmann, *op. cit.*, pp. 216 f. from other religions which would lead to the conclusion that there was such a permanent duty to be discharged: the *'utfa* of the modern Bedouin tribes, which otherwise has hardly anything in common with a tent (see below), was not occupied until immediately before the beginning of a battle (cf. *ibid.*, p. 220.). The sedan-type of *palladium* used by the Rwala-Bedouins, which is also quite different from a tent, was generally left empty according to all the evidence (cf. *ibid.*, pp. 220 f.) On the tent of the Qarmaṭi, cf. below n. 457.

[449] This cultic centre must have accommodated the central shrine of the amphictyony for a short period (cf. A. Alt, 'Die Wallfahrt von Sichem nach Bethel', *Kleine Schriften* I, pp. 85 f.; M. Noth, *The History of Israel*, pp. 49 f.) and therefore the Ark also (cf. M. Noth, *Das System der zwölf Stamme Israels*, *BWANT* IV, 1, pp. 95 f.).

[450] On its reliability see O. Eissfeldt, 'Der geschichtliche Hintergrund der Erzählung von Gibeas Schandtat (Richter xix.–xxi)', *Beer-Festschrift*, pp. 38 f.

[450a] Cf. E. Sellin, 'Das Zelt Jahwes', *Kittel-Festschrift*, pp. 168-192; G. von Rad, *Theology of the Old Testament* I, p. 235 f.; A. Kuschke, *Z.A.W.* 63 (1951), p. 88; H-J. Kraus *Gottesdienst in Israel*, p. 34.

[451] Cf. the tradition of the grave in Joshua xxiv. 30.

[452] Cf. M. Noth, *The History of Israel*, p. 93.

(see above), it is probable that it was not the Elohist but the pre-Elohistic nucleus of this tradition that first assumed the Ark stood in the Tent.

There is no reason to doubt the possibility that Tent and Ark may have been thought of as connected in this way at this early period. The Elohist and the tradition edited by him are not alone in holding this view. There is a further pre-exilic[453] example in Ps. xcix: in vv. 6 and 7 the pillar of cloud which appeared at the Tent of Meeting and out of which Yahweh spoke to Moses and Aaron (cf. Exod. xxxiii. 9, 11a; Num. xii. 5) is thought of in connection with the Ark from which God spoke to Samuel (cf. 1 Sam. iii. 3 f).[454] 1 Sam. ii. 22, obviously under the impression of the traditional connection of Tent and Ark, calls the temple at Shiloh, which now shelters the Ark (probably instead of the Tent—cf. 1 Sam. iii. 3), the Tent of Meeting.[455] There is a similar situation in Ps. lxxviii. 60.[456] Even if these passages do not permit any definite conclusion about the *original* relationship of Tent and Ark,[457] they make it quite certain that the opinion was widely held in the pre-exilic period that the Ark stood in the Tent of Meeting.[458] In view of these circumstances it is quite credible that Exod. xxxiii. 7–11 also assumes the Ark to be in the Tent.

The objection that the two objects are incompatible because Yahweh only appeared from time to time in the Tent of Meeting in conjunction with the cloud, whereas he was always present above the Ark,[459] does not hold good: the epithet *yōšēḇ hakkᵉrûḇîm* (1 Sam. iv.

[453] Cf. Verses 1, 5.

[454] Cf. also A. Weiser, *The Psalms*, pp. 643 f.

[455] The fact that LXX—B does not give the last part of the sentence is not important.

[456] Cf. A. Weiser, *The Psalms*, p. 29, n. 1; further H-J. Kraus, *Gottesdienst in Israel*, pp. 35 f.

[457] Cf. particularly E. Sellin, 'Das Zelt Jahwes', *Kittel-Festschrift*, pp. 168 f.; R. Hartmann, 'Zelt und Lade', *ZAW* 37, 1917/18, pp. 216 f. The material drawn from other religions by which Hartmann seeks to establish the theory of the empty tent of revelation among the southern tribes (cf. pp. 239 f.) is not convincing. It is quite clear that no revelations of God took place in the *'uṭfa* of the Bedouins (cf. pp. 219 f.). According to the account of Ibn al-Gauzi the commander of the Qarmati (about 900 A.D.) concealed himself in a tent with a reserve force of his warriors ready for the battle's crisis. That this tent was a place of inspiration is pure conjecture (cf. pp. 217 f.). Only through the *palladium* of the Rwala did Allah reveal his will. This wooden frame, however, would resemble the *Ark* more than the Tent (cf. pp. 220 f.). Nor is the *'uṭfa*, which was made of 'solid wood', had four corners, was shaped like a rectangle, open on top and fastened to a camel, like a tent.

[458] If the Ark existed in the wilderness (apart from the cherubim, cf. section III, 1) to which there is no really valid objection (cf. also M. Buber, *Moses*, pp. 149 f. and the literature cited there), then it could hardly have existed without the protection of a tent (so also M. Haran, *op. cit.*, pp. 50 f.). According to 2 Sam. vi. 17, at any rate, David immediately prepared a tent for it, which was probably a return to older usage.

[459] So G. von Rad, 'Zelt und Lade', *Gesammelte Studien*, pp. 122 f.; W. Rudolph, *op. cit.*, p. 55; A. Kuschke, *op. cit.*, p. 87; and others.

4; 2 Sam. vi. 2)[460] which occurs in texts which are undoubtedly very ancient, cannot on purely linguistic grounds mean the One who is seated permanently on the throne of the cherubim; it can only mean the One who sits there from time to time.[461] A human king does not usually sit on his throne permanently: he sits on it whenever he wishes to give expression to his task of ruling.[462] The invocation of Yahweh in Ps. lxxx. 2 is entirely similar: 'Thou who art enthroned upon the cherubim, appear!' Here, too, the *yōšēḇ hakkᵉrûḇîm* is not permanently seated on the throne; he is the One who in the context of the cultic festivals is constantly appearing afresh on the cherubim.[463] This was how the presence of the God of the Ark was understood in Shiloh. Otherwise how could 1 Sam. iii. 21 say: 'and the Lord appeared again at Shiloh '(*wayyōsep̄ yhwh lᵉhērā'ōh bᵉšilōh*)? There is no thought here of a permanent presence above the Ark. The ancient battle-cries in Num. x. 35 f. also make the Ark-shrine the place of theophany: the cry 'Arise, Yahweh!', to which the imperative 'Mount, Yahweh!'[464] probably runs parallel, calls upon God to take his place on the throne of cherubim.[465] The 'infallible cue' for Yahweh's epiphany is the appearance of the cloud (*'ānān*),[466] in which the Invisible is concealed. For the author of Ps. xcix the pillar of cloud (*'ammuḏ 'ānān*) in which God spoke when he appeared was certainly not incompatible with the Ark (cf. v. 6 f. and 1 Sam. iii.). Since the cherubim are probably to be understood as the cultic symbol representing the cloud of the theophany this is not surprising.[467] There is also a further, early pre-exilic text[468] attesting the union of Ark and cloud: in the call-vision of Isaiah (ch. vi.) the Temple and its Holy of Holies (where this vision was always

[460] On the primitiveness of this epithet in the accounts mentioned, cf. M. Dibelius, *Die Lade Jahwes*, pp. 21 f. The attempt of M. Haran, 'The Ark and the Cherubim', *IEJ* 9, 1959, pp. 32 f. to prove that the oldest stories about the Ark assume the Ark and the cherubim to be two separate symbols is not convincing. Do 1 Sam. iv. 3, 4, 7, for instance, still make sense if Yahweh was not enthroned above the Ark but above the statues of the cherubim in the temple at Shiloh?

[461] Cf. C. Brockelmann, *Hebräische Syntax*, § 44, p. 45: M. Buber, *op. cit.*, p. 157; and W. Caspari, *KAT* 7, p. 59, on *yōšēḇ 'ōhᵒlîm* in Gen. xxv. 27.

[462] With M. Buber, *ibid.*

[463] See v. 3. Cf. A. Weiser, 'Theophanie in den Psalmen und im Festkult', *Bertholet-Festschrift*, pp. 518 f.

[464] In Num. x. 36 *šᵉḇâh* should be read for *šûḇâh*. See above, n. 418.

[465] Cf. A. Weiser, *op. cit.*, p. 521.

[466] With H. Torczyner, *Die Bundeslade und die Anfänge der Religion Israels*, 2nd ed., pp. 44 f.: A. Weiser, *op. cit.*, pp. 520 f. See especially Ps. xviii. 10 f.; Ezek. i. 4 f.; x. 1 f., 18 f.

[467] So G. von Rad, *op. cit.*, p. 122.

[468] The account of the Ark being brought into the Temple of Solomon in 1 Kings viii may be left on one side since it is not a literary unity and the important verses 10 f. seem to have been added later. Cf. M. Noth, *Überlieferungsgeschichtliche Studien*, 2nd ed., p. 70 (esp. n. 5).

received)[469] form the background.[470] Even if the vision cannot be contained within the earthly shrine and a 'high and lofty' throne replaces the Ark-throne (vi. 1), the prophet sees and thinks in the categories of Temple and Ark. The cloud of smoke[471] which accompanies God's theophany is linked with these. Everything suggests, therefore, that even in early, pre-exilic times the Ark was regarded as a shrine for theophanies. The cloud which accompanied the theophany did not stand in opposition to it in any way.[472]

There is a great deal of evidence, therefore, for assuming that in Exod. xxxiii. 7–11 the Ark and Tent were connected with each other: 1. the observation that Exod. xxxiii. 3b f. and Exod. xxxiii. 7–11 have been edited as belonging together. 2. the expression *weنāṭâh-lô* (in Exod. xxxiii. 7). 3. Joshua's unbroken service in the Tent (Exod. xxxiii. 11b). 4. the fact that in the pre-exilic period others also were of the opinion that the Ark stood in the Tent of Meeting (cf. Ps. lxxviii. 60; xcix. 6 f.; 1 Sam. ii. 22). And 5. the compatibility of the Ark as a shrine for theophanies and the Tent which was described as the 'Tent of Meeting' and the pillar of cloud which appeared at its door.[473] There are, therefore, good grounds for thinking that Exod. xxxiii. 7–11 presupposes the Ark was in the Tent.[474]

If this is so, then we are not dealing here with a special tradition observed in southern Israel (early Judah),[475] but with a tradition which belonged to the tribal confederacy of all Israel set up at

[469] Cf. for instance E. J. Kissane, *The Book of Isaiah* I, p. 74.

[470] Cf. I. Engnell, 'The Call of Isaiah', *UUÅ* 1949/4, pp. 27 f., 31.; further M. Schmidt, *Prophet und Tempel*, p. 33.

[471] *'anan* and *'ašan* (Isa. vi. 4) are synonyms. Cf. Exod. xix. 16, 18; further I. Engnell, *op. cit.*, pp. 37 f.

[472] If the ancient stories of the Ark sometimes think of Yahweh as tied to the Ark inseparably (cf. for instance 1 Sam. iv. 3), they are resorting to crude, popular notions (cf. M. Buber, *op. cit.*, p. 160). *Abusus non tollit usum.*

[473] We must take into consideration the question whether the Ark, which, so far as we know, was first housed in a temple-shrine not in Shechem or Bethel or Gilgal but in Shiloh (cf. M. Noth, *The History of Israel*, p. 95), could have existed without the protection of a tent even in the period before it was brought to Shiloh. David, at any rate, immediately prepared a tent for it in Jerusalem, as stated earlier (cf. 2 Sam. vi. 17).

[474] If A. Kuschke, *op cit.*, pp. 82 f. proves that P, in making the Tent of Meeting the centre of his camp, went back to the old tradition which also underlies Exod. xxxiii. 7–11, then in view of the conclusion we have just arrived at above (sc. the Ark was in the tent) it should be asked whether this does not suggest that the combination of Tent and Ark which is found in P was also based on this old tradition rather than P's own free construction. As H-J. Kraus, *Gottesdienst in Israel*, p. 29 remarks: 'We are too hasty in explaining the author of the late passages of the Pentateuch as a fabricator'. Meanwhile K. Koch (*Die Priesterschrift von Exodus 25 bis Leviticus 16*, *FRLANT*, 71, p. 97, 10–16) has established that Tent and Ark were linked together in the cultic-aetiological rituals taken over by P.

[475] Cf. G. von Rad, *Studies in Deuteronomy*, p. 43; *Theology of the Old Testament* I, p. 238, n. 114.; A. Kuschke, *op. cit.*, p. 103.

Shechem. For the Ark which it presupposed[476] was really the central shrine of this tribal union.[477] It is true that it is not attested for Shechem,[478] but it is well attested for the succeeding amphictyonic centres at Bethel, Gilgal and Shiloh.[479] On the other hand, it was at Shiloh that the Tent of Meeting also still possessed importance. That it was, in fact, pitched there cannot be proved for certain.[480] It seems certain, however, that here in Shiloh the function of the Tent was taken over by the temple-shrine.[481] Otherwise it is impossible to understand the Psalmist's apostrophe of the temple there as a tent (Ps. lxxviii. 60) or the way it is called 'tent of meeting' by the narrative of 1 Sam. 2, 22. From all the evidence it seems likely that the Tent of Meeting did, in fact, exist *prior* to the removal of the central shrine of the amphictyony to Shiloh. If it is remembered, on the other hand, that although there was no temple-shrine for the Ark at the amphictyonic shrines which preceded Shiloh (i.e. Gilgal, Bethel and probably Shechem) it needed some shelter,[482] this strongly suggests that at this period the Ark stood in the Tent of Meeting. Exod. xxxiii. 7–11, therefore, would reflect the order of things at the central shrine of ancient Israel in the period when Shechem and Shiloh were prominent amphictyonic centres.

This historical judgement is, furthermore, confirmed by the text of this piece of tradition in two respects: 1. The youth, Joshua, from a historical point of view, certainly never played the rôle ascribed to him by Exod. xxxiii. 11b.[483] Most probably he was the man who, as victor in a battle against the Canaanites and as mediator of claims between the tribes, laid the foundation of Israel's history by the union round the shrine at Shechem.[484] Joshua may well have played the leading rôle in the assembly at Shechem and in the cult for the

[476] With M. Noth, *Das System der zwölf Stämme Israels*, *BWANT* IV. 1, pp. 95 f.

[477] The theory (revived by K. Koch, *op. cit.*, p. 17) that there were several copies of the Ark in Israel lacks convincing evidence. Cf. for a different view the instructively worded statement in Judges xx. 27b and M. Noth, 'Jerusalem und die israelitische Tradition', *Gesammelte Studien*, pp. 184 f.

[478] For the explanation of this cf. M. Noth, *The History of Israel*, p. 93.

[479] On this sequence cf. A. Alt, 'Die Wallfahrt von Sichem nach Bethel', *Kleine Schriften* I, pp. 85 f.; H-J. Kraus, 'Gilgal. Ein Beitrag zur Kultusgeschichte Israels', *VT.* 1, 1951, pp. 184 f.; M. Noth, *op. cit.*, pp. 94 f.

[480] Joshua xviii. 1 cannot be used for literary-critical reasons. Cf. M. Noth, *Das Buch Joshua*, 2nd ed., *HAT* 1/7, p. 108. R. Kittel, *Geschichte des Volkes Israel* II, 3rd ed., p. 136, n. 1, seeks to conclude from 2 Sam. vii. 6 f. that the *temple-shrine* at Shiloh was also only temporary.

[481] Cf. also H-J. Kraus, *Gottesdienst in Israel*, pp. 35 f.

[482] *Vide supra*, n. 473.

[483] Cf. in this connection also K. Möhlenbrink, 'Josua im Pentateuch', *ZAW* 59, 1942/3, pp. 14 f. and esp. pp. 28 f.

[484] Cf. A. Alt, 'Josua', *Kleine Schriften* I, p. 192; M. Noth, *The History of Israel*, p. 93 f.

renewal of the covenant which was linked with Shechem.[485] This is the only sufficient reason for the later choice of Joshua ben Nun to be on permanent duty in the Tent of Meeting. The tradition underlying Exod. xxxiii. 7–11, therefore, cannot have taken shape very far away from the Shechemite field of tradition. 2. Joshua's continuous service in the shrine, as mentioned earlier in another context, has clear parallels in the service before the Ark in the temple at Shiloh ascribed to Samuel (1 Sam. iii. 3.) and in the office discharged by Phinehas ben Eleazar at the cult-centre of Bethel (Judges xx. 27b). These two reflections on Exod. xxxiii. 11b taken together favour the view that the tradition underlying Exod. xxxiii. 7–11 is to be connected with the amphictyonic shrines of the pre-monarchic period.

In short, the tradition of the Tent of Meeting edited by the Elohist most probably had its *Sitz im Leben*, judging by Exod. xxxiii. 7–11, in the amphictyonic cult during the period bounded by Shechem and Shiloh, when the Ark and the Tent of Meeting were living realities and there was always someone on duty before the Ark.

In what follows we shall take up the question of whether any other features of the tradition reproduced in Exod. xxxiii. 7–11 have their *Sitz im Leben* in this sphere.

One feature in the tradition about the Tent of Meeting is especially marked: the Tent is linked with the *camp* of Israel. The Tent where Yahweh appears stands in full view of the tents of the camp; they are visibly turned towards it (Exod. xxxiii. 8). What happens at the door of the Tent of Meeting provokes its reaction at the doors of the tents of the camp (Exod. xxxiii. 10). Whenever the Tent of Meeting is spoken of in the Pentateuch the camp is always mentioned (cf. Num. xi. 16, 24–30; xii. 4, 14 f.—E) or at least presupposed (cf. Deut. xxxi. 14 f.—E). Even in the Priestly Source the sacred Tent is very closely connected with Israel's camp.[486] Everything suggests that the Tent of Meeting and Israel's camp belong indissolubly together.[487] If this Tent, as attested by Exod. xxxiii. 7–11, had its *Sitz im Leben* in all probability in the central shrines of the amphictyony in the pre-monarchic period, the same might be assumed for the camp which was always linked with it in the tradition. This much, at any rate, is certain: every year at Shiloh in the autumn after the

[485] Cf. Joshua xxiv. and on this A. Alt, *Die Ursprünge des israelitischen Rechts* (= *Kleine Schriften* I, p. 325); G. von Rad, *Das formgeschichtliche Problem des Hexateuch* (= *Gesammelte Studien*, p. 44).

[486] Cf. A. Kuschke, *op. cit.*, pp. 79 f. See also L. Rost, 'Die Wohnstätte des Zeugnisses', *Baumgärtel-Festschrift*, *EF.*, A. 10, 1959, p. 162.

[487] With H-J. Kraus, *op. cit.*, p. 28; G. von Rad, *Theology of the Old Testament* I, p. 236

harvest there took place the festival of Yahweh (*ḥag-yhwh*), to which all Israel went in pilgrimage (cf. Judges xxi. 19 f.; 1 Sam. 1).[488] It is unlikely that this festival of Yahweh for all Israel should have been introduced solely at Shiloh.[489] There is a great deal to be said for the view that similar pilgrimages to the festival of Yahweh took place at the amphictyonic centres which were chronologically prior to Shiloh.[490] In Deut. xvi. 13; Lev. xxiii. 39–44 this autumnal festival of Yahweh is described as 'the feast of booths', corresponding to the cultic practice of dwelling in booths during the days of the festival. It is rightly assumed[491] that behind this practice is the still older custom of dwelling in *tents* during the days of the festival (cf. Hos. xii. 10). This suggests that it was the autumnal *festival of Yahweh* that was later celebrated in the tent-camp.[492] The influx of pilgrims from all the tribes must have confronted the pre-monarchic central shrines of Israel periodically with a situation that could only be solved by the official deputations of the tribes[493] and the crowds of pilgrims to the festival finding accommodation at these cult-places in tents (or booths).[494] There are numerous parallels to this cultic practice in other religions also.[495] At panegyric, annual festivals in connection with the Greek cults it was quite common to dwell in tents or booths. The great Muslim festival held every autumn at the shrine of nebi Rubin (to the north of Jaffa) is still held even today in a tent-camp.[496] It is not impossible, therefore, that at the central shrines of the tribal confederacy in the pre-monarchic period not only was the Tent of Meeting (with the Ark and its cultic servant) a living reality but it was also still the custom here to dwell in tents when on pilgrimage to a festival of Yahweh.[497] Accordingly, the

[488] Cf. P. Volz, *Das Neujahrfest Jahwes* (*Laubhüttenfest*), *SGVS*, 67, pp. 7 f., 22 f.

[489] Cf. W. F. Albright, *Archaeology and the Religion of Israel*, pp. 105 f.

[490] Cf. P. Volz, *op. cit.*, pp. 23, 53, n. 43; A. Alt, *Die Ursprünge des israelitischen Rechts* (= *Kleine Schriften* I, pp. 325 f.); *idem*, 'Die Wallfahrt von Sichem nach Bethel', *Kleine Schriften* I, pp. 87 f.; G. von Rad, *Das formgeschichtliche Problem des Hexateuch* (*Gesammelte Studien*, pp. 42 f.); M. Noth, *History of Israel*, p. 98. Other pilgrimages to the great central shrines also took place throughout the ancient Orient. Cf. on this W. F. Albright, *Archaeology and the Religion of Israel*, p. 103 f.

[491] Cf. above all P. Volz, *op. cit.*, p. 20, and H-J. Kraus, *op. cit.*, pp. 26 f.

[492] So also W. Eichrodt, *Theology of the Old Testament* I, pp. 122 f.

[493] Cf. M. Noth, *op. cit.*, p. 98.

[494] Cf. also P. Volz, *op. cit.*, p. 21.

[495] Further details in P. Volz, *op. cit.*, pp. 20 f.

[496] Cf. A. Alt, 'Das Institut im Jahre 1924', PJ, 21, 1925, pp. 14 f.; H-J. Kraus, *op. cit.*, p. 31; W. Eichrodt, *op. cit.*, p. 122, n. 7.

[497] If the fact that the camp in P is composed of the twelve tribes (cf. A. Kuschke, *op. cit.*, pp. 78, 93–98) is not a free construction of P but, as is far more probable (cf. H-J. Kraus, *op. cit.*, p. 29), has been elaborated in connection with ancient tradition, then it would appear here too that the camp once had something to do with the institution of the tribal confederacy.

tradition underlying Exod. xxxiii. 7–11 would reflect the picture which the amphictyonic shrines of ancient Israel (prior to Shiloh) offered to pilgrims attending the autumnal festival of Yahweh: the covenant-people came to the Tent of Meeting, in which the Ark stood, with their tents.

This piece of tradition clearly corresponds to such a cultic situation in another respect also: the event of Yahweh's epiphany obviously constitutes the focal point of interest. The sacred tent is seen and understood in terms of nothing else. Its very description as 'Tent of Meeting' emphasises the theophany. The theophany, on the other hand, occupied a central position in the cult of the amphictyony in ancient Israel. This may be inferred from the fact that the Ark, with which the theophany was connected, undoubtedly played an important part at the pre-monarchic central shrines of Bethel, Gilgal and Shiloh.[498] Further, the address to the assembly at Shechem (Joshua xxiv. 2 f.), for instance, which is worded as if it were an utterance of God in the first person and recounts Israel's salvation-history, makes it clear that Yahweh's cultic epiphany is presupposed here also.[499] Lastly, the Song of Deborah, a liturgical complex, which had its *Sitz im Leben*[500] in a festival of Yahweh in the tribal union of the pre-monarchic period, is a clear illustration of the outstanding importance of the theophany in the early Israelite worship of Yahweh. The central position, therefore, which the epiphany of Yahweh occupies in Exod. xxxiii. 7–11, corresponds perfectly with conditions at the amphictyonic centres of the pre-monarchic period.

According to Exod. xxxiii. 10, Israel prostrates itself in awe at the sight of the theophany. This feature, too, is evidenced in the festival-cult of ancient Israel: Elkanah, the father of Samuel, went as a pilgrim to the annual festival of Yahweh at Shiloh with the express purpose of doing homage to Yahweh Seba'oth (1 Sam. i. 3). This prostrate homage before the God who appears above the Ark—a fact referred to on several occasions (cf. for instance Ps. xcix. 5, 9; cxxxii. 7)—was doubtless a well-established practice in the early Israelite cult of Yahweh. Thus, this feature of the old Tent of Meeting tradition in Exod. xxxiii also corresponds to a firmly established cultic form of the festival of Yahweh in the pre-monarchic period.

In Exod. xxxiii. 7b anyone who has recourse to the Tent of Meet-

[498] Cf. Judges xx. 27 f.; Joshua iii f. (cf. on this H-J. Kraus, 'Gilgal', *VT*, 1, 1951, pp. 191 f.); 1 Sam. iii. f. (esp. 1 Sam. iii. 21).

[499] With A. Weiser, *Introduction to the Old Testament*, pp. 88 f. Cf. also A. Alt, *Die Ursprünge des israelitischen Rechts* (= *Kleine Schriften* I, pp. 324 f.).

[500] Cf. on this A. Weiser, 'Das Deboralied', *ZAW*, 71, 1959, pp. 67 f.

ing is called 'one who seeks Yahweh' (*mᵉḇakkēš yhwh*). It is questionable whether the tradition is referring to the obtaining of an oracle as is often assumed.[501] Such an undertaking is almost always described by the phrase *šā'al bᵉyhwh*[502] occasionally by the words *dāraš 'eṯ-yhwh*. Since *biḳḳeš ('eṯ-)yhwh*, on the other hand, usually means to 'seek Yahweh' in a comprehensive sense and in all sorts of ways,[503] sometimes accompanied by sacrifice,[504] and since it means 'to seek Yahweh's epiphany' quite often,[505] it seems easier to believe that *mᵉḇakkēš yhwh* in Exod. xxxiii. 7b also referred to Yahweh's epiphany, which occupies such a dominant position in this whole strand of tradition. The phrase means, then, everyone who seeks to meet with the One who appears. To that extent, therefore, this feature also can quite well be understood against the background of the festival of Yahweh, in which the theophany is central.

It goes without saying, however, that the God who appears in the Tent of Meeting can make his will known whether asked[506] or not.[507] Hence, the possibility should not be excluded that *mᵉḇakkēš yhwh* in Exod. xxxiii. 7b also incidentally included the expectation that God would manifest his will when he appeared[508] In this respect, too, the tradition would have a cultic parallel—in a ceremony which was undoubtedly performed at amphictyonic centres in the premonarchic period. According to Judges xx. 18 f. the Israelites, in connection with an expressly amphictyonic action,[509] turn to the central shrine of the sacral tribal union at that time in Bethel with a question. They do this—as stated specifically in Judges xx. 27 f.—because the Ark of Yahweh, which was served by Phinehas ben Eleazar, stood there at that time. Such situations (which also seem to correspond to Exod. xxxiii. 11b) could well be envisaged in Exod. xxxiii. 7b.

Finally it should be added that the *pillar of cloud* at the door of the

[501] Cf. for instance R. Brinker, *The Influence of Sanctuaries in Early Israel*, p. 76; A. Kuschke, *op. cit.*, p. 84; H-J. Kraus, *op. cit.*, p. 31 (esp. n. 47); G. von Rad, *Theology of the Old Testament* I, p. 236; W. Eichrodt, *Theology of the Old Testament* I, p. 110.

[502] Cf. Judges xx. 18; I Sam. xxiii. 2, 4; xxviii. 6; xxx. 8; 2 Sam. ii. 1; v. 19, 23; Num. xxiii. (see App. BH.); cf. Hos. iv. 12 (tree-oracle).

[503] Cf. Deut. iv. 29; Isa. li. 1; lxv. 1; Jer. xxix. 13; 1, 4; Hos. iii. 5; v. 6; Zeph. i. 6; ii. 3; Zech. viii. 21 f.; Mal. iii. 1; Ps. xl. 7; lxix. 7; lxx. 5; cv. 3 f.; Prov. xxviii. 5; 1 Chron. xvi. 10 f.; 2 Chron. vii. 14.

[504] Cf. Hos. v. 6; 2 Chron. xi. 16.

[505] Cf. 2 Sam. xxi. 1 (on the technical term *pᵉnē yhwh* see section II, 9 above); Hos. iii. 5; Mal. iii. 1; Ps. xxiv. 6; xxvii. 8; lxix. 7; lxxxiii. 17; cv. 3 f.; 1 Chron. xvi. 10 f.

[506] Cf. Num. xxvii. 1–11 (P!); also 2 Sam. xxi. 1, which has been displaced from its original context.

[507] Cf. Num. xii. 5 f.–E.

[508] Cf. in this connection Amos viii. 12 also.

[509] Further details in M. Noth, *History of Israel*, p. 105.

Tent of Meeting (v. 9) was also probably influenced by the pattern of the cult. According to the directions for the great Day of Atonement in Lev. xvi, which are based on an old ritual,[510] it may be assumed that the cloud concealing God's epiphany was indicated by a corresponding cloud of incense (v. 13 and 2; further Isa. vi. 4; 1 Kings viii. 10 f.).[511] The fact that this pillar of cloud descended at the *door* of the sacred tent (Exod. xxxiii. 9 f.) is undoubtedly connected with the idea of the door into the shrine which is also to be found in other connections in the early Israelite amphictyony: according to 1 Sam. ii. 22 a special service was discharged in Shiloh 'at the entrance to the sacred tent'. And according to 1 Sam. i. 9; iv. 18 it was at the door of the temple at Shiloh that Eli, the priest, also discharged a permanent duty.[512] Thus, the old tradition of the Tent of Meeting seems to have been influenced in this respect also by a definite cultic situation.

Finally, we must consider by what motives *the Elohist* was determined in formulating the tradition underlying Exod. xxxiii. 7–11. As stated at the beginning, it may have been he who removed the tent of God's epiphany from the camp and made Moses instead of the people approach the sacred tent alone—Moses who is more than a prophet. The fact that the Tent of Meeting was put at a distance from Israel's camp can hardly have been inspired by 'the position of the cult-places on a height outside the encampment in Palestine'.[513] Rather, this attempt to preserve a distance between God and the people, which is certainly not a peculiarity of Exod. xxxiii. 7–11 but is characteristic of E (cf. especially Exod. xx. 18–21), corresponds to the basic experience of the Holy (the wholly other),[514] which found frequent expression and consistent encouragement in the sphere of the cult.[515]. To that extent the Elohist's motive is also connected with the sphere of the cult. The prominence of *Moses* in the tradition about the Tent of Meeting may be partly the result of the fact that the Elohist has woven this piece of tradition into the

[510] Cf. K. Koch, *Die Priesterschrift von Exodus 25 bis Leviticus 16*, *FRLANT*, 71, pp. 92 f.

[511] With A. Weiser, 'Theophanie in den Psalmen und im Festkult', *Bertholet-Festschrift*, p. 523

[512] Cf. further Ps. xxiv. 7, 9. The pillars Jachin and Boaz, set up in front of Solomon's Temple (1 Kings vii. 21; 2 Chron. iii. 15, 17) perhaps presuppose a similar view about the entrance to the shrine. W. F. Albright (*Archaeology and the Religion of Israel*, pp. 144–148), referring to Robertson Smith, regards Jachin and Boaz as incense-holders and considers it possible that the clouds of incense rising from them were meant to represent the pillars of fire and smoke which led the Israelites through the desert (p. 148).

[513] G. Beer, *HAT*, 1/3, p. 158; cf. also B. Baentsch, *HK*, 2/1, p. 276.

[514] Cf. for instance S. Mowinckel, *Religion und Kultus*, pp. 31 f.

[515] Cf. for instance W. Eichrodt, *op. cit.*, p. 273.

context of his account of Sinai, in which the figure of Moses, the mediator of the revelation, was firmly anchored (cf. for instance Exod. xix. 17, 19; xx. 18–21; xxiv.). E may have been determined by another motive at this point however: in 1 Sam. iii. 20 f. it is strongly emphasised that all Israel knew that Samuel had been appointed Yahweh's prophet. And this appointment is then regarded as the reason for Yahweh's continued appearances in Shiloh. May not the thought of the Elohist have been similar? Israel itself should not come too near to Yahweh (cf. Exod. xxxiii. 7, 10); the people make it difficult for God to appear in their midst (cf. Exod. xxxiii. 3b. 5a). But there is Moses, who is more than a prophet—Moses, with whom Yahweh speaks face to face, as a man speaks to his friend (Exod. xxxiii. 11a), and because *Moses* intervenes and undertakes to mediate between Israel's camp and the tent of the theophany (Exod. xxxiii. 8 f.) Yahweh can continue to appear in the Tent of Meeting. These were the thoughts which most probably influenced the Elohist in his interpretation of the tradition about the Tent of Meeting. It should be clear, however, how keenly interested he was in the problem of God's presence among his people. This, judging by all the evidence, was the aim animating the Elohist when he took up this material and worked it into his account of Sinai. Since the neighbouring fragments of tradition in Exod. xxxiii. 3b–4, 5–6 (E) bear witness to the same aim it is probable that the whole Elohistic complex of tradition in Exod. xxxiii. dealt with the question of God's presence among his people on their way to Canaan. At the same time it is clear that the Jehovistic edition of Exod. xxxiii. has linked this E-tradition with the later Yahwistic tradition of vv. 12b–17 extremely appropriately.[516]

Summary. Exod. xxxiii. 7–11 embraces a tradition which exhibits various links with the central shrines (preceding Shiloh) of the pre-monarchic union of the twelve tribes and it should most probably, therefore, be associated with this field of cultic history. (Obviously it was here, for instance, that the Tent of Meeting and the Ark were joined together. There was always someone on duty before the Ark here. Israel assembled here at the autumnal pilgrim-festival of Yahweh in a tent-camp. It was here that the theophany occupied the centre of the stage. The cultic community came here to do homage to Yahweh's epiphany. Israel came here with its questions.) In all these separate points the tradition has been influenced by

[516] Cf. section II, 9 above, esp. p. 110.

cultic patterns and circumstances (even in respect of the pillar of cloud which appeared at the door of the sacred Tent). And lastly, the Elohist was obviously dealing with a very important question for the cult of Yahweh in demonstrating how and why God could continue to appear to his people on their way to Canaan.

11. Exodus xxxii

There are many points of contact between the account in vv. 1–6 of the construction and cultic veneration of the image of the Golden Calf[517] and the account in 1 Kings xii. 25–33 of the cult of the image of the bull in the shrine at Bethel (and Dan.) In both accounts the calf-image made of gold occupies the centre of the stage. In both cases it is said of the image: 'this is your God, O Israel, who brought you up out of the land of Egypt'. In both cases an unusual plural form is used.[518] In both cases an altar stands in front of the calf-image. Both accounts refer to a feast of Yahweh (*ḥāg*) celebrated in connection with the 'golden calf'. In both cases sacrifice is offered in front of the image of the calf. The parallels between Exod. xxxii. 1–6 and 1 Kings xii. 25–33 are so numerous and obvious that one cannot refrain from suspecting a connection between the two texts.[519]

The connection certainly does not consist in the dependence of Exod. xxxii on the Deuteronomist, however.[520] The description of the calf in Exod. xxxii. 4 sounds more ancient than that in 1 Kings xii. 28 and the former can hardly have arisen from the latter.[521] Moreover, the idea of making the casting mould from the rings discarded by the Israelites (Exod. xxxii. 2–4a)[522] could hardly have been derived from the account of 1 Kings xii; in fact, it suggests the independence of the Exodus tradition. On the other hand there is nothing to indicate that the deuteronomistic narrative was dependent on the Exodus tradition; the parallel description of the calf-image in 1 Kings xii. 28 and Exod. xxxii. 4b is sufficiently explained

[517] On the unity of the section (in opposition to S. Lehming, 'Versuch zu Exod. xxxii', *VT*, 10, 1960, pp. 21 f., *inter al.*) cf. section I, 8a, above.

[518] Cf. Gesenius-Kautzsch, *HG* § 145 i, and the post-exilic reproduction of the passage in Neh. ix. 18.

[519] Cf. the literature cited in O. Eissfeldt, 'Lade und Stierbild', *ZAW*, 58, 1940/1, p. 200, n. 1.

[520] *Contra* M. Noth, *Überlieferungsgeschichte des Pentateuch*, p. 158, n. 408; *Exodus*, p. 246.

[521] Cf. M. Buber, *Moses*, pp. 147 f.

[522] On Exod. xxxii. 4a, cf. M. Noth, 'Zur Anfertigung des "Goldenen Kalbes" ', *VT*, 9, 1959, pp. 419 f.; cf. J. J. Petuchowski in *VT*, 10, 1960, p. 74.

if the same formula underlies both[523]. The connection between these two narratives seems to have been brought about through their both referring to the same cult of the calf-image at Bethel (and Dan). The cultic setting of the state-shrine of northern Israel at Bethel,[524] as it appears in 1 Kings xii. 25–33, also clearly forms the background to the account in Exod. xxxii. 1–6.

In what sense, however, does Exod. xxxii refer to the cult of the calf-image at Bethel? If one takes vv. 1–6 by themselves it is noticeable that there is little or no polemical emphasis. The people's request for an *'ᵉlōhîm* who would go before them need not have incurred reproach in the tradition from the very beginning.[525] Similarly, the fact that the calf-image was made out of the Israelites' jewels, which is regarded as un-Yahwistic in Gen. xxxv. 4,[526] need not imply condemnation of what happened, especially since Exod. xxxii. 5, judging by all the evidence, makes the same ornaments the source of a legitimate shrine.[527] Nor does the word *'ēgel* (calf)[528] necessarily imply contempt, as used to be thought.[529] At most, the verbal form *lᵉṣaḥēḳ* (v. 6) may contain a polemical note.[530] The way in which Exod. xxxii has been linked with the Elohistic account of Sinai (Exod. xxiv. 15a, 18b) by v. 1) also indicates a desire to set the following events in a negative light, by making the people proceed from a false assumption in their argument. But since this link has nothing to do with the original nucleus of the tradition in Exod. xxxii 1–6 and since the peripheral *lᵉṣaḥēḳ* may also be attributed to later editing, it follows that the original tradition of the verses referred to the cult of the calf-image at Bethel in a thoroughly *positive* sense.[531] If, for instance, the account makes Aaron agree to the wishes of the people without hesitation or demur and if in so doing his choice falls on the calf-image as if this were something

[523] *Contra* M. Buber, *ibid.*; S. Lehming, *op. cit.*, p. 25, n. 3.

[524] See Amos vii. 13. Cf. on this G. Widengren, *Sakrales Königtum im Alten Testament und im Judentum*, p. 14.

[525] Cf. B. Baentsch, *HK* 2/1, p. 269. For a different view cf. H. Junker, 'Traditionsgeschichtliche Untersuchung über die Erzählung von der Anbetung des Goldenen Kalbes Exod. xxxii.)', *TrThZ* 60, pp. 232 f., n. 2.

[526] Cf. P. Volz, *Die Biblischen Altertümer*, p. 183.

[527] Cf. for instance O. Eissfeldt, 'Lade und Stierbild', *ZAW*, 58, 1940/1, pp. 191 f.

[528] Cf. W. Baudissin in *RE*, 9, 3rd ed., p. 705, and W. F. Albright, *From the Stone Age to Christianity*, pp. 228–30.

[529] Cf. H. Holzinger, *KHC*, 2, p. 110, H. Gressmann, *Mose und seine Zeit*, *FRLANT*, 18, p. 204, n. 1.

[530] Cf. H. Gressmann, *op. cit.*, p. 201.

[531] In fact, 2 Kings x. 28 makes it unobjectionably clear that even avowed devotees of Yahweh (cf. 2 Kings x. 16) did not consider the cult of the calf-image incompatible with true worship of Yahweh.

quite natural, then it is clear we are dealing here with aspects of this old, pre-critical tradition.[531a]

Can its relation to the cult of the calf-image be determined more closely? The fact that this theme of discarding jewellery occurs twice in the old tradition in connection with an aetiology of cultic objects (cf. Judges viii. 24 f. and Exod. xxxiii. 3b ff.) strongly suggests that the tradition underlying Exod. xxxii. 1–6 should also be interpreted as a *cultic aetiology*. Just as Judges xvii f. offers reasons for the origin and introduction of a cultic image at the shrine of Dan, so the old tradition of Exod. xxxii. 1–6 explains the construction and cultic veneration of the calf-image at Bethel.[532] But since the cultic image at Dan in the pre-monarchic period was probably a bull (*pĕsĕl ûmassēkâh*),[533] the possibility that even in Bethel the cult of the calf-image was not first introduced by Jeroboam I should be reckoned with. It could well be that Jeroboam only confirmed existing relations at the shrines of Bethel and Dan and officially confirmed these through the institution of new cultic images.[534] Whatever the exact truth of this might be, the revised tradition in Exod. xxxii. 1–6 is probably seeking to give an account of the origins of the cult of the calf-image at Bethel which was in existence under Jeroboam I at the latest. The significant difference between this aetiology and the explanation given in Judges xvii f. lies in the fact that the former emerged from the sphere of family and tribal history and seeks to connect itself with the events which established the covenant-people of Israel, such as the revelation on Sinai and the deliverance from Egypt: when Israel asked for a god to lead them at Sinai, then Aaron made for it the image of a calf, erected an altar in front of it, and did and said for the first time what the priesthood made a practice of doing and saying later in the cult of the calf-image at Bethel. If the old tradition underlying Exod. xxxii. 1–6 referred to the cultic situation in the southern

[531a] With R. Dussaud, *Les origines cananéenes du sacrifice israélite*, 1st ed., p. 244. Cf. on the other hand H. Junker, *op. cit.*, p. 234. (According to Junker Exod. xxxii. is 'genuine, reliable, ancient tradition . . . which may naturally be understood at all points from the historical situation of Israel in the Mosaic period'. p. 240.)

[532] Further details in R. Dussaud, *op. cit.*, pp. 243 f. Cf. also G. Widengren, *op. cit.*, p. 9.

[533] Cf. R. Kittel, *Geschichte des Volkes Israel*, 3rd ed., II, pp. 129 f.; R. Dussaud, *op. cit.*, p. 243.

[534] Cf. for instance J. Wellhausen, *Prolegomena to the History of Israel*, pp. 282 f.; W. Baudissin, *op. cit.*, p. 711 f.; R. Dussaud, *ibid.*; G. Widengren, *ibid.*; and S. Talmon, 'Divergences in Calendar-Reckoning in Ephraim and Judah', *VT*, 8, 1958, p. 50, who notes with justice, 'that dissenters, political and religious alike, will as a rule not proclaim themselves innovators. They will, on the contrary, always try to appear as champions of time-honoured ideas and institutions that, according to their contentions, have been desecrated by the leaders of the community from which they strive to detach themselves.'

Ephraimite shrine at Bethel, then it might owe its origin to the priesthood there. The priests obviously tried, when the amphictyonic traditions of the revelation at Sinai and the deliverance from Egypt proved popular at their shrine,[535] to base the cultic image of their shrine and the cultic ordinances and usages associated with it on these traditions.[536]

A final reason for accepting that the tradition revised in Exod. xxxii. 1–6 is, in fact, connected with the cult at Bethel and goes back to the priesthood there is the rôle played by *Aaron* in this old narrative.[537] According to Judges xx. 27 f. the Ark was tended by Phinehas, a grandson of Aaron,[538] when it was in Bethel.[539] In the comparatively short time during which this cult-place was the centre of the union of the twelve tribes and the headquarters of the Ark, it would hardly have been possible for a priestly family from *outside* Bethel to find entrance there. It is more likely that the local priesthood sought to maintain their position unmolested and, on the instructions of the tribal union, discharged their duties before the Ark. In that case, Phinehas, Aaron's descendant, belonged to the priesthood resident at Bethel, and this priesthood, judging by all the evidence, regarded Aaron as their tribal father.[540] If this is so it explains immediately why Aaron plays the chief rôle in the aetiology on which the cult of the calf-image at Bethel is based: it was at that time on Sinai that the ancestor of the priesthood at Bethel inaugurated the cult which his descendants practised afterwards.[541]

[535] This was certainly true after Bethel became the central shrine of the amphictyony (cf. M. Noth, *History of Israel*, pp. 94 f.).

[536] Perhaps this was how the calf-image was given the *rôle* of the Ark, which was previously stationed in Bethel (Judges xx. 27), and was interpreted accordingly. This would explain why the calf-image is described as 'God who goes before us' (Exod. xxxii. 1) and as the one who 'brought Israel out of the land of Egypt' (Exod. xxxii. 4). Cf. on the other hand, O. Eissfeldt, 'Lade und Stierbild', *ZAW*, 58, 1940/41, pp. 200 f., who thinks the description of the bull as a *leader*-symbol is to be explained differently. See below.

[537] The suspicion that Aaron was not originally mentioned (so M. Noth, *Exodus*, p. 244, and following him S. Lehming, *op. cit.*, p. 45) seems unfounded. Cf. section I, 8a.

[538] Cf. however R. Smend, *Die Erzählung des Hexateuch*, p. 358, n. 3.

[539] On the reliability of these verses cf. n. 450.

[540] Cf. also H. Oort, 'De Aäronieden', *ThT*, 18, 1884, pp. 289 f.; B. Stade, *Geschichte des Volkes Israel*, p. 583, n. 2; A. von Gall, *Altisraelitische Kultstätten*, *BZAW*, 3, p. 101; R. H. Kennett, 'The origin of the Aaronite priesthood', *JThSt*, 6, 1905, pp. 166 f.,; G. Westphal, 'Aaron und die Aaroniden', *ZAW*, 26, 1906, p. 202; R. Smend, *ibid.*; F. S. North, 'Aaron's rise in prestige' *ZAW*, 66, 1954, p. 192; Y. Kaufmann, *Tol^{e}dot Ha'^{e}muna Hajisra'elit* IV, pp. 261, 264. Cf. now also S. Lehming (*op. cit.*, pp. 46 f.) who reaches a similar conclusion by a different path.

[541] Since the sons of Aaron probably did not count as Levites originally (cf. especially Num. xvi. 17 and on this F. S. North, *op. cit.*, p. 192), the critical note of the Judaean historian in 1 Kings xii. 31 f. that Jeroboam allowed non-Levitical priests to hold office in Bethel, is quite compatible with the above hypothesis. (Cf. on the other hand S. Talmon, *op. cit.*, p. 53, who locates a Levitical priesthood both in Bethel and in Dan. (Judges xviii. 30) and recommends that the reference in 1 Kings xii be taken 'with a grain of salt').

Everything points to the probability at least, that an old aetiological narrative underlies Exod. xxxii. 1–6, reflecting the cult of the calf-image at the southern Ephraimite shrine and seeking to base it on what happened at the Exodus and Sinai. The question whether this derivation is pure fiction or whether it corresponds to an actual historical situation[542] may be left undecided in the present context.

The Elohist,[543] at any rate, vigorously condemned the cult of the calf-image at Bethel[544] (and Dan[545] or wherever else in Israel it was able to find expression[546]) by the way he introduced this old Ephraimite cultic aetiology into the context of his account of Sinai. He deliberately makes the creation of the Golden Calf conflict with the revelation of God's will on Sinai and the delivery of the tables of the covenant to Moses (cf. Exod. xxiv. 12, 13b, (15a), 18b; xxxi. 18b). According to Exod. xxxii. 1, Israel considers that Moses' approach to Yahweh has already failed and it turns its back on what happened at Sinai. What was considered legitimate worship of Yahweh in this old cultic aetiology is now regarded as a breach of the covenant which the Elohist indicates by the smashing of the tables of the covenant (cf. Exod. xxxii. 15, 16, 19).[547] According to Exod. xxxii. 20 (cf. Deut. ix. 21) Moses finally destroys the pernicious calf-image. In all this the Elohist gives eloquent expression to a determined opposition to the cult of the calf-image in the northern kingdom, a cult which had been above suspicion even in circles loyal to Yahweh (cf. 2 Kings x. 28 f.).[548] To engage in such worship meant to break the Sinaitic covenant. Since the Elohist in Exod. xxxiii. 3b f., 7 f.

[542] On this last possibility cf. O. Eissfeldt, *op. cit.*, pp. 199 f., who would prefer to see the calf-symbol at Bethel as a sort of bull-shaped pedestal stemming from Israel's pre-Canaanite period.

[543] Cf. section I, 8b above.

[544] It appears to have lasted up to the destruction of the northern kingdom. Cf. 2 Sam. x. 28 f.; xvii. 16 f.

[545] Cf. on the one hand Judges xviii. 30 f., on the other 1 Kings xii. 29 f.; 2 Kings x. 28 f.; xvii. 16 f.

[546] Cf. W. Baudissin, *op. cit.*, pp. 712 f.

[547] In vv. 17 f. an older fragment (belonging with Exod. xxiv. 13a, 14 and Exod. xvii. 8–16) has obviously been worked into the narrative. Cf. section I, 8b above.

[548] A further representative of this opposition was Hosea (viii. 5 f.; x. 5 f.; xiii. 2) and perhaps also Amos (v. 5; viii. 14), who were both active in the northern kingdom and to that extent close to the Elohist. Cf. on this W. Baudissin, *ibid.*, and, as far as Hosea is concerned, H. W. Wolff, 'Hoseas geistige Heimat', *ThLZ*, 81, 1956, col. 91. It is impossible to believe that the source-author was concerned to illustrate the principle of Exod. xxxii. 33, 'Whoever has sinned against me, him will I blot out of my book', with the help of the narrative of the Golden Calf (so S. Lehming, *op. cit.*, p. 27), since this sentence, which has little in common with Exod. xxxiv. 11, 14, does not occupy a central position in its present context in the tradition and since the story of the Calf could not be recommended particularly as an illustration of this point.

acknowledges the Ark above which Yahweh is present,[549] his categorical rejection of the cult of the calf-image may spring from the conviction that Yahweh does not offer himself to his people in the guise of or in connection with the calf-image cult, but exclusively above the Ark, the central shrine of the tribal union.[550] Whatever the exact truth of this, the whole complex of tradition in Exod. xxxii. 1–6, 15–20 (+ 35) must have grown out of a definite, historical form of the cult of Yahweh.[551]

The distinct cultic orientation of this complex of traditions is not limited to content, however. The narrative follows certain cultic-ritual forms. Thus, the account of the destruction of the calf-image (Exod. xxxii. 20) has been modelled on a specific cultic procedure.[552] This cultic procedure was certainly not that of the ordeal,[553] for the question of guilt is not in doubt.[554] In fact, it is followed by the description of how the sin-offering (*ḥaṭṭā'ṯ*) was instituted.[555] It is not sufficient to destroy the casting-mould. The power residing in it must also be got rid of.[556] This favours the procedure of total destruction by burning—as in the case of purification, when the flesh of the sacrifice had to be destroyed since it was filled with sacred energy.[557] Because the gold of the calf-image could not be obliterated by fire the dust which remained was mixed with water and given to the Israelites to drink. In this way, it was intended, the idol would be 'disposed of'[558] without remainder and got rid of entirely.[559] The Deuteronomist, on the other hand, makes the remainder of the broken image be washed away by a brook (Deut. ix. 21), corresponding to the rite of purification in Deut. xxi. 6. Thus, both versions of this tradition follow definite cultic-ritual forms.

Attached to the older, Elohistic complex of tradition in Exod. xxxii.

[549] Cf. section II, 9 and 10.

[550] Cf. M. Noth, *Das System der zwölf Stämme Israels*, *BWANT*, IV, 1, pp. 95 f.

[551] It cannot be concluded from Exod. xxxii. 19a, 20, 35a (as S. Lehming, *op. cit.*, pp. 28 f. does), which does not specifically refer to a wooden calf-image (cf. M. Noth, *Exodus*, p. 249; S. Lehming, *op. cit.*, p. 20, n. 2) that there was an old text, now replaced by Exod. xxxii. 2–4a, which spoke of the 'veneration of a (wooden) calf image at a certain shrine (perhaps East of the Jordan)'.

[552] On the following cf. R. Dussaud, *op. cit.*, p. 245.

[553] Cf. Num. v. 11–31.

[554] *Contra* H. Holzinger, *KHC*, 2, p. 111; B. Baentsch, *HK*, 2/1, p. 272; H. Gressmann, *op. cit.*, pp. 204 f.; *et al.*

[555] Cf. also R. Dussaud, *op. cit.*, pp. 117 f.

[556] Cf. S. Mowinckel, *Religion und Kultus*, pp. 48 f.

[557] Cf. Th. Jacobsen in *Before Philosophy*, p. 147 (= *The Intellectual Adventure of Ancient Man*).

[558] With R. Dussaud, *ibid.*

[559] Since the destruction of the idol is clearly the sole issue there is no need to verify the effect of what was drunk on the bodies of the Israelites. Willingness to find a reference of this sort in Exod. xxxii. 35 has probably been a mistake. Cf. in this respect for instance H. Holzinger, *KHC*, 2; B. Baentsch, *HK*, 2/1; S. Lehming, *op. cit.*, pp. 19 f.

1–6, 15–20 (+ 35) are other pieces of tradition which seem to be mostly younger, Exod. xxxii. 7–14, 21–24, 25–29, 30–34.[560] Vv. 21–24 are clearly distinguished from the other verses by their effort to exonerate the person of Aaron, once regarded positively but later negatively in the E-tradition.[561] In fact, the excuse placed on Aaron's lips in Exod. xxxii. 22 and worded with reference to Exod. xxxii. 1–6 begins so seriously that it is difficult to believe these verses were really inserted here to tell against Aaron.[562] Reflection on the question of *who* could have been responsible for such a defence of Aaron suggests the tradition stems from circles which thought of Aaron as their ancestor (see above). The destruction of Solomon's Temple at Jerusalem may have created a situation in which the Aaronite priesthood obtained greater power and authority and the possibility of influencing the development of the tradition.[563] Whatever the exact truth, Exod. xxxii. 21–24, may well be an expression of priestly interests. Similarly the tradition of vv. 25–29 which has been added to the E-source has been determined by the group interests of the Levitical priesthood, which found in it the aetiological explanation and defence of their right to the priesthood.[564] Since this tradition has a parallel in the Blessing of Moses (cf. Deut. xxxiii. 8 f.), we should ask whether we are dealing here with a tradition which was originally independent and was only interwoven with the narrative of the 'Golden Calf' later.[565] A definite answer is not possible here. If, however, this piece of tradition was only set in this context at a later date, then it may have been done with the intention of defending the sole right of the Levites, who were loyal to Yahweh, to be priests in Israel, in opposition to the priests who regarded Aaron as their ancestor.[566] In that case this process in the composition would also have been determined by conflicts in the

[560] Cf. section I, 8a above.

[561] Perhaps this tendency has also been at work in the plural verbal forms of Exod. xxxii. 4, 6 (the LXX may have preserved the original wording here), which exonerate Aaron by making the *people* responsible for what happened. Thus also W. Rudolph, *Der 'Elohist' von Exodus bis Josua*, *BZAW*, 68, 1938, p. 49.

[562] With S. Lehming, *op. cit.*, pp. 48 f., *contra* W. Rudolph, *op. cit.*, pp. 51 f.

[563] Cf. R. H. Kennett, *op. cit.*, pp. 173 f., 184; and F. S. North, *op. cit.*, pp. 192 f.

[564] Cf. also H. Gressmann, *op. cit.*, pp. 211 f. S. Lehming, *op. cit.*, pp. 43 f. has rightly drawn attention to the apologetic aim of this unit of tradition. It may have suited those Levitical groups which had been excluded from the shrines of the northern kingdom (at least partly—Judges xviii. 30) by the measures of Jeroboam I (1 Kings xii. 31) to defend their priestly privileges (cf. H. W. Wolff, 'Hoseas geistige Heimat', *ThLZ*, 81, 1956, col. 91 f.). To that extent, therefore, the tradition of Exod. xxxii. 25–29 could have dealt with the hierarchical situation at these same northern shrines, whose calf-cult is opposed by the Elohist in Exod. xxxii.

[565] Further details in H. Gressmann, *op. cit.*, pp. 215 f.

[566] Cf. also W. Rudolph, *op. cit.*, p. 52.

history of the cult. The two passages Exod. xxxii. 7–14, 30–34 which culminate in Moses' prayer of intercession would finally explain why Yahweh permitted the continued existence of his people although they had broken the covenant and why he allowed the calf-cult to continue at the state-shrines in the northern kingdom.[566a] Some specific event in Israel's cultic history may have been responsible, in part at least, for the origin of these two pieces of tradition; at the same time a specific cultic form has been placed at the service of this interpretation—namely the prayer of intercession, which is undoubtedly a cultic practice of early Israel.[567] Moreover, the wording of Exod. xxxii. 7–14 also follows liturgical usage.[568]

Summary. It is evident that not only the older tradition in Exod. xxxii, which belongs to the E-source (vv. 1–6, 15–20, 35), stems from the attitude adopted towards a particular historical manifestation of the cult of Yahweh, but that the passages which were added later (like Exod. xxxii. 21–24, 25–29, 30–34) also grew out of certain contexts in the history of the cult. To this end the narrative uses well-established cultic forms in both cases. Finally, the fact that the whole complex of tradition in Exod. xxxii was composed in contrast to Exod. xxxiii was perhaps intended as a contribution to the question discussed in chap. xxxiii, namely how Yahweh was actually present in Canaan, making Israel's cult possible. Thus, even in its composition Exod. xxxii was regarded and used as an important complex for the cult of Yahweh in the period after the people settled in Canaan.

12. Exodus xix. 9–25; xx. 18–21; xxxiii. 18–xxxiv. 8

Now that Exod. xxxiii and xxxii[569] have been discussed in the light of the close literary connection that exists between them and Exod. xxxiv. 9,[570] we must turn our attention to those verses of

[566a] Cf. W. Rudolph, *op. cit.*, pp. 52 f.

[567] Cf. G. von Rad, 'Die falschen Propheten', *ZAW*, 51, 1933, p. 115; P. A. H. de Boer, *De voorbede in het Oude Testament*, *OTS*, 3, 1943; F. Hesse, *Die Fürbitte im Alten Testament*, pp. 5 f., 109; W. Eichrodt, *Theology of the Old Testament*, I, p. 167.

[568] It is well-known how much it has in common with the language of Deuteronomy (cf. the comparison in H. Holzinger, *KHC*, 2, p. 108). This need not indicate Deuteronomic origin, however. The vocabulary of Exod. xxxii. and the forms of expression used in Deuteronomy could both stem from the language of the cult (cf. S. Mowinckel, *Le Décalogue*, p. 7; G. von Rad, *Studies in Deuteronomy*; A. Weiser, *Der Prophet Jeremia*, *ATD*, 21, p. 482, n. 1). Details which tell in favour of this are the parallels between Exod. xxxii. 11b and the liturgy of Ps. cxxxvi. 11 f. and between Exod. xxxii. 12b and Ps. lxxxv. 4. On God's *yād* and on *kōaḥ* in the language of the Psalms and its prose-prayers cf. M. Tsevat, *A Study of the Language of the Biblical Psalms*, *JBL Monogr. Ser.* 9, p. 31.

[569] Cf. section II, 8 above.

[570] Cf. section II, 9–11 above.

chap. xxxiv which are concerned with the theophany on Sinai and its attendant circumstances (vv. 2–3, 5–8). At the same time it is also an appropriate moment to discuss the relevant parts of chaps. xix and xx.[571]

There is *one* feature which always occurs in all the theophanies described in the tradition: Yahweh appears hidden in *cloud* (*'ānān* Exod. xxxiv. 5; xxxiii. 9 f.; xix. 9, 16; *'āšan* Exod. xix. 18; xx. 18; *'ᵃrāp̱ĕl* Exod. xx. 21). The account obviously considers it important that Yahweh remains hidden to the human eye when he appears: he descends in the cloud (*bĕ'ānān* Exod. xxxiv. 5); he comes to Moses in a thick cloud (*bᵉ'aḇ hĕ'ānān* Exod. xix. 9). It is clear from the parallel *'āšan* that this cloud which covers Yahweh refers to a cloud of smoke.[572] The instructions for the great Day of Atonement, as already mentioned in passing,[573] do in fact refer to a cloud of smoke which conceals the place where God appears and hides it from men's eyes, lest they die (Lev. xvi. 2, 13). This cloud of smoke is derived from the 'censer full of coals of fire' in Yahweh's shrine (Lev. xvi. 12). Since an old ritual underlies the instructions for the Day of Atonement,[574] we are doubtless dealing here with a long-established incense-ceremony, attested also by Isa. vi. 4.[575] Since it very definitely serves the same end that is pursued so obviously by the stereotyped references to the cloud in the accounts of Sinai, namely to conceal God's appearance,[576] there was probably a close connection between the two: everything goes to suggest that in describing the smoke (and fire[577]) of the primordial theophany[578] the tradition had before it the incense-ceremony which served to hide

[571] On Exod. xix. 13b and Exod. xx. 2–17 see sections II, 2 and II, 5 above.

[572] Both nouns are to be found within the same source: Exod. xix. 9; xxxiv. 5 –J; and Exod. xix. 18 –J; cf. also I. Engnell, 'The call of Isaiah', *UUÅ* 1949/4, pp. 37 f.

[573] See above, p. 124.

[574] Cf. on this K. Koch, *Die Priesterschrift von Exodus 25 bis Leviticus 16*, *FRLANT*, 71, pp. 92 f.

[575] Cf. I. Engnell, *op. cit.*, pp. 27 f., 31; M. Schmidt, *Prophet und Tempel*, p. 33. On 1 Kings viii. 10 f. cf. M. Noth, *Überlieferungsgeschichtliche Studien*, 2nd ed., p. 70.

[576] Cf. also K. Galling, *ATD*, 12, p. 92 on the ancient Temple-dedication in 2 Chron. vi. 1 f.

[577] Cf. A. Jirku, *Die Ausgrabungen in Palästina und Syrien*, p. 90, on *ḥammān*.

[578] Since the function of concealing was probably characteristic of this cultic ceremony from the very beginning (corresponding to the ancient view that whoever sees God must die—Judges xiii. 22; vi. 22 f.; Exod. iii. 6; xxxiii. 20, 23) the prototype of the narrative is probably to be sought here rather than in the natural phenomena of the volcano (cf. apart from the literature cited by H. Gressmann, *Mose und seine Zeit*, *FRLANT*, 18, p. 192, n. 7 E. Auerbach, *Moses*, pp. 168 f.; M. Noth, *The History of Israel*, pp. 131 f.) to which this function could not have been ascribed until a later date. The attempt to locate Sinai in north-west Arabia because of its assumed volcanic character also seems questionable. The oldest element in the Sinai tradition, however, Exod. xxiv. 1a, 9–11, does not presuppose either smoke or fire on Sinai.

Yahweh in the festival-cult. Conversely, this cultic ceremony served to realise* in a dramatic way the Sinai theophany and its accompanying phenomena.[579]

Another element firmly rooted in the ancient Sinai tradition is the noise of thunder that accompanied Yahweh's epiphany (*ḳōlōṯ*—Exod. xix. 16; xx. 18, E). Contrasting yet combined with it in a peculiar way is the *sound of the trumpet* (*ḳôl hassōp̄ār*—Exod. xix. 16, 19; xx. 18, E), which grows louder and louder until finally it seems to drown even the thunder (v. 19a). There is no indication anywhere in the text of the tradition that the reference to the sound of this trumpet was only meant metaphorically. Quite clearly the sound of a real trumpet was thought of. Since there is no attempt by any part of the tradition to introduce the trumpet with an explanation we must be dealing with a phenomenon which was generally well-known at that time.[580] Undoubtedly, it is the same phenomenon that used to accompany Yahweh's cultic epiphany according to 2 Sam. vi. 2, 14 f.; Ps. xlvii. 6; lxxxi. 4 and xcviii. 6.[581] Thus, the Sinaitic tradition was obviously influenced by a definite cultic usage in this respect also. The custom of blowing the trumpet which belongs to the cultic theophany was given a central position in the picture of Yahweh's epiphany and the accompanying thunder and lightning: so much so, in fact, that the sound of the trumpet perceptibly assumes predominance over the other phenomena accompanying the theophany (cf. Exod. xix. 16, 19). On the other hand, this cultic usage probably gave dramatic realisation to this element in the account of Sinai.[582] According to Exod. xix. 19, God's voice was heard in the sound of the trumpet at the primordial theophany. It is a reasonable hypothesis, therefore, that the corresponding custom of blowing the trumpet during the cultic theophany was meant to indicate Yahweh's voice (cf. Isa. lviii. 1). The epiphany of the God whom no man could look upon (cf. Judges xiii. 22; vi. 22 f.; Exod. xxxiii. 20) and who remained hidden in the cloud of incense (*ʿanan haḳḳeṭōreṯ*—Lev. xvi. 13), could only be perceived by the cultic

[579] With A. Weiser, 'Theophanie in den Psalmen und im Festkult', *Bertholet-Festschrift*, p. 523.

[580] See also section II, 2 above on Exod. xix. 13b.

[581] Cf. in addition section II, 2 and S. Mowinckel, *Le Décalogue*, p. 120. On the pre-exilic application of these Psalms cf. H. Schmid, 'Jahwe und die Kulttraditionen von Jerusalem', *ZAW*, 67, 1955, pp. 185 f.

[582] Cf. A. Weiser, *ibid.*

* Tr. note: the German word is 'Vergegenwärtigung'. Cf. III. 4 below. 'Aktualisiering' is also translated 'realization', cf. II. 12 and III. 4 below. Literally, perhaps 're-present' or 'actualize'.

community in terms of such dramatic representation (cf. Deut. iv. 12).[583] The blowing of the trumpet cannot be properly understood apart from this cultic function which it had in the festival of Yahweh's theophany, where it symbolises the presence of the God who reveals himself in hiding himself.

This sign of the theophany in the Elohist is replaced in the narrative of the Yahwist by the *proclamation of Yahweh's name*, to announce his appearance. According to Exod. xxxiv. 5 f. (and xxxiii. 19) it is the Godhead concealed in the cloud (not Moses)[584] who proclaims Yahweh's name.[585] God goes past Moses and calls, 'Yahweh, Yahweh[586] . . . .' Thus, ancient Israel is assured of the presence of the One whom no man can see. [587] In fact, when invoked in prayer, which is its more normal usage, the name has the power to summon the bearer of the name.[588] But since Yahweh himself invokes his own name the effectiveness of this act of naming is rooted in the free-will of the God who reveals himself and not in magic.[589] Most peculiarly, what Yahweh does here is described by the formula *kārā' bešēm yhwh*, which otherwise always has man as its subject. It occurs frequently if not exclusively (cf. 1 Kings xviii. 24; Zeph. iii. 9) in the tradition of the Yahwist (Gen. iv. 26; xii. 8; xiii. 4; xvi. 13; xxi. 33; xxvi. 25) and generally denotes the invocation of Yahweh's name at a holy place where the cultic presence of the Godhead was discernible. (It is also used as a technical term, *pars pro toto*, for the cultic worship of Yahweh).[590] The application of this phrase in Exod. xxxiv. 5 (and xxxiii. 19) to Yahweh's designation of himself when he appeared on Sinai makes it quite clear that the Yahwistic account thought of this in terms of the cultic forms by which Yahweh's presence was usually recognised by the cultic community. The existence of such a proclamation of Yahweh's name in the cult—particularly in connection with the cultic theophany, in fact—can still be clearly

[583] Cf. in this connection M. Buber, *Moses*, p. 158 f.

[584] With O. Grether, 'Name und Wort Gottes im Alten Testament', *BZAW*, 64, 1934, p. 20, n. 2; J. Scharbert, 'Formgeschichte und Exegese von Exod. xxxiv. 6 f. und seiner Parallelen', *Bibl.* 38, 1957, p. 131 *Contra* W. Rudolph, *Der 'Elohist' von Exodus bis Josua*, *BZAW*, 68, 1938, p. 57, n. 2; *et al.*

[585] The phrase *kārā' bešēm yhwh* really means 'to call upon Yahweh by naming the name' (with Koehler-Baumgartner, *LVTL*, p. 984; cf. also O. Grether, *op. cit.*, p. 19).

[586] Since the second 'Yahweh' is only missing in LXX-B and is otherwise well attested, it should be retained.

[587] So also O. Grether, *op. cit.*, p. 20.

[588] Cf. *ibid.* pp. 18 f.; J. Pedersen, *Israel. Its Life and Culture I–II*, pp. 256 f.; J. W. Wevers, 'A Study in the Form-Criticism of Individual Complaint Psalms', *VT*, 6, 1956, pp. 82 f.; F. Giesebrecht, *Die alttestamentliche Schätzung des Gottesnamens*, pp. 42 f.

[589] On the latter cf. for instance, H. Bietenhard in *ThWBNT*, V, pp. 250 f.

[590] Cf. O. Grether, *op. cit.*, *p.* 19; H. Bietenhard, *op. cit.*, p. 254.

traced:[591] according to 2 Sam. vi. 2 the name, 'Yahweh Ṣeba'oth,[592] enthroned on the cherubim', was invoked[593] above the Ark, the place of the theophany.[594] According to Ps. xxiv. 8, 10 also the proclamation of Yahweh's name belonged to the liturgy of the Ark-cult. The connection of this act of naming with the cultic theophany[595] is further suggested by the way Yahweh introduces himself[596] in the preface to the Decalogue (Exod. xx. 2) and in Ps. l. 7 and lxxxi. 11) (cf. the context). Expressions in the Psalter like 'thy name is near' (lxxv. 2), 'seek thy name' (lxxxiii. 17) etc.[597] and Jeremiah's description of the Temple as the 'house which is called by my name' (Jer. vii. 10, 11 etc.) tell equally in favour of the view that the invocation of God's name belonged substantially to Yahweh's cultic presence.[598] At all events, the relevant Deuteronomistic terminology[599] can only be understood in the light of the central importance which the name of Yahweh had in the worship of the Temple. All in all we seem justified in assuming that the proclamation of the name in Exod. xxxiv. 5 f. corresponded to a custom of proclaiming Yahweh's name in connection with the cultic theophany. Everything suggests that the narrator had this liturgical practice before his eyes when he used the phrase *ḳārā' bᵉšēm yhwh* for his account of the theophany. And conversely the narrative obviously found its realization in this cultic practice.

Attached to Yahweh's name in Exod. xxxiv. 6 f. is a* *list of attributes*[600] developing it further: 'a God merciful and gracious, slow to

[591] Cf. on the following, A. Weiser, 'Theophanie in den Psalmen und im Festkult', *Bertholet-Festschrift*, pp. 521 f.

[592] On the question of its origin cf. O. Eissfeldt, 'Jahwe Zebaot', *Miscellanea Academica Berolinensia*, 1950, pp. 128 f.

[593] Cf. also the explanation of the passage in K. Galling, 'Die Ausrufung des Namens als Rechtsakt in Israel', *ThLZ*, 81, 1956, col. 68 f. See below, n. 598.

[594] Cf. section II, 10 above.

[595] Cf. also S. Mowinckel, *Le Décalogue*, pp. 125 f.; W. Zimmerli, *op. cit.*, pp. 207 f.

[596] Cf. on this W. Zimmerli, 'Ich bin Jahwe', *Alt-Festschrift*, *BHTh*, 16, pp. 179 f.

[597] Cf. on this A. Weiser, *The Psalms*, pp. 41 f.

[598] It is inconceivable that all these references to God's name could go back to the legal act of the roll-call associated with the transfer of property. Only their connection with Yahweh's cultic presence is common to all the references. It is questionable whether the invocation of God's name above the Ark in 2 Sam. vi. 2 is to be understood in the context of this legal act (K. Galling, *ibid.*) if for no other reason than that the Ark as such, apart from the cherubim placed on top, could have belonged to Yahweh in the desert-period (cf. M. Buber, *Moses*, pp. 149 f. and the literature cited there). It is unlikely that Jeremiah's description of the Temple of Solomon goes back to the cultic naming-ceremony which normally accompanied the transfer of property (K. Galling, *op. cit.*, col. 70); the Temple belonged to Yahweh and no one else from the very beginning.

[599] Cf. the summary in O. Grether, *op. cit.*, p. 31.

[600] Whether this list develops it in the sense advocated by S. D. Goitein '*YHWH* the passionate', *VT*, 6, 1956, pp. 1–9 (Yahweh = 'the passionate lover', derived from the Arabic root *hwy* = 'to be passionate') is a question that need not be decided here.

* Tr. note: the German word is 'Gottesprädikation'; cf. III. 3.

anger and abounding in steadfast love and faithfulness, keeping steadfast love for thousands, forgiving iniquity and transgression and sin, but who will by no means clear the guilty, visiting the iniquity of the fathers upon the children and the children's children to the third and fourth generation'. The appearance of such attributes alongside God's name[601] may be observed in ancient liturgical poetry.[602] Exod. xxxiv. 5 f. undoubtedly follows a well-established liturgical form in this respect. The list itself, which employs *parallelismus membrorum* and exalted language, may also have had its *Sitz im Leben* in Israel's festival-cult.[603] There is no other satisfactory explanation for the way in which these attributes are frequently reflected in the hymns of the cult (Ps. cxlv. 8; ciii. 8; cxi. 4; Neh. ix. 17, 31), in lament (Ps. lxxxvi. 15), in exhortation (Joel ii. 13) and in the recorded prayers of a later period (Jonah iv. 2; Num. xiv. 18).[604] The list of attributes which interprets Yahweh's name in Exod. xxxiv. 6 f. is thoroughly cultic and liturgical. To that extent it confirms once more that the name of God linked with it must have been constantly proclaimed anew in the festival-cult and that there must have been a cultic recapitulation corresponding to the Yahwistic account of the primordial theophany.[605]

This is also rendered probable by the *act of obeisance* described in Exod. xxxiv. 8 with which Moses greets Yahweh's epiphany.[606] It is self-evident that this is not a distinctive, individual reaction. According to Exod. xxxiii. 10, all Israel prostrates itself in awe when Yahweh appears in the Tent of Meeting. According to 1 Sam. i, 3 the annual pilgrimage to Shiloh culminates in the cultic act of obeisance before Yahweh Ṣeba'oth when he appears there (cf. 1 Sam. iii. 21). The firm connection between Israel's reverent obeisance and Yahweh's cultic epiphany is also apparent in Ps. xcix. 1, 5, 9; cxxxii. 7. Thus, this feature of the Sinai narrative also corresponds

[601] Cf. on this L. Köhler, *Deuterojesaja stilkritisch untersucht*, *BZAW*, 37, 1923, p. 120.

[602] Cf. for instance Ps. xxiv. 8, 10.

[603] Cf. also H. J. Stoebe, 'Die Bedeutung des Wortes *ḥäsäd* im Alten Testament', *VT*, 2, 1952, pp. 249 f., who considers Exod. xxxiv. 6 a revised and extended liturgical formula. The share of the Yahwist in the revision should not be overestimated, however, seeing that Ps. lxxviii, which antedates the division of the Kingdom (cf. O. Eissfeldt, *BSAW*, *Phil.-hist. Kl.*, 104/5, pp. 26–43), and which belongs to the covenant-festival (cf. A. Weiser, *The Psalms*, pp. 539 f.), declares God's mercy, patience and readiness to forgive (v. 38).

[604] Cf. also J. Scharbert, 'Formgeschichte und Exegese von Exod. xxxiv. 6 f. und seiner Parallelen', *Bibl.*, 38, 1957, pp. 132 f. See also the gloss in Nahum i. 3.

[605] The fact that the communication of the laws in Exod. xxxiv. 14 f. (cf. section, II 7 above) follows Yahweh's manifestation of himself and description of his attributes in Exod xxxiv. 6 f. likewise corresponds, judging by Ps. l and lxxxi *inter alia*, to a well-established liturgical sequence. Cf. on this for instance W. Zimmerli, 'Ich bin Jahwe', *Alt-Festschrift*, *BHTh*, 16, pp. 207 f. See also pp. 89 f. above.

[606] Cf. pp. 90 and 122 above.

to a well-established ceremony that was closely connected with the cultic theophany.

In Exod. xx. 18–21,[607] a passage which belongs to the E-source, neither Moses nor the people prostrate themselves before God at his epiphany. The people stand at a distance trembling (v. 18, 21). According to this piece of Elohistic tradition, this situation results in a conversation between Israel and Moses. This is all the more surprising since the parallel E-narrative of chap. xix (vv. 16aβ-17, 19, 25) does not seem to point to such a conversation. Moreover, the composed, prolix exhortation of Moses in Exod. xx. 20 is not particularly suitable for the situation. Altogether one is left with the impression that this conversation did not come to occupy its present position in the account of the theophany until a later date (which seems to have led to the break-away of a variant tradition from the material of chap. xix.) and that it is basically the product of later reflection. What caused this is not difficult to see: it was the question of why the voice of God himself was no longer heard by the cultic community at the cultic recapitulation of the Sinai-theophany and why the mediating word of a man issued forth instead.[608] Exod. xx. 18–21 gives the answer: a human *mediator* speaks in the name of God at his epiphany because even at that time Israel asked Moses to act as mediator. These verses simply contain the aetiology of the office of cultic spokesman.[609] The fact that a description of the creation of this cultic mediating agency which is to establish God's word is inserted in the course of the theophany indicates how much the account of the revelation on Sinai is seen from and shaped by the view-point of its cultic realisation.[610] The Yahwistic tradition in Exod. xix. 9a also takes account of this aspect. The Godhead concealed in the cloud appears and speaks to Moses in order that 'the people may hear when I speak with you, and may also believe you for ever' (Exod. xix. 9b). Accordingly the theophany is here *con-*

[607] See sections I, 2 and I, 5 above.

[608] With G. von Rad, *Das formgeschichtliche Problem des Hexateuch* (= *Gesammelte Studien*, p. 37).

[609] With G. von Rad, *ibid.*; cf. H-J. Kraus, *Gottesdienst in Israel*, pp. 60–66, who maintains that Exod. xx. 18–21 is proof of the individual office of a covenant-mediator.

[610] The tradition of Exod. xx. 18–21 shows traces of priestly terminology: the words, 'Do not fear!' in v. 20 correspond to the phrase used to introduce a favourable priestly oracle (cf. J. Begrich, 'Das priesterliche Heilsorakel', *ZAW*, 52, 1934, pp. 81–92; but see also S. Mowinckel, *Le Décalogue*, p. 127, and A. Weiser, *Der Prophet Jeremia*, *ATD*, 21, p. 278, who points out that the phrase 'fear not' usually occurs in connection with the theophany. See also O. Kaiser, *Der Königliche Knecht*, *FRLANT*, 70, p. 45). The expression *niggaš 'el* in v. 21 is a technical priestly term (cf. also for instance Exod. xix. 22; Lev. xxi. 21; Num. xvii. 5 and Exod. xliv. 13; see also G. von Rad, ' "Gerechtigkeit" und "Leben" in den Psalmen', *Bertholet-Festschrift*, p. 429).

firming Moses' office as *mediator*;[611] not only in respect of his contemporaries but '*for ever*' (*l*ᵉ'*ôlām*). The horizon of the historically unique situation of the primordial theophany is here unmistakably opening out, and the attention is directed to the future mediation of God's revelation of himself to the cultic community through all those who share in Moses' work of mediation.[612] This is yet another instance, therefore, of the tradition of God's appearance on Sinai being drawn up in the light of its later cultic realisation.

According to the tradition of Exod. xix. 10 f., 15 f.; xxxiv. 2, 4 (after a period of preparation), Yahweh's epiphany takes place *at the appointed time:* again a marked cultic point of view may be observed. It is characteristic of what happens in the cult that it can only succeed if it is performed *rite*—at the appointed time, at the time of the festival.[613] And on the other hand, the fact that the tradition of Exod. xix. 12–13a, 20–24; xxxiv. 3 marks out a *holy place* for the theophany, also satisfies a characteristically cultic requirement.[614] Add, too, the fact that the tradition regarding the theophany thought it important (as shown above) to introduce and attest a mediator of God's revelation, and it becomes clear that this tradition unites in itself all the chief features of a cultic event: the time, the place and the person are all appointed.[615] This general affinity with the cultic sphere is another reason for assuming that the tradition of the theophany on Sinai was in fact recapitulated in Israel's festival-cult.

At the time appointed for God's appearance the people are to *make themselves holy*[616] *and wash their garments*[617] according to Exod. xix.

611 Cf. ch. I, n. 27 above.

612 Cf. for instance A. S. Herbert, *Worship in Ancient Israel*, pp. 33–42.

613 Cf. for example the festival-calendar *l*ᵉ*mō'ēd ḥōdeš hā'abîḇ* (Exod. xxiii. 15; xxxiv. 18). Cf. above all S. Mowinckel, *Religion und Kultus*, pp. 53, 58 f.; G. van der Leeuw, *Religion in Essence and Manifestation*, pp. 388 ff.

614 Cf. for instance Lev. xvi. 1 f.; Num. i. 51; 1 Kings ix. 3; Ps. ii. 6; xv. 1; xxiv. 3; Isa. xlviii. 2. Cf. further S. Mowinckel, *op. cit.*, pp. 53, 57; G. van der Leeuw, *op. cit.*, pp. 393 f. Exod. xix. 20–24 is a late midrashic addition to Exod. xix. 12–13a; it discusses the validity of the stipulated separation of the holy place with reference to the privileged position of the priesthood at the shrine and doubtless, in view of this special interest, it originated in priestly circles (cf. W. Rudolph, *op. cit.*, p. 41). The latter point also seems to be indicated by the language of the section: *ha'ed b* . . . in v. 21, 23 refers to the admonition of the priest or cult-prophet (cf. Ps. l. 7.) affirming the divine commandment. On the technical priestly term *ngš* (v. 22) see n. 610, above. On the declaratory use of *ḳdš* (piel) in v. 23 see G. von Rad, *Theology of the Old Testament* I, pp. 261 f., where the declaratory tasks of the priests are dealt with.

615 With C. Westermann, *Das Loben Gottes in den Psalmen*, p. 70. On this however, cf. A. Weiser, *The Psalms*, p. 38, n. 2.

616 Apparently not only was everyone to consecrate himself, but Moses was to do so on behalf of the whole community (*piel* of *ḳdš*). Cf. also the wording of the commission given to Joshua (Joshua vii. 13): 'Up, sanctify the people, and say, "Sanctify yourselves for tomorrow"'. See M. Noth, *Das Buch Josua, HAT*, 1/7, p. 45 on this.

617 On the way in which person and clothes were regarded as a unity cf. for instance Exod. xxix. 21 and A. Jirku, 'Zur magischen Bedeutung der Kleidung in Israel', *ZAW*, 37, 1917/18, pp. 110 f.; J. Pedersen, *Israel. Its Life and Culture*, I–II, p. 170 etc.

10–11a. According to Exod. xix. 14–15a this also happened in accordance with a command. It may be concluded from Exod. xix. 15b that sexual abstinence also belonged to the required holiness. Everything suggests, therefore, that we are concerned here with the observation of ritual regulations concerning purity and abstinence. It is interesting to find that a regular, ritual purification which included clothes (Gen. xxxv. 2) also took place within the cult at Shechem.[618] This makes it clear that this act of purification was connected with the renunciation of foreign gods. According to Joshua xxiv. 23 this renunciation of foreign gods and these rites of purification may have belonged to the ritual of the cult for the renewal of the covenant at Shechem.[619] This, in its turn, included Yahweh's epiphany.[620] It seems, therefore, that here in the context of the covenant-cult at Shechem the rites of purification, on the one hand, and the theophany on the other were linked together. If, then, it is probable that a definite cultic ordinance corresponded to the account of the theophany on Sinai in Exod. xix in view of the preparations for consecration mentioned there, this impression is strengthened by numerous other examples of the fact that Israel always prepared to consecrate itself when it was about to meet its God. According to Num. xi. 18 and Joshua iii. 5 the people consecrated themselves before a mighty act of Yahweh, according to Joshua vii. 13 before a judgement of God, according to 1 Sam. xvi. 5 before a sacrificial meal, according to 1 Chron. xv. 12, 14 before the transfer of the Ark to Jerusalem,[621] according to 2 Chron. xxix. 3 before a renewal of the Sinaitic covenant[622]. Moreover, whenever Yahweh came into the battle-camp (Deut. xxiii. 14) the men of Israel consecrated themselves according to the regulations laid down for the Holy War and exercised continence in sexual matters (2 Sam. xi. 11).[623] In short, before every meeting with the holy God who revealed himself in salvation-history and in the cult, Israel made itself holy.[624] This established cultic-sacral regulation

[618] Cf. A. Alt, 'Die Wallfahrt von Sichem nach Bethel', *Kleine Schriften* I, pp. 80 f.; H-J. Kraus, *op. cit.*, pp. 58 f. The difference between washing and changing clothes is insignificant.

[619] Cf. G. von Rad, *Das formgeschichtliche Problem des Hexateuch* (= *Gesammelte Studien*, p. 44 f.).

[620] This may be concluded from Joshua xxiv. 2 f. where God's word is given in the first person. With A. Weiser, *Introduction to the Old Testament*, pp. 88 f.

[621] See also Ps. cxxxii. 9, 16.

[622] Cf. H-J. Kraus, *Gottesdienst in Israel*, pp. 85 f.

[623] Cf. G. von Rad, *Der Heilige Krieg im alten Israel*, p. 7. See also 1 Sam. xxi. 5 f.

[624] Cf. also S. Mowinckel, *op. cit.*, p. 47.

corresponds to the preparatory act of consecration described in the account of the theophany on Sinai in Exod. xix. It was also one of the factors influencing the form of this account. If, on the other hand, there was an act of purification and clothes were changed in connection with Yahweh's epiphany in the cult of the renewal of the covenant at Shechem (see above), then this indicates that the passage in the account of Sinai dealing with the act of consecration was given concrete expression in a corresponding rite belonging to the cultic celebration of the theophany.

Summary. All the important elements of the Sinaitic tradition in Exod. xix. 9–25; xx. 18–21 and xxxiii. 18–xxxiv. 8 clearly had an exact parallel in the Israelite festival-cult. The cloud which concealed God at his epiphany was, judging by all the evidence, described in the light of the incense-ceremonial, which served the same purpose in the cultic theophany—namely, to conceal—and which certainly had to serve the cultic-dramatic realisation of the phenomena accompanying the theophany on Sinai. The sound of the trumpet, in which Israel heard the voice of its God, corresponded to the practice of blowing the trumpet at the cultic theophany, which in turn seems to have had the task of indicating the voice of God. The account of the proclamation of Yahweh's name has been influenced by the cultic practice of calling Yahweh's name to help realise his theophany; equally, the account finds its cultic embodiment in this practice. The list of attributes which explains Yahweh's name is obviously cultic-liturgical in style and origin. The fact that Yahweh's manifestation and description of himself is followed by the communication of his commands also corresponds to a well-established liturgical sequence. Everything suggests that the account of the way they bowed down before God when he appeared had an exact parallel in the cultic theophany. Likewise the account of the purificatory rites preparatory to Yahweh's epiphany corresponded to a fixed cultic-sacral regulation which has clearly moulded the tradition. Since this regulation may also be observed in connection with the theophany in the covenant-cult at Shechem, this feature of the Sinaitic tradition may also have found embodiment in Israel's festival-cult. In that the tradition gives a fixed time and a well-marked place for Yahweh's epiphany and is at pains to explain the institution of a mediator of God's revelation and confirm it 'for ever', it shows all the basic features of a cultic event and in view of this marked affinity with the cultic sphere was almost certainly recapitulated in Israel's festival worship. It follows from all this that the older tradition of the theophany on Sinai stood in a close reciprocal relationship with a cultic festival corresponding to it.[625]

[625] Further justification of this view may be seen in the fact that it does not select disparate elements in the cultic parallels referred to but deals with related elements that occur together in groups. Cf. for instance Lev. xvi.: theophany (v. 2)—cloud (v. 2, 13)—consecration (*passim*). 2 Sam. vi.: theophany (v. 2, cf. also 1 Sam. iii. 21)—proclamation of name (v. 2)—blowing of the trumpet (v. 15)—consecration (1 Chron. xv. 12, 14). Ps. l: theophany (v. 1 f.)—Yahweh's manifestation of himself (v. 7)—commands (v. 16 f.). Ps. lxxxi: theophany (v. 6 f.)—Yahweh's manifestation of himself (v. 11)—blowing of the trumpet (v. 4)—commands (cf. v. 10). Ps. xcix: theophany (v. 1)—proclamation of name (v. 3)—cloud (v. 7)—homage (v. 5, 9).

III

SUMMARY AND CONCLUSIONS

The final task is to attempt a synthesis of what we have discovered about the pre-literary growth of the Yahwistic and Elohistic Sinaitic traditions: (1) in the desert-period, (2) in the period between the invasion of Palestine and the formation of a state, (3) in the period of the monarchy.

1. The Development of the Tradition in the Desert-period

All the formal elements which are characteristic of the Decalogue (Exod. xx. 2–17) correspond to a covenant-form which is well-known from Hittite state-treaties (II, 5, especially pp. 51–55, 63 f.). There is also a formal parallel (pp. 52 f.) in the outline of these treaties to the introductory reference to Yahweh's saving-act in delivering the Israelites from Egypt (Exod. xx. 2): just as the historical prologue of the Hittite state-treaties gives the reasons for the vassal's oath of obedience to the author of the covenant, so the preface to the Decalogue puts Yahweh's community under an obligation to obey the covenant by its reference to God's previous activity in history. Since this covenant-outline, which was used by the Hittites in the 14th and 13th century B.C. (p. 51), had long been familiar in the time of Moses and was geographically within the reach of Yahweh's people (pp. 51 f.), we are justified in assuming that a primordial form of the Decalogue, as the tradition asserts (Exod. xxxiv. 27 f.; xxiv. 4, 7, 12; xx. 1), had in fact arisen in the Mosaic period through the use of this treaty form.

This could only happen, however, where there was a living knowledge of Yahweh's saving-act in delivering the Israelites from Egypt as well as an experience of the revelation on Sinai with its climax in the making of the covenant. It may be assumed, therefore, that the Decalogue originated somewhere where we can count on the presence of those who experienced *both* the Exodus *and* the meeting with God on Sinai.[1] The first place which calls for consideration in this respect is *Kadesh*,[2] where according to Judges xi. 16 f.; Exod. xv–xviii the

[1] On the disagreement with G. von Rad, *Das formgeschichtliche Problem des Hexateuch*, (= *Gesammelte Studien*, pp. 20 f., and M. Noth, *Überlieferungsgeschichte des Pentateuch*, pp. 63 f.; *History of Israel*, pp. 127 f., 134 f., see section III, 4 below.

[2] On the texts which permit this conclusion cf. for instance J. Welhausen, *Prolegomena to the History of Israel*, pp. 353 f.; H. Gressmann, *Mose und seine Zeit*, *FRLANT*, 18, pp. 123 f.; S. Mowinckel, 'Kadesj, Sinai, og Jahve', *Norsk Geografisk Tidsskrift*, 11, 1942, pp. 1 f.; R. Brinker, *The Influence of Sanctuaries in Early Israel*, pp. 136 f.; E. Auerbach, *Moses*, pp. 74 f.; J. Gray, 'The Desert Sojourn of the Hebrews and the Sinai-Horeb Tradition', *VT*, 4, 1954, pp. 148 f.

groups that escaped from Egypt and that were one day to constitute Israel made their way. Since Sinai-Horeb, which should be eleven days' journey[3] from Kadesh according to Deut. i. 2, could be identified with the sacred mountain to which the Nabataeans, following an ancient custom, made pilgrimages,[4] it is quite conceivable that the groups of the future Israel that sojourned in Kadesh came to Sinai on a pilgrimage from Kadesh.[5] Their stay in the region of the oasis there[6] must have lasted a fairly long time. This is indicated by Exod. xvi. 35; Deut. i. 46; Amos v. 25, as well as by the fact that not a few of the traditions in Exod. xv.–xviii are to be located in this area.[7] Exod. xviii. 13–27 makes it probable that the method of administering justice and the social organisation of the Yahwistic community[8] were instituted during this stay at Kadesh;[8a] equally probably the basic ordinance of the covenant with Yahweh, the *Decalogue*, may have been first composed in this area. The community of those who had experienced Yahweh's saving activity in the deliverance from Egypt and had encountered his sovereign will at Sinai and had pledged themselves to obey him understood their tie with Yahweh on the analogy of a vassal-covenant. The same treaty-form which the Hittite kings had used to make their covenant-will law now became the vehicle for expressing something quite new and unique—the majestic revelation of the nature and will of the God of Sinai (pp. 74 f.). The historical prologue of the Decalogue reminded the Yahwistic community of Yahweh's saving-act in delivering them from Egypt and their corresponding obligation of gratitude and obedience; the Ten Commandments themselves contained the demands of the covenant-God.

As long as Yahweh's people were conscious of being geographically

[3] Cf. F. M. Abel, *Géographie de la Palestine* I, pp. 393 f.

[4] Cf. B. Moritz, *Der Sinaikult in heidnischer Zeit*; A. Alt, *Der Gott der Väter* (= *Kleine Schriften* I, pp. 5 f.).

[5] With J. Gray, *op. cit.*, p. 151.

[6] Cf. (in connection with H. C. Trumbull, *Kadesh Barnes*, 1884) H. Gressmann, *op. cit.*, pp. 419 f.; E. Auerbach, *Moses*, p. 76.

[7] See H. Gressmann, *op. cit.*, pp. 121 f., 422; E. Auerbach, *op. cit.*, pp. 77 f.; for a different view see M. Noth, *Überlieferungsgeschichte des Pentateuch*, pp. 181 f. It is quite misleading to think of the Israelites wandering aimlessly for forty years in the desert. As ass-using nomads these groups could never have been more than a short day's march from water. Cf. on this W. F. Albright, *Archaeology and the Religion of Israel*, pp. 97 f.

[8] It can hardly be doubted that this tradition conceals a historical nucleus (cf. H. Gressmann, *op. cit.*, pp. 174 f.) even if its present form presupposes that Israel has become a settled community (cf. M. Noth, *Exodus*, p. 150).

[8a] On the determination of this locality cf. H. Gressmann, *op. cit.*, pp. 164 f.; E. Auerbach, *op. cit.*, pp. 99 f.

near their God (i.e. during their stay at Kadesh),[9] *Yahweh's epiphany and presence* will hardly have presented itself as a problem. There could be no objection, therefore, to using this covenant-outline and publishing the treaty framed in accordance with it, although it presupposes the presence of the author of the covenant (p. 53). Thus, there is no difficulty in explaining the I-thou style of the Ten Commandments from the situation of the Kadesh-community. The presence of the God of Sinai is probably discernible in the ceremonial invocation of Yahweh's name. The phrase *ḳārā' ḇešēm yhwh*, which subsequently in Exod. xxxiv. 5 and xxxiii. 19 is related so distinctively to Yahweh's description of himself (pp. 136 f.), is rooted in the practice of proclaiming Yahweh's name. The *place* of God's appearance was probably the Tent of Meeting (Exod. xxxiii. 7 f.), the origins of which must go back to the time in the desert rather than Canaan.[10] Finally, then, the tradition in Exod. xxxiii. 7–11 reflects a cultic arrangement from the earliest period of the Yahwistic community.

The covenant-treaty of the Ten Commandments must have been given *written form* from the very beginning (pp. 55f.). This was in accord with the view which was fairly widespread throughout the Ancient Orient that the written record of a treaty contributed to its realisation and served to attest its conclusion (pp. 55, 57). In view of the fact that the covenant-form underlying the Hittite state-treaties of the 14th and 13th centuries B.C. provided for the treaty to be set down in writing (p. 55), the tradition in Exod. xxxiv. 1a, 4, 27 f.; xxiv. 4, 7, 12; xxxi. 18b, according to which the Decalogue was already written down in Mosaic times, seems quite reliable. In the elements of tradition just referred to, it is clearly expressed that similar written records of the covenant-treaty existed in the oldest cult of Yahweh. They were probably *deposited* in some holy place (p. 57). In the case of the Hittite state-treaties also the written record which was made had to be deposited in the shrine (p. 57). While the community of Yahweh was still in the desert, however, there was no question of the Decalogue being deposited in anything

[9] The introduction to the Blessing of Moses in Deut. xxxiii. 2, when amended on the basis of the LXX and the double *parallelismus membrorum*, speaks of Yahweh coming from Sinai, from Se'ir, from Mt. Paran and from *meribat kadeš*.

[10] The theory now put forward by M. Haran ('The nature of the "'Ohel Mo'edh" in Pentateuchal sources', *JSSt* 5, 1960, pp. 50 f.), that this tent was not a shrine for theophanies but a prophetic-nabiistic institution separate from the camp of the people for the purpose of meditation and preparation for inspiration, cannot be accepted for the reasons given in section II, 10: the older stratum of tradition in Exod. xxxiii. 7–11 assumes the Tent of Meeting was still in the centre of the camp (pp. 113f.); the connection of Tent and Ark can hardly be doubted (pp. 114–116).

but a movable shrine.[11] Accordingly, the tradition preserved by Deuteronomy (x. 1–5), which makes Moses deposit the Tables of the Law in the Ark of Yahweh (cf. 1 Kings viii. 9), carries greater weight. As a container serving this purpose the Ark can be fully relied on for the desert period. In fact, its box-like form[12] does not make sense otherwise. On the other hand, at this early period when the God of Sinai was not yet felt by the Yahwistic community to be geographically distant (see above) the Ark could hardly have had the task of embodying his presence (cf. p. 106 f.). It is significant that the part of the Ark formed by the cherubim, which is connected with the cultic theophany, was made with reference to Syro-Canaanite forms and ideas (p. 108). Accordingly, its origin in Israel's desert period is unlikely, apart from the fact that it would hardly have been possible technically. Since the Ark with the texts of the Decalogue could hardly have remained without the protection of a tent[13] and since, moreover, the tablets of the treaty, as in the case of the Hittite state-treaties, were best guarded in the presence of the deity who was responsible for the alliance, this strongly suggests that even in this early period of the Yahwistic community the Ark was housed in the Tent of Meeting. This physical connection of Ark and Tent would also help to explain how the Ark eventually came to be positively related to the cultic theophany, as is assumed in Exod. xxxiii. 7–11, 12–17 (section II, 9, 10).

It goes without saying that the first proclamation of the covenant-treaty when the community of Yahweh was established could not have been the end of the matter. A *repetition of the public recital of the treaty* was perhaps made necessary by the fact that freshly incoming groups of Hebrews were admitted into the Sinaitic covenant. A regular, recurrent recital was chiefly required, however, because in the view of antiquity this was the only way the validity of the treaty could be actively preserved and because it served to prevent the covenant-law falling into oblivion during the decades which the community of Yahweh seems to have spent at Kadesh[14] and to

[11] The remains of a fortification (cf. K. Galling, *BRL*, col. 192 f.) discovered by C. L. Wolley—E. T. Lawrence (*The Wilderness of Zin*, *Palestine Exploration Fund Annual*, 3, 1914/15) at 'Ain Qderat (Kadesh Barnea) probably date from the 10/9th. cent. B.C. It was probably a Judaean border-fort built by David, Solomon or Rehoboam (cf. M. Burrows, *What Mean These Stones?*, § 101, p. 143).

[12] Hebr. *'aron*, Akkad. *arānu* = chest, ark, coffin. Cf. for instance Meissner-v. Soden, *Akkadisches Handwörterbuch*, p. 65.

[13] Similarly also M. Haran, *op. cit.*, pp. 50 f.

[14] Cf. Deut. i. 46; Exod. xvi. 35; Amos v. 25. For the explanation of the number 40 see for instance H. Gressmann, *op. cit.*, p. 422; G. Ricciotti, *The History of Israel*, I, p. 188 par. 225.

impress it on the younger members of the community. These necessary repetitions led to well-established forms and the beginnings of a cultic *tradition*. Belief in a regular, public recital of the covenant during the Mosaic period is based on the fact that the covenant-form underlying the Hittite state-treaties also provided for these treaties to be written down and deposited in the cultic centre expressly in order that they might be recited there in public at regular intervals (p. 58 f.). The Tables of the Decalogue were also probably kept in the Ark of Yahweh with this intention. The form and contents of the apodeictic clauses of the Ten Commandments correspond at any rate to the requirements of such a regular, recurrent cultic recital (p. 58 f.). Everything suggests, therefore, that the tradition of the covenant made on Sinai, when it describes a proclamation of the Law in Exod. xxiv. 3, 7; xix. 7, reflects a cultic practice which began in the time of Moses.

Such a practice is inconceivable without the figure of a *covenant-mediator:* just as the reading of the law of the covenant was taken care of by someone who spoke in Yahweh's name and at Yahweh's bidding, so the Sinaitic covenant as a whole can only have come about through the mediation of a particular person who knew how to explain to the community Yahweh's revelation of himself on Sinai and in the events of the Exodus and to bring home the obligations imposed by this. According to Joshua xxiv. 15b, 24 f. and Judges v. 2, 3b, 9 the covenant with Yahweh even in pre-monarchic times was obviously made or renewed in such a way that the community participated only indirectly in the covenant made or renewed by the leader with Yahweh (pp. 78 f.). This, too, could point to the fact that even in the desert God's people did not have a direct share in the making of the covenant. It is quite likely, therefore, that the tradition in Exod. xxxiv. 27, according to which Yahweh makes the covenant with Moses and only secondarily with Israel (p. 78), refers to a procedure which was in fact adopted in Mosaic times. Since all these considerations involve the assumption of a covenant-mediator and since the Yahwistic-Elohistic tradition of Sinai ascribes this rôle to *Moses* not only in Exod. xxxiv. 27 but throughout, there is no need to doubt the correctness of this view,[15]

[15] *Contra* M. Noth, *Überlieferungsgeschichte des Pentateuch*, pp. 172 f., 177 f. The basic assumption made by Noth in coming to the conclusion that the figure of Moses was only linked with the Sinaitic tradition at a later date, the assumption, namely, of separate 'Pentateuchal themes' (cf. *op. cit.*, pp. 63 f., 172), seems untenable according to the interpretation we have given evidence for above, at least as far as the traditions about Sinai, the Exodus and the desert-wanderings go. See section III .4 below.

and certainly no proof that the oldest stratum of the tradition did not mention Moses.[16]

Just as everything points to the basic law of the Sinaitic covenant, the Decalogue, having been first composed in Kadesh and having begun to fashion its own cultic tradition in connection with its regular, recurrent recital of the law, and just as the social organisation and administration of justice in the Yahwistic community probably originated in the same place (Exod. xviii. 13–27), so also the *sacrificial cult* found its way into the worshipping life of the covenant-community at this early period (cf. pp. 37 f.). According to the Elohistic tradition in Exod. xviii. 12 the first sacrifices were probably offered to the God of Sinai at Kadesh.[17] The fact that a Midianite priest, the father-in-law of Moses, played an important part in them (Exod. xviii. 1),[18] not only tells in favour of the report being reliable but also permits the conclusion that these sacrifices represented a tradition which stemmed from the environment of the covenant-community intruding into the worship of Yahweh.[19] According to Exod. xviii. 12 burnt-offerings and sacrifices were introduced into the worship of Yahweh at that time. The tradition of the making of the covenant in Exod. xxiv. 5, in describing the sacrifice of similar burnt-offerings and peace-offerings (see p. 37, n. 64 f.), is probably referring to the cultic situation of the Kadesh-community. In connection with these sacrifices Exod. xviii. 12 also mentions a communal sacrificial-meal in the presence of the deity. It was, in fact, at such meals according to Gen. xxxi. 44, 54 and xxvi. 26–31 that the conclusion of covenant-treaties was sealed even in the days of the patriarchs (pp. 33 f.). The evidence suggests, therefore, that the tradition of the covenant-meal on the mount of God in Exod. xxiv. 11b was rooted in a practice of the desert-period. The Yahwistic community of this period (perhaps through contacts with its Bedouin environment) was also probably familiar with the rite of the twofold application of blood, which was practised in a corresponding manner by the pre-Islamic Arabs (p. 38). It is quite probable, therefore, that the tradition of the sprinkling of blood when the covenant was made at Sinai in Exod. xxiv. 6, 8 grew out of the conditions of the desert-period. Thus, it is probable that several

[16] Even in Exod. xxiv. 1a, 9–11 there is nothing to suggest this. See ch. I, n. 7 above.

[17] With H. Gressmann, *op. cit.*, pp. 164 f.; E. Auerbach, *op. cit.*, pp. 97 f.

[18] Cf. on this H. H. Rowley, 'Mose und der Monotheismus', *ZAW*, 69, 1957, pp. 11 f.

[19] Even if *contra* R. Dussaud (*Les origines cananéennes du sacrifice israélite*, 1921) pre-Canaanite influence on the origin of an 'Israelite' sacrificial cult should be emphasised more, Dussaud is absolutely right in tracing back Israel's sacrificial cultus to a foreign origin.

elements in the Yahwistic-Elohistic tradition of Sinai had their origin in the initial stages of the cult of Yahweh, which everything points to having first developed at Kadesh.

2. The Development of the Tradition in the Period between the Invasion of Canaan and the Establishment of the Monarchy

The invasion of Canaan by the Israelite tribes and clans was of the greatest importance and consequence for the further development of the Sinaitic tradition. In the course of this complicated and somewhat protracted process[20], among those who entered Palestine were those groups which had united at Kadesh to form the covenant-community of the God of Sinai. Chiefly because they came into contact with the other Israelite tribes and groups, that had settled in Canaan at the same time as or even before them, these other groups also became familiar with the (Exodus)-Sinai tradition.[21] Under the influence of this tradition and carried along by the enthusiasm of the old Yahwistic community the incoming tribes bound themselves together into a sacral *tribal union*[22] bearing the name Israel.[23] According to Joshua xxiv this took place at the assembly at Shechem.[24] The central point of this Israelite tribal union was primarily the *festival-cult* which was celebrated by all the tribes in concert in the shrine at Shechem, as may be inferred from Joshua xxiv.; Deut. xxvii. 11, 29 f. and Joshua viii. 30 f. (p. 40).[25]

(a) It is not surprising to find the *tradition of the Kadesh-community* re-appearing in the forms it once had previously and had in fact maintained throughout the desert-period; nor should it surprise us to find this tradition coming to occupy a dominant position. The same Sinaitic covenant by which the desert-community was con-

[20] Cf. M. Noth, *History of Israel*, pp. 68–97.

[21] The possibility that influences proceeding from the not too distant Kadesh community and its special Yahwistic tradition had already been at work in the region occupied by the southern tribes and especially the tribes coming from the Negeb—which like the Midianites had perhaps worshipped a God Yahweh from the very beginning (cf. H. H. Rowley, 'Mose und der Monotheismus', *ZAW*, 69, 1957, pp. 13 f.)—is not of course to be excluded. Cf. also W. F. Albright, *Archaeology and the Religion of Israel*, p. 99.

[22] Cf. M. Noth, *Das System der zwölf Stämme Israels*, *BWANT*, IV 1, 1930.

[23] Cf. M. Noth, *The History of Israel*, pp. 3 f.

[24] On the text of Joshua xxiv. 1, 25 see ch. I, n. 4 above.

[25] The fact that this particular cultic centre (and the Ephraimite Joshua) played a leading rôle in establishing the amphictyony of ancient Israel seems (together with other factors) to indicate that the event was connected with the immigration of the house of Joseph (with O. Kaiser, 'Stammesgeschichtliche Hintergründe der Josephsgeschichte. Erwägungen zur Vor- und Frühgeschichte Israels', *VT*, 10, 1960, pp. 12 f.). In that case it is also probable that the groups coming from Kadesh were already united in this way when they entered Canaan and thus had a decsive influence on future development.

scious of being bound to Yahweh is renewed at Shechem with reference to the tribal union. The tradition of the assembly at Shechem (Joshua xxiv) makes it clear that the covenant was constantly understood as a vassal-covenant and was drawn up according to the relevant covenant-outline.[26] Insofar as this reflects the cultic ritual of a regularly celebrated renewal of the covenant in all probability (see p. 40, n. 78 above), it may be assumed that the use of this treaty-form was not confined to the assembly at Shechem but continued to be active in the consequent Shechemite covenant-cult.

Since the majority of the members of the Israelite amphictyony were unfamiliar with the clauses of the covenant, and since their ordinary mode of life in Canaan disposed them to follow quite different ordinances[27] and since new generations were constantly having to be instructed in the covenant-law, the repeated, regular proclamation of the clauses of the covenant was one of the most important tasks of the central cult of the amphictyony. It is evident from Joshua xxiv. 25; Deut. xxvii. 9 f., 15 f. that the practice followed in the desert of publishing the law regularly was continued in the covenant-cult at Shechem. (It may be taken as certain that the reading of the Decalogue played a prominent part here also). It was in connection with this practice that the tradition of Moses' recital of the commandments when the covenant was made at Sinai (Exod. xxiv. 3, 7; xix. 7) was handed on and given shape (pp. 40 f.).

It may be inferred from Joshua xxiv. 26 that there was a written copy of the law in the covenant-shrine at Shechem. It is probable that there was a similar *written document* underlying the proclamation of the law in ancient Israel as in the case of the recital of the commandments in the Kadesh community's worship of Yahweh. When the tradition records how Moses committed the commandments to writing in Exod. xxiv. 4, 12; xxxi. 18b; xxxiv. 1a, 4, 27 f., then this is an aetiological reference to the document at Shechem, which influenced the transmission of the tradition (pp. 43 f.).

The community of Yahweh in the desert-period probably partici-

[26] In the preface Yahweh, the God of Israel, is named (v. 2). There follows a historical prologue (vv. 2 f.; especially vv. 5 f.) in the I-thou style. Then Israel is summoned to obey Yahweh and his will (v. 14). Only a single—but fundamental—clause of the covenant is emphasised, namely, to put away foreign gods (v. 14). Yahweh makes exclusive claims upon his people (vv. 15 f., 19 f.). Sanctions to be applied in the event of the treaty being broken are announced (v. 20). God's law is written down (v. 26). Witnesses to the covenant are brought in (vv. 26 f.–cf. v. 22), and an affirmation of covenant-obligation made. See pp. 52–63 above. Cf. G. E. Mendenhall, 'Covenant forms in Israelite Tradition' *BA*, 17/3, 1954, p. 67; J. Muilenburg, 'The Form and Structure of the Covenantal Formulations', *VT*, 9, 1959, pp. 358 f.

[27] Cf. for instance G. von Rad, *Theology of the Old Testament* I, pp. 20 f., 30 f.

pated in the covenant between Moses and the God of Sinai only *indirectly*, and a similar procedure was followed according to Joshua xxiv. 15b, 24 f. when the assembly at Shechem made a covenant and also, according to Judges v. 2, 3b, 9, in the subsequent period of the tribal union prior to the monarchy (pp. 79 f.). The tradition in Exod. xxxiv. 27, according to which Yahweh makes the covenant on Sinai with Moses and only secondarily with Israel (p. 78), has been transmitted, it would seem, in accordance with this method of making or renewing a covenant.

(b) Just as these particular forms and practices, which were important for the cult of Yahweh in the desert-period, were maintained in the covenant-cult of ancient Israel and important elements of the Sinai tradition were shaped and handed on in connection with them, so in the new historical situation after the invasion of Canaan and the establishment of the tribal union of Israel *new* problems, adjustments and circumstances arose in the amphictyony's festival-cult and these were the prelude to further developments of tradition.

According to Joshua xxiv it was *Joshua* who performed the duties of covenant-mediator in the assembly at Shechem and hence also in the cult for the renewal of the covenant which was linked with the assembly (pp. 48 f., 115, 120). The tradition of the making of the covenant on Sinai in Exod. xxiv. 13a, 14 has been influenced by this circumstance in making room for Joshua by the side of Moses (II. 4, pp. 48 f.). For the same reason probably Joshua is the first to be entrusted with the office of serving before the Ark in the tradition of the Tent of Meeting (Exod. xxxiii. 7–11; pp. 115 f., 120).

Close to the shrine at Shechem there stood by all accounts a *pillar*, which is probably mentioned in Gen. xxxiii. 20 and Judges ix. 6 and which is explained in Joshua xxiv. 26 as a witness of the covenant-oath sworn by the tribal union at Shechem (p. 45 f.). A similar stone was probably spoken of by an earlier form of the tradition of the covenant made at Sinai in Exod. xxiv. 4 (p. 61 f.). According to Joshua iii f. there were *twelve stones* in Gilgal, which seems to have been the amphictyonic centre at the end of the pre-monarchic period (p. 46, n. 105). They no longer acted as covenant-witnesses but they were symbols of the twelve tribes which made up Israel. Just as they stood in Gilgal 'according to the number of the tribes of the Israelites', (Joshua iv. 8), so the tradition in Exod. xxiv. 4 recalls that at the place where the Sinaitic covenant was made there were 'twelve pillars according to the twelve tribes of Israel' (pp. 45 f.).

Just as there was an attempt at Shechem to *bind* all the members of the Israelite amphictyony to the Sinaitic covenant even though they had not shared in the events of the desert-period which brought about the covenant, so now, if not before, a form must have been found which would allow the rising generations of Israel to have a vital share in the covenant with God. This was probably the context for the growth of the practice of assigning the task of offering sacrifice at the annually celebrated festival for the renewal of the covenant to a new generation of young Israelites each year (pp. 38 f.). The tradition of Exod. xxiv. 5, which speaks so naturally of the sacrificial service of Israel's young men, is best explained as a reflection of this practice. According to Joshua xxiv. 16 f., 24 f. those who were received into the covenant with Yahweh made an express affirmation of their obligations in the assembly at Shechem and hence also, it is certain, in the cult for the renewal of the covenant at Shechem: Israel answered with its confession of faith and promise of obedience. Likewise, according to the tradition of Exod. xix. 8; xxiv. 3, 7 the people of Yahweh responded with an oath of obedience at Sinai (pp. 38 f.). Seeing that the amphictyonic cult-liturgy of the Song of Deborah contains the brief, formal covenant-vow *'ānōkî layhwh* (Judges v. 3b. Cf. p. 68, n. 219) it may be that there was an affirmation of covenant-obligation not only in the cult at Jerusalem under the monarchy but also in the pre-monarchic period and perhaps even in the festival-cult at Shechem: Yahweh (in the manner of Deut. xxvi. 17–19) would promise to be Israel's God and Israel would promise to be his people (pp. 69 f.). The tradition of Exod. xix. 5, which bases its exhortation on the concept of 'the people for Yahweh's own possession' (II. 6; pp. 67 f.), has been conceived and worded with reference to an affirmation of covenant-obligation and its attendant formula, such as may be assumed for the festival-cult of the pre-monarchic period.

Not only the reciprocal cultic acts of covenant-vow and proclamation of the commandments but the cult of Yahweh in itself presupposes *Yahweh's presence* and cannot be celebrated without it. The transplantation of the covenant-cult to Canaan, however, renders it problematical. The God of Sinai is now a long way from his people. He has to come from Sinai, from Se'ir, from Mt. Paran, from Meribat Kadesh,[28] if he is to be present with the community of Israel's tribes (Deut. xxxiii. 2 f.; Judges v. 4). The tradition in Exod. xxxiii. 12–17, which does, it is true, belong to the later strand of

[28] See ch. III, n. 9 above.

Yahwistic tradition but which, as far as content goes, has its origin not in the period of the monarchy but in the situation after the invasion of Canaan (as the passages from the Blessing of Moses and the Song of Deborah show), grew out of the attempt to grapple with this problem (II. 9). In the passage which deals with the procuring of a leader for the journey through the desert (Exod. xxxiii. 12a) a passionate argument breaks out to establish that the God of Sinai has, in fact, accompanied his people to Canaan (pp. 99–112). Not as the ever-present One who is not tied to any place (p. 107) but as the One whose *face* is turned to the covenant-people, now settled in Canaan, in the cultic theophany (pp. 103–107) in connection with the Ark (p. 109–112). The fact that the God of Sinai is present in his *panim* makes Israel's cult in Palestine possible (pp. 103 f., 112).

The *Ark*, which served to protect the tables of the covenant in the desert-period (III. 1), obviously now became the shrine above which the God of Sinai, thought of as 'Cloud-Rider' in connection with Syro-Canaanite forms and ideas (Ps. xviii. 10 f.; lxviii. 5, 34; civ. 3; Deut. xxxiii. 26; Isa. xix. 1; p. 109), appears (pp. 116 f.). Accordingly the *kapporeṯ* with the winged *cherubim*, a copy of Yahweh's chariot of clouds, is now combined with the Ark (p. 108). In this way the Ark now serves the theophany in which the God of Sinai overcomes the geographical barrier and comes to his people in Canaan. The making of this Ark was described in a piece of tradition which evidently stood between Exod. xxxiii. 1–6 and xxxiii. 7–11 but was finally excised in view of the later parallel account in P. (pp. 112 f.). The old, cultic and aetiological material in Exod. xxxiii. 3b–6 has clearly been linked with the shrine of the Ark and been placed at the disposal of the account of its creation: the tradition which was originally intended to explain the amphictyonic rite in which jewellery was discarded (see below) now has the task of making it possible to understand how the metal required for making the Ark or the *kapporeṯ* was obtained (pp. 110 f.). It was, then, the conviction of Israel that God's appearance was connected with the Ark, its *kapporeṯ* and its cherubim. Yahweh's *kāḇôḏ* shone above them (1 Sam. iv. 21; 1 Kings viii. 11; Ps. xxiv. 7–10; xcvii. 1–6; Ezek. i. 4–28; x. 1) (pp. 30 f.). The tradition of the covenant-meal on the mount of God (Exod. xxiv. 1a, 9–11) is shaped accordingly: the appearance of the 'God of Israel' is linked with the phenomenon of light; his feet rest on a plate-shaped structure (v. 10). By all accounts, therefore, the ideas which were associated with Yahweh's epiphany above the covering of the Ark have been at work here (pp. 29–33). After the Ark of the covenant became the shrine for the theophany there was always someone on duty before it (Judges xx. 27 f.; 1 Sam. iii. 3; vii. 1) (p. 115). Hence the tradition of Exod. xxxiii. 11 reports that Joshua the son of Nun kept constant watch in the Tent before the Ark (pp. 115–118, esp. pp. 115 f., 120).

In view of the fact that the Israelite *cult of the calf-image* in Bethel and Dan may not have been first introduced by Jeroboam I (1 Kings xii. 25–33) but may have grown up in the pre-monarchic period under the influence of Canaanite cultic forms and may simply have been officially recognised by Jeroboam by the erection of new cultic images (cf. Judges xvii. f. and p. 128, n. 534), Yahweh's appearance was probably expected and celebrated as represented by and connected with the calf-image[29] at these shrines in northern Israel in the period between the invasion of Canaan and the establishment of the monarchy (pp. 128–131). The tradition which has been revised in Exod. xxxii. 1–6 probably grew out of the attempt to relate this cult of the calf-image to the events on which the covenant-community was based, namely the revelation on Sinai and the deliverance from Egypt, and thus to make it legitimate[30] (pp. 126–129).

The covenant-people recognised from an early period in their history (Judges xiii. 22; vi. 22 f.; Exod. iii. 6; xxxiii. 20, 23) that no one who sees the God of Israel appear can continue to live. Hence the place of God's epiphany is wrapped in a *cloud of smoke* according to the ritual underlying Lev. xvi. (cf. vv. 12 f.; p. 134). Since this ritual is best understood in the time of the monarchy[31] and since Yahweh's epiphany is surrounded with smoke in the account of the call of the prophet Isaiah (Isa. vi. 4) (p. 134), it may be assumed that by the time Israel became a monarchy the cult included an incense ceremonial which served to conceal the theophany.[32] On the other hand, the discovery of incense-altars and receptacles from the Bronze Age in Syria and Palestine[33] demonstrates the cultic use of incense in pre-Israelite Canaan. It seems quite likely, therefore, that pre-monarchic Israel, in accordance with its conviction that Yahweh must remain hidden from human view, utilised this practice of

[29] It was probably not a question of a bull-shaped image, but rather of a pedestal (or support) and attribute for the deity whose appearance was invisible. Cf. on this K. Galling, *BRL*, col. 202–205.

[30] See n. 542.

[31] Cf. K. Koch, *Die Priesterschrift von Exodus 25 bis Leviticus 16*, *FRLANT*, 71, p. 97.

[32] Cf. in this connection also W. F. Albright, *Archaeology and the Religion of Israel*, pp. 144 f.

[33] Cf. A. Jirku, *Die Ausgrabungen in Palästina und Syrien*, pp. 90 f. (+ plate 20).

burning incense to conceal the cultic theophany.[34] The traditions of the primordial theophany on Sinai and of the Tent of Meeting were then influenced by the pattern of this rite which probably grew up soon after the invasion of Canaan:[35] in both cases Yahweh's epiphany was hidden in a cloud of smoke (Exod. xix. 9, 16, 18; xx. 18, 21; xxxiv. 5 and Exod. xxxiii. 9 f.) (pp. 124 f., 134 f.).

Just as ancient Israel was conscious that the naked epiphany of Yahweh was unbearable, so too it felt the necesssity of preparing for the meeting with its God by a *ritual consecration* (Num. xi. 18; Joshua iii. 5; vii. 13; 1 Sam. xvi. 5 *et passim*; cf. pp. 141 f.). According to Gen. xxxv. 2 (and Joshua xxiv. 23) there was a regular, ritual purification, which applied above all to clothing, in the covenant-cult at Shechem (pp. 140 f., 111). In accordance with this practice the Sinaitic tradition in Exod. xix. 10, 14–15b describes a ceremony of consecration and washing of clothes prior to the making of the covenant.

Yahweh did not tolerate the worship of other gods when he vouchsafed his cultic appearance and presence (Exod. xx. 3). His people had to renounce foreign gods in a cultic act of *renunciation*, such as is attested for Shechem in Gen. xxxv. 2 f. and Joshua xxiv. 19 f., and to renew their oath of allegiance to the one Lord (pp. 29 f.). The tribal union which was joined together under the name 'Israel' did not belong to foreign gods; it belonged exclusively to its own God, the *God of Israel*. Accordingly, this name for God, which is rooted in the cultic act of renunciation, subsequently appears in the tradition of the making of the covenant on Sinai: it is now the 'God of Israel' who is seen by the participants in the covenant-meal on the mount of God (Exod. xxiv. 10a) (pp. 28 f.).

According to Gen. xxxv. 2–4 (and Joshua xxiv. 23) the rites of purification and the rejection of foreign gods at the shrine of Shechem were connected with the cultic practice of *discarding ornaments* (see *LXX*), which at that time were thought of as protective charms that could ward off evil (p. 111, n. 431). The fragments of tradition represented by Exod. xxxiii. 3b–4, 5–6 probably originated as aetiologies of this practice. Before they could be utilised in another context (see above), however, it was obviously necessary that, like Gen. xxxv. 2–4 (see *LXX*), this cultic practice should be derived

[34] On the polemic of the prophet againsts the *ḥammānīm* (Isa. xvii. 8; xxvii. 9; Ezek. vi. 4, 6) which was certainly not directed against *this* use of incense but only against the incense-sacrifice, cf. M. Burrows, *What Mean These Stones?*, p. 234, 48.

[35] It is significant that the oldest and most original fragment of tradition, Exod. xxiv. 1a, 9–11, knows nothing of a mount of God wrapped in smoke.

from what happened at Sinai (pp. 110 f.): this was what was done in Israel 'from Horeb onwards' (Exod. xxxiii. 6).

The cultic acts of renouncing foreign gods and discarding jewellery played an important part in separating Israel from its Canaanite environment (even if this was not the only reason for their growth) and the debate of the Yahwistic community with Canaanite practice in the matter of festivals and sacrifices led to a further development of the tradition,[36] which subsequently found literary expression in Exod. xxxiv. 14–26 (xxiii. 12–19) (pp. 85 f.). Thus, in the transition to an agricultural way of life Israel also took over the calendar of festivals used by the Canaanites (Exod. xxxiv. 18a, 22), modifying it in particular details (p. 87). The date of the Feast of Unleavened Bread (*maṣṣot*), for instance, which had previously been a purely astronomical affair, was now brought into connection with the salvation-history of the covenant-people and based on it (Exod. xxxiv. 18b). The prohibition in Exod. xxxiv. 26b resulted from the position adopted by Israel in opposition to a magical rite[37] practised among its neighbours: 'You shall not boil a kid in its mother's milk'. The stipulation that every male Israelite should make a *pilgrimage* three times each year to the place where Yahweh, the God of Israel, was present (Exod. xxxiv. 23), grew out of the attempt to strengthen the ties between the Israelite tribes that had settled in the different parts of the land of Canaan and at the same time to make the central cult of the Yahwistic amphictyony effective in the midst of its Canaanite surroundings (p. 87). All these determined attempts to absorb and master Canaanite practice in the matter of festivals and sacrifices probably came from those Yahwistic shrines where these cultic stipulations later made their home and were put into operation (p. 86). There is a great deal of evidence that points to the temple at Shiloh as the source and shelter of the cultic law attested in Exod. xxxiv. 14–26 (xxiii. 12–19) (pp. 88 f.). Not only its composition but also its insertion into the context of the account of Sinai took place in the course of the debate which the tribal union had to wage with its Canaanite environment and its ordinances right up to the period of the early monarchy, when with the incorporation of the remaining Canaanite areas into the Davidic Empire, the danger of Israel becoming Canaanite was renewed in an acute form (p. 88, n. 322 and p. 85, n. 309). In order to give the greatest possible weight to this

[36] On the long duration and the local differences of this process cf. for instance G. von Rad, *Theology of the Old Testament* I, p. 23.

[37] It is attested in the texts from Ras Shamra. Cf. for instance G. R. Driver, *Canaanite Myths and Legends*, p. 121 (Shachar and Shalim, col. 14).

cultic law in the debate with Canaanite practice, Exod. xxxiv. 14–26 has been put in the place of the original 'ten words' in Exod. xxxiv., just as the Book of the Covenant with *its* cultic stipulations (Exod. xx. 22–xxiii. 19) has taken the place of the Decalogue (Exod. xx. 2–17). This new cultic law which grew out of the situation in Canaan was most likely to succeed if it was regarded as the covenant-document, on the basis of which the Sinaitic covenant was concluded and the regular reading of which introduced the cultic renewal of the covenant (pp. 88 f.). It is significant that after its insertion into this liturgical context its form was influenced by the frequently mentioned covenant-outline of the vassal-treaties, which was also the formal model of the Decalogue and which had a decisive influence on Exod. xxxiv. 1a, 4, 27 f. also (pp. 89 f.). A historical prologue seems to have been added to the cultic law in Exod. xxxiv. 10 as a result of this influence (pp. 89 f.); this makes it clear that this covenant-outline retained its vitality in the cult of Yahweh even beyond Shechem (p. 90).

Even if Israel could not avoid becoming acquainted with Canaanite practice under the changed conditions of life in Palestine, it was nevertheless marked off from its Canaanite environment. The beginnings of this are to be found in its new cultic stipulations. The cultic acts of renouncing foreign gods and discarding jewellery also played an important part here. In this way the people chosen by Yahweh for his own possession knew they were separate from the nations round about them. The nature of Israel is described in the tradition of Exod. xix. 5, 6; it is a *holy nation*. This description also reflects the distinctive organisation of the pre-monarchic tribal union: unlike all other nations, it was not subject to a king (1 Sam. viii. 5, 20), but to the kingly office and kingly rule of priests, a rule which was, in turn, subject to Yahweh (pp. 71 f.).[38] It is also characteristic of the social organisation of the tribal union in ancient Israel that it was represented by a college of elders (pp. 27 f.). The *elders of Israel* were only displaced from their position as representatives of all Israel by the growing civil service of the kings (p. 28). The representation of the people of Yahweh at the covenant-meal on the mount of God by the 'elders of Israel' in Exod. xxiv. 1a, 9 indicates

[38] Moreover the context of this passage (Exod. xix 3b–8) has been influenced by the same covenant-form that the fundamental law of the people of Yahweh was modelled on, and that governed the renewal of the covenant at Shechem. See above, pp. 67 f. and ch. III, n. 26. Cf. also J. Muilenburg, 'The Form and Structure of the Covenantal Formulations', *VT*, 9, 1959, pp. 356–360.

that at this point also the old Israelite amphictyony and its organisation have contributed to the shape of the Sinaitic tradition.

3. The Development of the Tradition under the Monarchy

In order to win over Israel's tribes in the North and South to his kingdom's new capital, David had the Ark, the central shrine of the tribal confederacy, brought to Jerusalem.[39] This ancient Jebusite city, however, which had had no relations with Israelite tradition up till then,[40] would not have become the recognised centre of the Yahwistic amphictyony, to which even after its capture in 587 B.C. members of northern Israelite tribes still made their pilgrimage,[41] simply by the transfer of the Ark. But with the Ark came the cultic practices and traditions associated with it.[42] It was only through these being taken over into the newly established state-shrine that Jerusalem became recognised as the new amphictyonic centre among the tribes of Israel.[43]

(a) According to Deut. x. 1–5 a *written copy* of the Decalogue was kept in the Ark until the late monarchical period (p. 55). It may also be inferred from Deut. xxvii. 1 f. and xxxi. 9, 24 f. that the recording and deposition of a covenant-law was still a palpable reality in the state-cult at Jerusalem (pp. 44 f.). Linked, therefore, with the tradition of Moses making a written record of the commandments in Exod. xxiv. 4, 12; xxxi. 18b; xxxiv. 1a, 4, 27 f. were corresponding circumstances in the Temple at Jerusalem that were explained by this tradition in the light of the revelation on Sinai.

Corresponding to these written copies of the law there was a periodic *proclamation of the law* in the cult under the monarchy. Evidence for this is to be found in Ps. l and lxxxi, the late pre-exilic ordinance Deut. xxxi. 9–13, the covenant-renewals of the kings of Judah and Jerusalem (see especially 2 Kings xxiii. 2), the promise in Isa. ii. 1–4 and, the traditio-historical analysis of the message of Micah (pp. 42 f.). Thus, in the festival-worship of the Jerusalem Temple there existed a parallel cultic practice to the tradition of

[39] See 2 Sam. vi; Ps. cxxxii. Cf. for instance M. Noth, *Die Gesetze im Pentateuch* (= *Gesammelte Studien*, pp. 44 f.), 'Jerusalem und die israelitische Tradition', *Gesammelte Studien*, pp. 174 f.

[40] See Judges xix. 11 f. Cf. M. Noth, *op. cit.*, pp. 172 f.

[41] See Jer. xli. 5. Cf. M. Noth, *op. cit.*, pp. 177 f.

[42] Cf. M. Noth, *Die Gesetze im Pentateuch* (= *Gesammelte Studien*, pp. 46 f.); 'Jerusalem und die israelitische Tradition', *Gesammelte Studien*, pp. 175, 179 f.; A. Weiser, 'Theophanie in den Psalmen und im Festkult', *Bertholet-Festschrift*, pp. 528 f.

[43] Cf. also S. Talmon, 'Divergences in Calendar-Reckoning in Ephraim and Judah', *VT*, 8, 1958, p. 50 (see n. 534 above).

Moses' proclamation of the commandments in Exod. xix. 7 f.; xxiv. 3, 7 (pp. 40 f.).

It may be concluded from the message of Jeremiah (vii. 23; xi. 4; xxiv. 7; xxx. 22; xxxi. 1, 33; xxxii. 38) and Deuteronomy (vii. 6; xiv. 2; xxvi. 17–19) that there was an *affirmation of obligation* in the cult of the monarchical period, in which the covenant-formula 'I will be their God, and they shall be my people' seems to have had its *Sitz im Leben* (pp. 67 f.). Everything points to the tradition in Exod. xix. 5, in which Yahweh's covenant-promise, with hortatory qualifications, is employed, having been transmitted with reference to this affirmation and this formula and possibly also having been assimilated to them (p. 68f.). This same affirmation of covenant-obligation and its formal expressions have also been emphasised apparently by the Jehovistic redactor in the words which conclude the prayer for the forgiveness of sins in Exod. xxxiv. 9, 'and take us for thine inheritance' (pp. 98 f.).

It may be gathered from 2 Kings xxiii. 3 and 2 Chron. xxix. 10 that in the state-cult at Jerusalem (at least as *one* of several possibilities) the covenant could still be made in such a way that a *mediator* concluded the treaty with God and the people were only admitted later (pp. 78 f.). Thus, the tradition of Exod. xxxiv. 27, according to which Moses mediated the covenant between the God of Sinai and his people (p. 78), continued to agree with a corresponding cultic practice, even into the late pre-exilic period (p. 79).

As in the desert-period and the pre-monarchical period, so also under the monarchy the covenant-cult presupposes *Yahweh's cultic presence*. Proclamation of the law, affirmation of covenant-obligation and covenant-renewal would have been inconceivable without it. For instance, the cultic act which is reflected in the words, 'You have made Yahweh declare this day that he is your God . . . , and Yahweh has made you declare this day that you are a people for his own possession' (Deut. xxvi. 17, 18a; p. 67), undoubtedly presupposes the cultic epiphany of the God of Sinai. It was no more self-explanatory in the state-cult at Jerusalem, however, than in the cult of Yahweh at Shechem or another amphictyonic shrine of the pre-monarchic period. Accordingly, the tradition of Exod. xxxiii. 12b–17, the nucleus of which certainly goes back to the early history of Israel and which strives to establish that the God of Sinai did, in fact, go in person with his people to Canaan (pp. 99–112), remained alive right up to the period of the monarchy, and indeed it was first given literary expression in the later Yahwistic source (pp. 100 f.). In connection with Exod. xxxiii. 12b–17, and xxxiii. 3b–4, 5–6 the Jehovistic redaction has been at pains to establish that Yahweh did not only then appear on Sinai (xxxiv. 5 f.) but, thanks to Moses' prayer of intercession (pp. 92 f.), appears even now in the midst of the stiff-necked people in Canaan and shows himself as Israel's living God (II. 8; pp. 90–98, 110f.). The cardinal cultic question, whether, and if so how, Yahweh is present in Canaan, making possible the cult of his community, did not simply create and sustain individual elements of the tradition, however. It was also responsible for the composition of Exod. xxxii–xxxiii. as a whole (pp. 125f., 133): Exod. xxxii contests the validity of God's epiphany being represented by or in connection with the calf-image (pp. 130 f.), whereas Exod. xxxiii exhibits—what Moses implored and Yahweh himself granted—the true manner of his cultic epiphany.[44] The account of the dedication of the Temple in 1 Kings viii. 1 f. makes it clear that the first appearance of Yahweh there took place in connection with the transfer of the *Ark* into the Temple of Solomon. This corresponds to the tradition of Exod. xxxiii. 12b–17, which links God's presence in his *panim* with the Ark (pp. 109–111). Similarly, the Elohist also saw the threat of God's remoteness (Exod. xxxiii. 3b, 5a) alleviated in the Ark-shrine p. 110); this was the reason why he apparently described how the Ark was made (p. 110, n. 425; pp. 114 f.) after Exod. xxxiii. 3b–6.

As 1 Kings viii. 10 f. (p. 117, n. 468–70) and Isa. vi. 4 (p. 134, n. 575) show, the incense-ceremonial, which was probably practised in the pre-monarchic period and which according to Lev. xvi. 12, 13 served to conceal God's epiphany (p. 134), was also practised in the worship of the Temple at Jerusalem.[45] The tradition in Exod. xix. 9, 16, 18; xx. 18, 21; xxxiv. 5, therefore, according to which the original theophany on Sinai was concealed by a cloud of smoke, continued to be linked with the corresponding cultic ceremony in the Temple of Solomon and was given concrete expression in it (pp. 134 f.). Thus Yahweh's cultic appearance remains hidden from human view (cf. Judges xiii. 22; vi. 22 f.; Exod. xxxiii. 20), but it was indicated and realised (for instance, according to Ps. xxiv. 8, 10; lxxv. 2; lxxxiii. 17; Jer. vii. 10 f.) in the cult of the Temple at

[44] The tradition of the Tent of Meeting also bears witness to this (Exod. xxxiii. 7–11). To that extent the passage is not misplaced, as thought by K. Möhlenbrink ('Josua im Pentateuch', *ZAW*, 59, 1942/3, p. 30 f.), who from a historico-chronological point of view wanted to see it grouped with the saga of the desert-wanderings.

[45] The ritual underlying Lev. xvi also clearly derives from the period of the kings. Cf. K. Koch, *op. cit.*, p. 97.

Jerusalem and probably also in the covenant-cult of the desert-period and the pre-monarchic period (2 Sam. vi. 2; p. 137) by the ceremonial *proclamation of Yahweh's name.* The tradition of Exod. xxxiv. 5 f.; xxxiii. 19, which describes Yahweh's manifestation of himself on Sinai with the help of the formula belonging to this cultic practice *ḳārā' ḇešēm yhwh* (pp. 136 f.), was taken up and fulfilled, therefore, in the time of the kings by the parallel practice of proclaiming Yahweh's name.

(b) The further development of the Sinai tradition, which was transmitted in close connection with the customs, circumstances and problems which were passed on from Israel's pre-monarchic period to the cult of the Temple at Jerusalem, was influenced by forms and practices which only emerged in the festival-cult under the monarchy. The practice of indicating Yahweh's cultic appearance by the *blowing of the trumpet,* in which it was obviously believed that Yahweh's voice was heard (cf. Exod. xix. 19; Isa. lviii. 1), cannot be attested outside the sphere of the cult at Jerusalem, at any rate (2 Sam. vi. 15; 1 Chron. xiii. 8; xv. 28; 2 Chron. v. 11b–13a; vii. 6; Ps. xlvii. 6; lxxxi. 4; xcviii. 6), even if the possibility that the way for the custom was already paved in the pre-monarchic period should not be excluded. The tradition in Exod. xix. 13b, 16, 19; xx. 18 has been influenced by the cultic blowing of the trumpet in making the original theophany on Sinai be accompanied by the sound of the trumpet (pp. 36 f.; 135 f.). Ancient liturgical poetry, which had its source in the Temple-cult, connected Yahweh's name with a *list of divine attributes* (Ps. xxiv. 8, 10). Accordingly, such a description is now added to the tradition of the calling of Yahweh's name in Exod. xxxiv. 5 f. (Exod. xxxiv. 6 f.; pp. 138 f.). The description of Yahweh as a 'merciful and gracious God, slow to anger and abounding in steadfast love and faithfulness . . .' is reflected in these or similar words in the cultic poetry of the Temple at Jerusalem.[46] Hence it also found its way into the tradition of the theophany on Sinai (p. 138). Judging by Ps. l and lxxxi, for instance, there was also a fixed *liturgical sequence* consisting of a proclamation of Yahweh's name and his divine attributes and the revelation of his will. In accordance with this liturgical arrangement, the act of naming God and predicating his attributes in Exod. xxxiv. 5 f. was followed by a recital of the law in Exod. xxxiv. 14–26 (p. 138, n. 605). The prayer-language of the Temple-cult includes *prayer for the forgiveness of sins* couched in

[46] Cf. J. Scharbert, 'Formgeschichte und Exegese von Exod. xxxiv. 6 f. und seiner Parallelen' *Bibl.* 38, 1957, pp. 132 f.

stereotyped, formal phrases (1 Kings viii. 34, 36, 30, 39; cf. 2 Chron. vi; p. 97 f.). The Jehovistic redaction in Exod. xxxiv. 9 has obviously worded Moses' prayer of intercession in Exod. xxxiv. 9 in the light of this (p. 98).

The worship of the calf-image in northern Israel, exalted to the position of the official state-cult by Jeroboam I (1 Kings xii. 25–33; p. 127), gave rise to a further development in the tradition: the older Elohistic tradition in Exod. xxxii. 1–6, 15–20 (+ 35), (pp. 127–130; see below), in which the aetiology of the northern Israelite worship of the calf-image was taken up and refuted, grew out of the opposition to this cult. According to 1 Kings xii. 31, Jeroboam clearly excluded the *Levitical priesthood*, or at least a part of it (cf. Judges xviii. 30), from the shrines of his kingdom in the course of his cultic-political measures. The later Elohistic tradition in Exod. xxxii. 25–29, which defends the priestly privilege of the Levites, seems to have developed from this historical context (p. 132, n. 564). Finally, the tradition of Exod. xxxii. 21–24, which minimises Aaron's share in making the calf-image condemned by the Elohist, also stemmed from the group-interests of a priesthood which was conscious of its obligation to Aaron and was, therefore, bound to exonerate him (pp. 131 f.).

(c) All things considered, it is clear to what extent the Sinaitic tradition continued to be determined by Israel's festival-cult right into the monarchical period and to what degree its late developments were inspired by cultic forms and practices and evoked by certain cultic-historical connections; the literary work of the source-authors, on the other hand, contributed only a little to the final shaping of this tradition.[47] Substantial as were the literary interventions of the *Yahwist* in other Pentateuchal traditions, it is clear that the traditions about Sinai which he received were left untouched (apart from his characteristic linguistic usage), as far as may be judged by the comparatively small amount of Yahwistic material that found its way into the Sinai-pericope. Moreover, what has been considered as the distinctive contribution of Yahwistic theology, as for instance the description of God in Exod. xxxiv. 6 f. which begins with the promise of grace,[48] seems rather to have been modelled on the cultic poetry of the Jerusalem Temple and to have made its way into the Sinai tradition from there (cf. for instance Ps. lxxviii. 38; cxlv. 8 f., 20; pp. 138 f.). It is equally mistaken to ascribe the combination of

[47] On the dating of these literary forms to Israel's monarchical period cf. the Introductions to the O.T.

[48] Cf. H. J. Stoebe, 'Die Bedeutung des Wortes *häsäd* im Alten Testament', *VT*, 2, 1952, pp. 249 f.

the Sinai tradition and the Exodus-Conquest tradition to the literary initiative of the Yahwist; we shall say more of this presently (see III. 4e below). Nor can it be said that the Yahwist let the cultic origin of the tradition and its themes fade into the background.[49] Even if the Yahwistic form of the tradition dealing with the making of the covenant in Exod. xxxiv. 1–28 does not describe any rites of covenant-making, it is, nevertheless, connected with the cult in many respects: there was a mode of making a covenant still practised under the monarchy that corresponded to it (xxxiv. 27 f.; pp. 79 f.). It contains an aetiology of the written records of the commandments which were deposited in the Temple of Solomon (vv. 1a, 4, 27 f.; pp. 44 f., 55 f.). Insofar as it follows the proclamation of Yahweh's name and description of him with the revelation of his will it corresponds to a firmly established liturgical order of the festival-cult at Jerusalem (p. 138, n. 605). The description of God is also derived from this source (xxxiv. 6 f.; pp. 138 f.). Its account of Yahweh's introduction of himself is realised in the cultic proclamation of the name (xxxiv. 5 f.; pp. 136 f.). Its account of the theophany is connected with the incense-ceremonial which conceals God's epiphany (xxxiv. 5 f.; pp. 136 f.). In order to meet with Yahweh Moses had to prepare himself by cultic rites (v. 2a).[50] This ritual purification which preceded the theophany also occupies a large space in the Yahwistic tradition Exod. xix. 10, 14–15 (pp. 141 f.). A marked cultic requirement is satisfied in the tradition preserved by J: in Exod. xix. 10–11a, 15 f.; xxxiv. 2, 4 God's epiphany takes place at a definite time and, according to Exod. xix. 12–13a, (20–24); xxxiv. 3, at a definite place (p. 140). Everything points to the Yahwist not only having taken up the cultic origin of his Sinaitic traditions but also having valued them. According to J's description, which differs from the Elohistic version, Yahweh appears to Moses and talks with him, in order that the people might trust him, 'for ever' (Exod. xix. 9a): the Yahwist is obviously concerned to accredit the institution of the cultic spokesman by which the Sinaitic revelation was to be mediated to the cultic community henceforth (p. 139f.).

The *Elohist*, too, considered why this institution was established (pp. 139 f.): Exod. xx. 18–21 (pp. 12 f. and p. 26, n. 159) is meant to explain why the voice of God himself is no longer heard by the cultic community when he appears but instead only a mediating human

[49] *Contra* M. Noth, *Exodus*, p. 15.
[50] With M. Noth, *op. cit.*, p. 261.

word; this tradition is none other than the aetiology of the cultic office of mediator in Israel. This in itself may serve to indicate the interest the Elohist had in the covenant-cult: but this impression is strengthened when it is realised how important the problem of the presence of God with his people was to E (pp. 124 f.). According to Exod. xxxiii. 3b, 5a it must have been his conviction that the covenant-people themselves made it hard for God to appear in their midst. Hence, throughout the Sinai tradition which he received the Elohist has removed the people from the place of God's epiphany and introduced Moses as mediator: in Exod. xxiv. 1b–2 he corrects the old tradition to this effect—only Moses drew near to God; the others remained at a distance. This is also stressed in the Elohistic verses Exod. xx. 18b, 19, 21. In accordance with this the Elohist has altered the tradition handed down to him in Exod. xxxiii. 7–11 and placed the Tent of Meeting outside the camp, away from the people; entrance into the Tent of the theophany is reserved for Moses (pp. 112 f.). Only under such circumstances can Israel's God continue to appear. Again, the fact that the Elohist regards Moses as the one who is more than a *prophet* (xxxiii. 11a) was basically meant to secure the continuance of Yahweh's appearances, similar to the way in which 1 Sam. iii. 20 f. regards Samuel's appointment as prophet as a pledge that God's appearances will continue (p. 122f.). If E was so vigorously concerned with the cardinal question of God's cultic presence with his people, there is no doubt that he stood in a positive relationship to the covenant-cult. This is also shown by the way in which the cultic origin of the Sinaitic tradition which was handed down to the Elohist was clearly left untouched in the literary form he gave it. Moreover, the tradition of Exod. xxxii. 1–6, 15–20 (+ 35), a passage peculiar to the Elohist, which condemns the cult of the calf-image in the northern kingdom as a breach of the covenant made on Sinai (pp. 130 f.), was basically concerned with the problem of the cultic theophany: the appearance of Israel's God is not represented by or connected with the calf-image, as even circles loyal to Yahweh had assumed till now (2 Kings x. 28 f.); he appears exclusively above the Ark, the central shrine of the tribal confederacy (Exod. xxxiii. 3b f., 7 f.; p. 130f.). This opposition to a northern Israelite form of the worship of Yahweh (p. 130, n. 548), the use of the category of the prophet (pp. 113 f.) and the other alterations which were determined by concern for the continuance of God's appearances reveal the distinctiveness of the Elohistic author and his literary revision of the Sinaitic traditions more sharply than that of the Yahwist, who seems to have shaped his traditional material with greater reserve.

4. Conclusions

(a) The Sinai traditions and their individual elements differ from one another in many respects: they stem from quite different, and in part widely separated, historical situations and consequently their motives and aims are very different. Different forms and ideas were used to give them shape and they were finally given literary expression in two different sources. Yet, in spite of all this variety all the pieces and elements of the Sinai tradition have *one Sitz im Leben: the history of the sacral tribal confederacy of Israel.* Substantial elements of this tradition, amongst them the original nucleus of the Decalogue, very probably go back to the historical beginnings of the covenant with Yahweh in the desert-period (probably in Kadesh) (III. 1). Subsequently, it was chiefly the tribal union constituted at Shechem that promoted the further development of the Sinai tradition by its cultic ordinances, practices and institutions and by its constitution (III. 2). But the other centres of the pre-monarchic tribal union which succeeded Shechem also contributed to the form and development of the Sinai tradition. Fresh developments of this tradition came about chiefly in the course of the struggle which the tribal confederacy had to wage in Canaan with the ordinances of its neighbours and with the Canaanite elements which found their way even into the cult of Yahweh. And finally, the influence and interests of the festival-cult of the covenant-people in the period of the monarchy can be traced in not a few elements in the Sinai tradition (III. 3).

(b) If, then, the Sinai tradition had its *Sitz im Leben* in the history of Israel's tribal confederacy, it must have been linked with its *cult* to a special degree and the course of its development must have been determined by it. Not only the cult of the renewal of the covenant at Shechem influenced it and left its mark on it in many respects, however (III. 2). Even its oldest elements, with their roots in the desert-period, were of a thoroughly cultic, ritual nature (insofar as they relate to rites of sacrifice and covenant-making practised at that time and presuppose the deposition and regular recital of the covenant-document at a holy place) (III. 1). The post-Shechemite development of the Sinai tradition also continued to be connected with the Israelite cult:[51] the cultic arrangements and ordinances of the central shrines which succeeded Shechem in the pre-monarchic period undoubtedly contributed to the further development of the tradition. The conflicts with the cultic ordinances of the surrounding Canaanite world emanated from the shrines of Yahweh, at which the cultic laws resulting from this process were then domiciled and applied. The cult of the Temple at Jerusalem under the monarchy also had many points of contact with the Sinai tradition: it was based on the model of its festival-cult, the liturgical sequences employed in it and the forms and customs practised in it (III. 3). In the middle of the Sinai-account the interest in its cultic realisation is apparent; fresh developments in the tradition have been inspired by it (Exod. xix. 9a; xx. 18–21). The later Yahwistic tradition in Exod. xxxiii. 12b–17 also grew out of a marked cultic question, the question of the presence of the God of Sinai in Canaan, without which the cult of Yahweh after the conquest would have been impossible. Moreover, the Jehovistic redaction in Exod. xxxiv. 9 still seems to have been concerned with the cultic recapitulation of the tradition of the theophany and the making of the covenant.

(c) Although the traditions about Sinai in J and E try to give a historical outline they do not reveal any strong interest in the actual history. Thus, the speech of Moses in Exod. xxxiii. 12a, which originally sought to procure a leader for the journey through the desert (II. 9), is broken off in the middle of the sentence; the narrative of the Midianite Ḥobab ben Re'uel is abruptly set aside. In its place, attached to the request for a guide, is a passionate argument which is concerned with nothing less than Yahweh's cultic presence with his people in Canaan. In the middle of his account of the theophany and the making of the covenant in chap. xxxiv the Jehovistic redactor reassures himself that the God of Sinai is present with his cultic community in Palestine by referring expressly to Exod. xxxiii. 12 f. in a prayer of intercession by Moses (xxxiv. 9); this makes it clear that he wants the continuing power of the account of what happened on Sinai to be safeguarded (II. 8). Exod. xix. 9a, a Yahwistic verse, concerned for the later cultic realisation of the tradition, uses the event of Yahweh's epiphany to attest the office of mediator 'for ever' (II. 12); similarly, the Elohistic tradition in Exod. xx. 18–21 uses the material in the account of the theophany to compose an aetiology for the institution of a cultic spokesman

[51] *Contra* G. von Rad, *Das formgeschichtliche Problem des Hexateuch* (= *Gesammelte Studien*, pp. 55 f.).

(II. 12). All things considered, it is clear that the traditions of the Sinai-event (particularly as they developed later) were not so much concerned to relate history as to re-present what had happened for the salvation of later generations in Israel. This re-presentation was not sought in a 'spiritual' realisation, of course, but always in cultic experience.

(d) However much the growth of the Sinaitic tradition was determined by its cultic associations, which lasted into the period of the kings, the history of the beginning of the tradition certainly did not *originate* in the cult.[52] Rather, it was God's activity in *history* that gave the impulse to the formation of this tradition and had a decisive influence on its content and character. The part played by the cult of Yahweh in developing the Sinaitic tradition should not cause us to overlook the impulses which proceeded from *historical* circumstances, among which—as demonstrated—special importance attaches to the conquest of Canaan. All this confirms the necessity of investigating the historical circumstances from which the Sinaitic tradition grew.

(e) As far as its relation to the Exodus-tradition goes, it remains to confirm that the two traditions were linked together from the very beginnings of the covenant with Yahweh: the covenant-form attested in Hittite state-treaties of the 14th and 13th centuries B.C., which also underlies the Decalogue, the basic law of the Sinaitic covenant (II. 5), contains a historical prologue which describes the beneficent acts of the author of the covenant. If this treaty-form was already in use in Mosaic times, as may be assumed, it must have referred in its preface to Yahweh's saving act in delivering the Israelites from Egypt (III. 1). Again, in the passage Exod. xix. 3b–8, which has its roots in the pre-monarchical tribal union of Israel, the traditions about the Exodus and Sinai, which are held together by the same covenant-form, are combined (II. 6). Finally, under the influence of this treaty-form, a historical prologue telling of Yahweh's acts of saving-history was attached in v. 10 to the cultic law in Exod. xxxiv. 14–26, which was a product of the conflict with Canaanite practices (II. 7; pp 87 f.). We may conclude, therefore, that the traditions of the deliverance from Egypt and of the events on Sinai were connected at a very early date under the influence of an old covenant-form going back to the pre-Mosaic period. This is true, of the

[52] *Contra* S. Mowinckel. *Psalmenstudien II*, pp. 24 f.; 'Kadesj, Sinai og Jahve', *Norsk Geografisk Tidsskrift*, 11, 1942, p. 19.

earliest stages of the growth of Israel's tradition and not simply of the later period of literary fixation,[53] and is the reason for the union of history and law which is characteristic of the Old Testament.[54]

[53] *Contra* G. von Rad, *Das formgeschichtliche Problem des Hexateuch* (= *Gesammelte Studien* pp. 60 f., 55 f.).
[54] Cf. the Introduction, pp. xxv. f.

BIBLIOGRAPHY

Biblia Hebraica, ed. by R. Kittel, 6th ed., Stuttgart, 1950.

Der hebräische Pentateuch der Samaritaner, ed. by A. Frhr. v. Gall, Pt. II: Exodus, Giessen 1914.

The Old Testament in Greek, ed. by A. E. Brooke-N. McLean, Vol. I, pt. 2, Cambridge, 1909.

Septuaginta, ed. by A. Rahlfs, 3rd ed., Stuttgart 1949.

Catalogue of the Greek and Latin Papyri in the John Rylands Library Manchester, Vol. 3, ed. by C. H. Roberts, Manchester, 1938.

Biblia Sacra juxta Vulgatam Clementinam . . . denuo ediderunt complures Scripturae Sacrae Professores Facultatis theologicae Parisiensis et Seminarii Sancti Sulpitii, Rome-Turin-Paris, 1947.

Abel, F. M., *Géographie de la Palestine* I, *Géographie physique et historique*, Paris, 1933.

Albright, W. F., Review of Harris's 'Development of the Canaanite Dialect', *JAOS* 60, 1940, pp. 414–22.

From the Stone Age to Christianity, Baltimore, 1946 (2nd ed.).

Archaeology and the Religion of Israel, Baltimore, 1942.

'Some remarks on the Song of Moses in Deuteronomy xxxii', *VT* 9, 1959, pp. 339–46.

'The Hebrew expression for "Making a Covenant" in pre-Israelite documents', *BASOR*, 121, 1951, pp. 21 f.

'The Song of Deborah in the Light of Archaeology', *BASOR*, 62, 1936, pp. 26–31.

Allegro, J. M., 'Uses of the Semitic Demonstrative Element z in Hebrew', *VT*, 5, 1955, pp. 309–12.

Alt, A., *Der Gott der Väter*, *BWANT*, III, 12, 1929 (=*Kleine Schriften*, I, München 1953, pp. 1–78).

Die Staatenbildung der Israeliten in Palästina 1930 (=*Kleine Schriften* II, München, 1953, pp. 1–65).

Die Ursprünge des israelitischen Rechts 1934 (=*Kleine Schriften*, I, München, 1953, pp. 278–332).

'Josua', *Kleine Schriften*, I, pp. 176–92.

'Die Wallfahrt von Sichem nach Bethel', *Kleine Schriften*, I, pp. 79–88.

'Gedanken über das Königtum Jahwes', *Kleine Schriften*, I, pp. 345–57.

'Zelte und Hütten', F. Nötscher-Festschrift, *BBB*, I, 1950, *Kleine Schriften*, III, pp. 233–42.

'Hettitische und ägyptische Herrschaftsordnung in unterworfenen Gebieten', *Kleine Schriften*, III, pp. 99–106.

Arnold, W. R., *Ephod and Ark*, *HThSt*, 3, 1917, pp. 1–170.

Auerbach, E., *Moses*, Amsterdam, 1953.

'Die grosse Überarbeitung der biblischen Bücher', *VTS*, 1, 1953, p. 1–10.

'Die Feste im alten Israel', *VT*, 8, 1958, pp. 1–18.

'Neujahrs- und Versöhnungs-Fest in den biblischen Quellen', *VT*, 8, pp. 337–43.

Bach, R., 'Josua', *RGG*, 3, 3rd ed., col. 872 f.

Baentsch, B., *Exodus-Leviticus*, *HK*, 2/1, Göttingen 1903.

Numeri, *HK*, 2/2, Göttingen, 1903.

Baltzer, K., 'Das Bundesformular. Sein Ursprung und seine Verwendung im Alten Testament', *ThLZ*, 83, 1958, col. 585 f.

Baudissin, W. W., ' "Gott schauen" in der alttestamentlichen Religion', *ARW*, 18, 1915, pp. 173–239.

'Kalb, goldenes', *RE*, 9, 3rd ed., col. 704–13.

BAUER, J. B., 'Könige und Priester, ein heiliges Volk (*Exodus* xix, 6)', *Biblische Zeitschrift N.F.*, 2, 1958, pp. 283–286.

BAUMGÄRTEL, F., 'Zur Liturgie in der "Sektenrolle" vom Toten Meer', *ZAW*, 65, 1953, pp. 263–5.

BEER, G., *Mose und sein Werk*, Giessen, 1912.

Steinverehrung bei den Israeliten. Ein Beitrag zur semitischen und allgemeinen Religionsgeschichte. Schriften der Strassburger Wissensch. Gesellschaft in Heidelberg, N.F., 4, Berlin-Leipzig, 1921.

Exodus, *HAT*, 1/3, Tübingen, 1939.

BEER, G.-Meyer, R., *Hebräische Grammatik I–II*, Berlin, 1952–5.

BEGRICH, J., 'Das priesterliche Heilsorakel', *ZAW*, 52, 1934, pp. 81–92.

BENZINGER, I., *Die Bücher der Könige*, *KHC*, 9, Freiburg i. Br., 1899.

BERNHARDT, K-H., *Gott und Bild. Ein Beitrag zur Begründung und Deutung des Bilderverbotes im Alten Testament.* Diss. Greifswald, 1952, Selbstanzeige in *ThLZ*, 79, 1954, col. 173–5.

BERTHOLET, A. *Deuteronomium*, *KHC*, 5, Freiburg i. Br., 1899.

'Zum Verständnis des alttestamentlichen Opfergedankens', *JBL*, 49, 1930, pp. 218–33.

BEYERLIN, W., *Die Kulttraditionen Israels in der Verkündigung des Propheten Micha*, *FRLANT*, 72, Göttingen, 1959.

BIETENHARD, H., *onoma*, *ThWBNT*, 5, pp. 242–83.

BIKERMANN, E., 'Couper une alliance', *Arch. d'hist. du droit oriental*, 5, 1950/51, pp. 133–56.

BIRKELAND, H., 'Hebrew *zae* and Arabic *dū*', *St.Th.*, 2, 1950, p. 201 f.

BOEHMER, J., "Gottes Angesicht', *BFChTh*, 12, 1908, pp. 323–47.

DE BOER, P. A. H., *De voorbede in het Oude Testament*, *OTS*, 3, 1943.

BORNKAMM, G., *presbys*, *ThWBNT*, 6, p. 651 f.

BRIGHT, J., 'The date of the prose sermons of Jeremiah', *JBL*, 70, 1951, pp. 15–35.

Early Israel in Recent History Writing, *StBTh*, 19, London, 1956.

BRINKER, R., *The influence of sanctuaries in early Israel*, Manchester, 1946.

BROCKELMANN, C., *Hebräische Syntax*, Neukirchen, 1956.

BUBER, M., *Moses*, Oxford and London, 1946 (ET).

Königtum Gottes, 3rd ed., Heidelberg, 1956.

BUDDE, K., 'Die Gesetzgebung der mittleren Bücher des Pentateuchs, insbesondere der Quellen J und E', *ZAW*, 11, 1891, pp. 193–234.

BURROWS, M., *What mean these stones?* New York, 1957.

CASPARI, W., *Die Samuelbücher*, *KAT*, 7, Leipzig, 1926.

'Kultpsalm 50', *ZAW*, 45, 1927, pp. 254–66.

'Das priesterliche Königreich', *ThBl*, 8, 1929, col. 105–10.

CASSUTO, U., *The Documentary Hypothesis and the Composition of the Pentateuch*, Jerusalem (1941), 1953.

CORNILL, C. H., 'Zum Segen Jacobs und zum jahwistischen Dekalog', *Wellhausen-Festschrift*, *BZAW*, 27, Giessen, 1914, pp. 101–113.

DIBELIUS, M., *Die Lade Jahwes. Eine religionsgeschichtliche Untersuchung*, *FRLANT*, 7, Göttingen, 1906.

DRIVER, G. R., *Canaanite Myths and Legends*, *Old Testament Studies No.* 3, Edinburgh, 1956.

DUHM, B., *Israels Propheten*, Tübingen, 1916.

DUSSAUD, R., *Les origenes cananéennes du sacrifice israélite*, Paris, 1921.

EERDMANS, B. D., *Alttestamentliche Studien* 3, *Das Buch Exodus*, Giessen, 1910.

EHRLICH, A. B., *Randglossen zur hebräischen Bibel I*, Leipzig, 1908.

EHRLICH, E. L., *Kultsymbolik im Alten Testament und im nachbiblischen Judentum* (*Symbolik der Religionen, ed. by F. Herrmann*), Stuttgart, 1959.

EICHRODT, W., *Theology of the Old Testament I*, London, 1961 (ET).

EISSFELDT, O., *Hexateuch-Synopse*, Leipzig, 1922.
'Der geschichtliche Hintergrund der Erzählung von Gibeas Schandtat Richter 19–21)', *Beer-Festschrift*, Stuttgart, 1935, pp. 19–40.
'Lade und Stierbild', *ZAW*, 58, 1940–41, pp. 190–215.
Einleitung in das Alte Testament, 2nd ed., Tübingen, 1956.
'El and Yahweh', *JSSt*, 1, 1956, pp. 25–37.
'Die Umrahmung des Mose-Liedes Dtn. xxxii, 1–43 und des Mose-Gesetzes Dtn. i–xxx in Dtn. xxxi. 9–xxxii 47', *Wissenschaftliche Zeitschrift der Martin-Luther-Universität Halle-Wittenberg*, 4 Jg., Heft 3, pp. 411–17.
Das Lied Moses Deuteronomium xxxii, 1–43, *und das Lehrgedicht Asaphs Psalm* 78 *samt einer Analyse der Umgebung des Mose-Liedes, Berichte über die Verhandlungen des Sächs. Akademie der Wissenschaften zu Leipzig*, Phil.-histor. Klasse, 104/5, Berlin, 1958.
ELLIGER, K., *Das Buch der zwölf Kleinen Propheten II, ATD*, 25, 2nd ed., Göttingen, 1956.
'Ich bin der Herr—euer Gott', *Heim-Festschrift 'Theologie als Glaubenswagnis'*, Hamburg, 1954, pp. 9–54.
ENGNELL, I., *Gamla Testamentet. En traditionshistorisk inledning*, I, Stockholm, 1945.
'The Call of Isaiah. An Exegetical and Comparative Study', *UUÅ*, 1949/4, Uppsala-Leipzig 1949.
FITZMYER, J. A., 'The Aramaic Suzerainty Treaty from Sefire in the Museum of Beirut', *CBQ*, 20, 1958, pp. 444–76.
FOHRER, G., 'Der Vertrag zwischen König und Volk in Israel', *ZAW*, 71, 1959, pp. 1–22.
FRANKFORT, H. and H. A., *Before Philosophy* (*The Intellectual Adventure of Ancient Man*), London, 1949.
FRIEDRICH, J., *Staatsverträge des Ḫatti-Reiches in hethitischer Sprache* (Hethitische Texte, ed. by F. Sommer), *Pt. I, MVÄG*, 1, 1926, Leipzig, 1926; *Pt. II, MVÄG* 1930, 1, Leipzig.
VON GALL, A., *Altisraelitische Kultstätten, BZAW*, 3, Giessen, 1898.
Die Herrlichkeit Gottes, Giessen, 1900.
'Uber die Herkunft der Bezeichnung Jahwes als König', *Wellhausen–Festschrift*, Giessen, 1914, pp. 145 f.
GALLING, K., *Biblisches Reallexicon, HAT*, 1/1, Tübingen, 1937.
Die Bücher der Chronik, Esra, Nehemia, ATD, 12, Göttingen, 1954.
'Die Ausrufung des Namens als Rechtsakt in Israel', *ThLZ*, 81, 1956, col. 65–70.
GEMSER, B., 'The importance of the motive-clause in Old Testament Law', *VTS*, 1, 1953, pp. 50–66.
'Bilder und Bilderverehrung II. Im AT und NT', *RGG*, 1, 3rd ed., col. 1271–3.
GESENIUS, W., and Kautzsch, E., *Hebräische Grammatik*, 26 ed., Leipzig, 1896.
GESENIUS, W., and Buhl, F., *Hebräisches und aramäisches Handwörterbuch über das Alte Testament*, 17th ed., Berlin–Göttingen–Heidelberg, 1949.
GIESEBRECHT, F., *Die alttestamentliche Schätzung des Gottesnamens und ihre religionsgeschichtliche Grundlage*, Königsberg, 1901.
GOITEIN, S. D., 'Yhwh the passionate. The monotheistic meaning and origin of the name Yhwh', *VT*, 6, 1956, pp. 1–9.
GORDON, G. H., *Ugaritic Manual, An Or*, 35, Rome, 1955.
GÖTZE, A., *Das Hethiter-Reich, AO*, 1928, 2, Leipzig, 1928.
GRAY, G. B., *Sacrifice in the Old Testament*, Oxford, 1925.
GRAY, J., 'Cultic affinities between Israel and Ras-Shamra', *ZAW*, 63, 1949/50, pp. 207–20.
'The desert sojourn of the Hebrews and the Sinai-Horeb Tradition', *VT*, 4, 1954, pp. 148–54.
'The Hebrew Conception of the Kingship of God', *VT*, 6, 1956, pp. 268–85.
The Legacy of Canaan, VTS, 5, Leiden, 1957.

GREENBERG, M., 'Hebrew *s^egullā*: Akkadian *sikiltu*', *JAOS*, 71, 1951, pp. 172–4.
GRESSMANN, H., *Mose und seine Zeit. Ein Kommentar zu den Mose-Sagen*, *FRLANT*, 18, Göttingen, 1913.
Die Lade Jahves und das Allerheiligste des salomonischen Tempels, *BWAT N.F.*, 1, Berlin–Stuttgart–Leipzig, 1920.
Die Anfänge Israels (Vol. 2. Mose bis Richter und Ruth), *SATA*, 1/2, 2nd ed., Göttingen, 1922.
(ed.) *Altorientalische Texte zum Alten Testament*, 2nd ed., Berlin–Leipzig, 1926.
GRETHER, O., *Name und Wort Gottes im Alten Testament*, *BZAW*, 64, Giessen, 1934.
GROSS, H., *Weltherrschaft als religiöse Idee im Alten Testament*, *BBB*, 6, Bonn, 1953.
GULIN, E. G., *Das Antlitz Jahwes im Alten Testament*, *AASF*, 16, Helsingfors, 1922.
GUNNEWEG, A. H. J., *Mündliche und schriftliche Tradition der vorexilischen Prophetenbücher als Problem der neueren Prophetenforschung*, *FRLANT*, 73, Göttingen, 1959.
GUNKEL, H., *Genesis*, *HK*, 1/1, 5th ed., Göttingen, 1922.
HAELVOET, M., *La Théophanie du Sinai*, *ALBO*, II, 39, Louvain, 1953.
HARAN, M., 'The Ark and the Cherubim', *IEJ*, 9, 1959, pp. 30–38.
'The nature of the "'Ōhel Mô'edh" in Pentateuchal sources', *JSSt*, 5, 1960, pp. 50–65.
HARTMANN, R., 'Zelt und Lade', *ZAW*, 37, 1917/18, pp. 209–244.
HEMPEL, J., 'Priesterkodex', *Pauly-Wissowa, Realenzyklopädie des klassischen Altertums*, 22, 1954, col. 1943–1967.
HERBERT, A. S., *Worship in Ancient Israel* (*Ecumenical Studies in Worship*), London, 1959.
HERTZBERG, H. W., *Die Bücher Josua, Richter, Ruth*, *ATD*, 9, Göttingen, 1953.
Die Samuelbücher, *ATD*, 10, Göttingen, 1956.
HESSE, F., *Die Fürbitte im Alten Testament*, Diss. Erlangen, Hamburg, 1951.
'Herrlichkeit Gottes', *RGG*, 3, 3rd ed., col. 273 f.
HOLZINGER, H., *Einleitung in den Hexateuch*, Freiburg, i. Br.—Leipzig, 1893.
Exodus, *KHC*, 2, Tübingen, 1900.
Numeri, *KHC*, 4, Tübingen–Leipzig, 1903.
HUMBERT, P., 'Die literarische Zweiheit des Priester-Codex in der Genesis', *ZAW*, 58, 1940/1, pp. 30–57.
JACOBSEN, Th., Mesopotamia in: *Before Philosophy*, London, 1949, pp. 137–237 (= *The Intellectual Adventure of Ancient Man*, Chicago, 1946).
JEPSEN, A., *Untersuchungen zum Bundesbuch*, *BWANT*, III, 5, Stuttgart, 1927.
JIRKU, A., 'Zur magischen Bedeutung der Kleidung in Israel', *ZAW*, 37, 1917/18, pp. 109–25.
Altorientalischer Kommentar zum, AT., Leipzig–Erlangen, 1923.
Die Ausgrabungen in Palästina und Syrien, Halle (Saale), 1956.
JOHNSON, A. R., *Sacral Kingship in Ancient Israel*, Cardiff, 1955.
JUNKER, H., 'Traditionsgeschichtliche Untersuchung über die Erzählung von der Anbetung des Goldenen Kalbes (Ex. 32)', *TrThZ*, 60, vol. 5–8, pp. 232–242.
KAISER, O., *Der Königliche Knecht. Eine traditionsgeschichtlich-exegetische Studie über die Ebed-Jahwe-Lieder bei Deuterojesaja*, *FRLANT*, 70, Göttingen, 1959.
'Stammesgeschichtliche Hintergründe der Josephgeschichte', *VT*, 10, 1960, pp. 1–15.
KAUTZSCH, E., *Die Heilige Schrift des Alten Testaments*, I, 3rd ed., Tübingen, 1909.
KENNETT, R. H., 'The Origin of the Aaronite Priesthood', *JThSt*, 6, 1905, pp. 161–186.
KITTEL, R., *Die Bücher der Könige*, *HK*, 1/5, Göttingen, 1900.
Geschichte des Volkes Israel, 3rd ed., Gotha, 1916. 17.
KISSANE, E. J., *The Book of Isaiah*, I, Dublin, 1941.

KJAER, H., 'The excavation of Shilo', *JPOS*, 10, 1930, pp. 87–174.
KLOSTERMANN, A., *Der Pentateuch, Beiträge zu seinem Verständnis und seiner Entstehungsgeschichte*, *N.F.*, Leipzig, 1907.
KNUDTZON, J. A., *Die El-Amarna Tafeln*, I, (Text), *VAB*, 2, Leipzig, 1910.
KOCH, K., *Die Priesterschrift von Exodus 25 bis Leviticus 16. Eine überlieferungsgeschichtliche und literarkritische Untersuchung*, *FRLANT*, 71, Göttingen, 1959.
KÖHLER, L., *Deuterojesaja stilkritisch untersucht*, *BZAW*, 37, Giessen, 1923.
'Der Dekalog,' *ThR*, 1929, pp. 161–184.
Old Testament Theology, London, 1957 (ET).
'Die hebräische Rechtsgemeinde', in: *Der hebräische Mensch*, Tübingen, 1953, pp. 143–171.
KÖHLER, L.-BAUMGARTNER, W., *Lexicon in Veteris Testamenti Libros*, Leiden, 1953.
KOROŠEC, V., *Hethitische Staatsverträge. Ein Beitrag zu ihrer juristischen Wertung*, *Leipziger rechtswissenschaftliche Studien*, Heft 60, Leipzig, 1931.
KRAETZSCHMAR, R., *Die Bundesvorstellungen im Alten Testament in ihrer geschichtlichen Entwicklung*, Marburg, 1896.
KRAUS, H-J., 'Gilgal. Ein Beitrag zur Kultusgeschichte Israels', *VT*, 1, 1951, pp. 181–199.
Die Königsherrschaft Gottes im Alten Testament, *BHTh*, 13, Tübingen, 1951.
Gottesdienst in Israel. Studien zur Geschichte des Laubhüttenfestes, München, 1954.
Geschichte der historisch-kritischen Erforschung des Alten Testaments von der Reformation bis zur Gegenwart, Neukirchen, 1956.
Psalmen, *BK*, 15/1–11, Neukirchen, 1958 ff.
KUENEN, A., *Historisch-kritische Einleitung in die Bücher des AT*, 1/1, Leipzig, 1887.
KUSCHKE, A., 'Die Lagervorstellung der priesterlichen Erzählung', *ZAW*, 63, 1951, pp. 74–105.
KUTSCH, E., 'Feste und Feiern II. In Israel, '*RGG* 2, 3rd ed., col. 910–917.
LEEUW, G. van der, *Religion in Essence and Manifestation* (ET), London, 1938.
LEHMING, S., 'Versuch zu Ex. xxxii.', *VT*, 10, 1960, pp. 16–50.
LEVY, I., 'The story of the golden calf reanalysed', *VT*, 9, 1959, pp. 318–322.
LIDZBARSKI, M., *Handbuch der nordsemitischen Epigraphik*, I, Text, Weimar, 1898.
LISOWSKY, G., and Rost, L., *Konkordanz zum hebräischen Alten Testament*, Stuttgart, 1958.
LODS, A., 'Eléments anciens et éléments modernes dans le rituel du sacrifice israélite', *RHPhR*, 1928, pp. 399–411.
LOHSE, E., *prosopon*, *ThWBNT*, 6, pp. 769–781.
LOISY, A., *Essai historique sur le sacrifice*, Paris, 1920.
MANDELKERN, S., *Veteris Testamenti Concordantiae*. 2nd ed., Graz, 1955.
MENDENHALL, G. E., 'Covenant Forms in Israelite Tradition', *BA*, 17/3, 1954, pp. 50–76.
'Ancient Oriental and Biblical Law', *BA*, 17/2, 1954, pp. 26–46.
MICHEL, D., 'Studien zu den sogenannten Thronbesteigungspsalmen', *VT*, 6, 1956, pp. 40–68.
MÖHLENBRINK, K., 'Josua im Pentateuch', *ZAW*, 59, 1942/3, pp. 14–58.
MOORTGAT, A., 'Geschichte Vorderasiens bis zum Hellenismus', in: *Ägypten und Vorderasien im Altertum*, München, 1950.
MORGENSTERN, J., 'The Ark, the Ephod and the Tent of Meeting', *HUCA*, 17, 1942/3, pp. 153–165; *HUCA*, 18, 1944, pp. 1–52.
MORITZ, B., *Der Sinaikult in heidnischer Zeit, Abhandlungen d. königl. Gesellsch. d. Wissensch. zu Göttingen*, Phil.-Hist. Kl. N.F., 16/2, 1916.
MOWINCKEL, S., *Psalmstudien*, II, Kristiania, 1922.
Jesaja-Disiplene, Profetien fra Jesaja til Jeremia, Oslo, 1926.
Le Décalogue, Etudes d'Histoire et de Philosophie Religieuses, Paris, 1927.
'Wann wurde der Jahwäkultus in Jerusalem offiziell bildlos?', *AcOr*, 8, 1930, pp. 257–279.

'Kadesj, Sinai, og Jahve', *Norsk Geografisk Tidsskrift*, 11, 1942, pp. 1–32.
Religion und Kultus, Göttingen, 1953.
He That Cometh, Oxford, 1956.
MUILENBURG, J., 'The Form and Structure of the Covenantal Formulations', *M. Burrows-Festschrift*, *VT*, 9, 1959, pp. 347–365.
MUSIL, A., *The Manners and Customs of the Rwala Bedouins*, 1928.
NESTLE, E., Miscellen, *ZAW*, 24, 1904, pp. 122–138.
NICOLSKY, N. M., 'Pascha im Kulte des jerusalemischen Tempels', *ZAW*, 45, 1927, pp. 171–190, 241–253.
NORTH, C. R., 'Pentateuchal Criticism', in: *The Old Testament and Modern Study*, (ed. by H. H. Rowley), Oxford, 1952, pp. 48–83.
NORTH, F. S., 'Aaron's Rise in Prestige', *ZAW*, 66, 1954, pp. 191–199.
NOTH, M., *Die israelitischen Personennamen im Rahmen der gemeinsemitischen Namengebung*, *BWANT*, III, 10, Stuttgart, 1928.
Das System der zwölf Stämme Israels, *BWANT*, IV, 1, Stuttgart, 1930.
Die Gesetze im Pentateuch, Halle (Saale), 1940 (= *Gesammelte Studien*, pp. 9–141).
'Der Wallfahrtsweg zum Sinai (Num. 33)', *PJ*, 36, 1940, pp. 5–28.
Überlieferungsgeschichte des Pentateuch, Stuttgart, 1948.
'Jerusalem und die israelitische Tradition', *OTS*, 8, 1950, (= *Gesammelte Studien*, pp. 172–187).
'Gott, König, Volk im Alten Testament', *ZThK*, 47, 1950, pp. 157–191 (= *Gesammelte Studien*, pp. 188–229).
'Das alttestamentliche Bundschliessen im Lichte eines Mari-Textes', *Annuaire de l'Institut de Philologie et d'Histoire Orientales et Slaves*, 13, 1953. Mélanges Isidore Lévy. Pp. 433–444, Brussels, 1955 (= *Gesammelte Studien*, pp. 142–154).
Das Buch Josua, 2nd ed., *HAT*, 1/7, Tübingen, 1953.
Überlieferungsgeschichtliche Studien, 2nd ed., Darmstadt, 1957.
Die Welt des Alten Testaments, 3rd ed., Berlin, 1957.
Exodus, London, 1962 (ET).
The History of Israel (rev.), London, 1960 (ET).
'Zur Anfertigung des "Goldenen Kalbes" ', *VT*, 9, 1959, pp. 419–422.
NÖTSCHER, F., *Biblische Altertumskunde*, Bonn, 1940.
NYBERG, H. S., 'Deuteronomium 33, 2–3', *ZDMG*, 92, 1938, pp. 303–344.
OBBINK, H. Th., 'Jahwebilder', *ZAW*, 47, 1929, pp. 264–274.
OORT, H., 'De Aäronieden', *Theol. Tijdschrift*, 18, 1884, pp. 289–335.
PEDERSEN, J., *Israel. Its Life and Culture*, I–II, London–Copenhagen, 1926.
'Passahfest und Passahlegende', *ZAW*, 52, 1934, pp. 161–175.
PETUCHOWSKI, J. J., 'Nochmals "zur Anfertigung des Goldenen Kalbes" ', *VT*, 10, 1960, p. 74.
PRITCHARD, J. B., *Ancient Near Eastern Texts relating to the Old Testament*, 2nd ed., Princeton N.J., 1955.
PROCKSCH, O., *Das Nordhebräische Sagenbuch. Die Elohimquelle*, Leipzig, 1906.
QUELL, G., *diatheke*, *ThWBNT*, 2, pp. 106–127.
RAD, G. VON, 'Zelt und Lade', *NKZ*, 42, 1931, pp. 476–491 (= *Gesammelte Studien*, pp. 109–129).
'Die falschen Propheten', *ZAW*, 51, 1933, pp. 109 f.
Die Priesterschrift im Hexateuch, *BWANT*, IV, 13, Stuttgart–Berlin, 1934.
Das formgeschichtliche Problem des Hexateuch, *BWANT*, IV, 26, 1938 (=*Gesammelte Studien*, pp. 9–86).
Studies in Deuteronomy, *SBT*, 9, London, 1953 (ET).
'Die Stadt auf dem Berge', *EvTh*, 8, 1948/9, pp. 439–447 (= *Gesammelte Studien*, pp. 214–224).
' "Gerechtigkeit" und "Leben" in der Kultsprache der Psalmen', *Bertholet-Festschrift*, 1950, pp. 418–437 (= *Gesammelte Studien*, pp. 225–247).

Der Heilige Krieg im Alten Israel, 2nd ed., Göttingen, 1952.
Theology of the Old Testament, I, Edinburgh and London, 1963. (ET).
mal'akh im AT., *ThWBNT*, 1, pp. 75–79.
kabod im AT., *ThWBNT*, 2, pp. 240–245.
RENDTORFF, R., *Die Gesetze in der Priesterschrift. Eine gattungsgeschichtliche Untersuchung*, *FRLANT*, 62, Göttingen, 1954.
'Opfer', *EKL*, 2, col. 1691–1694.
'Pentateuch', *EKL*, 3, col. 109–114.
RICCIOTTI, G., *The History of Israel* I, Milwaukee, 1958.
ROST, L., 'Sinaibund und Davidbund', *ThLZ*, 72, 1947, col. 129–134.
'Die Wohnstätte des Zeugnisses', *Baumgärtel-Festschrift*, *Erlanger Forschungen* Series A, vol 10, 1959, pp. 158–165.
'Erwägungen zum israelitischen Brandopfer', *Eissfeldt-Festschrift*, *BZAW*, 77, 1958, pp. 177–183.
See also Lisowsky, G., and Rost, L.
ROWLEY, H. H., *From Joseph to Joshua* (*Schweich Lecture* 1948), London, 1952.
'The meaning of sacrifice in the O.T.', *BJRL*, 33/1, 1950, Manchester, 1950.
'Moses and the Decalogue', *BJRL*, 34/1, 1951, Manchester, 1951.
'Mose und der Monotheismus', *ZAW*, 69, 1957, pp. 1–21.
RUDOLPH, W., 'Der Aufbau von Exod. 19–34' in: *Werden und Wesen des Alten Testaments*, ed. by J. Hempel, *BZAW*, 66, Berlin, 1936, pp. 41–48.
Der 'Elohist' von Exodus bis Josua, *BZAW*, 68, Berlin, 1938.
Chronikbücher, *HAT*, 1/21, Tübingen, 1955.
See also Volz, P., Rudolph, W.
ŠANDA, A., *Die Bücher der Könige*, *Exegetishes Handbuch zum AT*. Münster 1911.
SCHARBERT J., 'Formgeschichte und Exegese von Exod. 34. 6 f. und seiner Parallelen', *Bibl.* 38, 1957, pp. 130–150.
SCHMID, H., 'Jahwe und die Kulttraditionen von Jerusalem', *ZAW*, 67, 1955, pp. 168–197.
SCHMIDT, H., 'Mose und der Dekalog', *Gunkel-Festschrift*, ('*Eucharisterion*'), *FRLANT*, 36, Göttingen, 1913, pp. 78–119.
'Kerubenthron und Lade', *Gunkel-Festschrift* ('*Eucharisterion*'), *FRLANT*, 36, Göttingen, 1923, pp. 120–144.
SCHMIDT, M., *Prophet und Tempel. Eine Studie zum Problem der Gottesnähe im Alten Testament*, Zollikon–Zürich, 1948.
SCHRADE, H., *Der verborgene Gott. Gottesbild und Gottesvorstellung in Israel und im Alten Orient*, Stuttgart, 1949.
SCHRADER, E., *Die Keilinschriften und das Alte Testament*, 3rd ed., Berlin, 1903.
SCOTT, R. B. Y., 'A Kingdom of Priests' (Exod. 19, 6)', *OTS*, 8, 1950, pp. 213–219.
SELLIN, E., 'Wann wurde das Moselied Deut. 32 gedichtet?', *ZAW*, 43, 1925, pp. 161–173.
'Das Zelt Jahwes', *Kittel-Festschrift*, *BWAT*, 13, Leipzig, 1913, pp. 168–192.
SIMPSON, C. A., *The Early Traditions of Israel*, Oxford, 1948.
SMEND, R., *Die Erzählung des Hexateuch auf ihre Quellen untersucht*, Berlin, 1912.
Das Mosebild von Heinrich Ewald bis Martin Noth, *BGBE*, 3, Tübingen, 1959.
SMITH, W. R., *The Religion of the Semites*, 3rd ed., London, 1897.
SODEN, W. v., *Grundriss der akkadischen Grammatik*, *AnOr*, 33, Rome, 1952.
STADE, B., *Geschichte des Volkes Israel*, I, Berlin, 1887.
STAERK, W., *Lyrik* (*Psalmen, Hoheslied und Verwandtes*), 2nd ed., *SATA*, 3/1, Göttingen, 1920.
STAMM, J. J., *Der Dekalog im Lichte der neuren Forschung*, *Studientage für die Pfarrer*, vol. 1, Bern, 1958.
STEUERNAGEL, C., 'Der jehovistische Bericht über den Bundesschluss', *ThStKr*, 72, 1899, p. 349.

'Jahwe, der Gott Israels. Eine stil-und religionsgeschichtliche Studie', *Wellhausen-Festschrift*, *BZAW*, 27, Giessen, 1914, pp. 329–349.
Lehrbuch der Einleitung in das Alte Testament, Tübingen, 1912.
Das Deuteronomium, *HK*, 3/1, 2nd ed., Göttingen, 1923.
STEVENSON, W. B., 'Hebrew 'Olah and Zebach Sacrifices', *Bertholet-Festschrift*, Tübingen, 1950, pp. 488–497.
STOEBE, H. J., 'Die Bedeutung des Wortes *häsäd* im Alten Testament', *VT*, 2, 1952, pp. 244–254.
TALMON S., 'Divergences in Calendar-Reckoning in Ephraim and Judah', *VT*, 8, 1958, pp. 48–74.
TORCZYNER, H., *Die Bundeslade und die Anfänge der Religion Israels*, 2nd ed., Berlin, 1930.
TSEVAT, M., *A Study of the Language of the Biblical Psalms*, *JBL Monograph Series* 9, Philadelphia, 1955.
DE VAUX, R., *Ancient Israel*, London, 1961 (ET).
VOLZ, P., *Das Neujahrsfest Jahwes* (*Laubhüttenfest*), *SGVS*, 67, Tübingen, 1912.
Die biblischen Altertümer, Calw–Stuttgart, 1914.
Mose und sein Werk, 2nd ed., Tübingen, 1932.
VOLZ, P., Rudolph, W., *Der Elohist als Erzähler. Ein Irrweg der Pentateuchkritik? BZAW*, 63, 1933.
VRIEZEN, TH. C., *Theologie des Alten Testaments in Grundzügen*, Wageningen–Neukirchen, 1957.
WEIDNER, E. F., *Politische Dokumente aus Kleinasien. Die Staatsverträge in akkadischer Sprache aus dem Archiv von Boghazköi* (*Boghazköi-Studien*, vol. 8, ed. by O. Weber), Leipzig, 1923.
WEISER, A., 'Zur Frage nach den Beziehungen der Psalmen zum Kult: Die Darstellung der Theophanie in den Psalmen und im Festkult', *Bertholet-Festschrift*, Tübingen, 1950, pp. 513–531.
Introduction to the Old Testament, London, 1961 (ET).
The Psalms, London, 1962 (ET).
Das Buch des Propheten Jeremia, *ATD*, 21, 4th ed., Göttingen, 1960.
'Das Deboralied. Eine gattungs-und traditionsgeschichtliche Studie', *ZAW*, 71, 1959, pp. 67–97.
'Samuels "Philister-Sieg". Die Überlieferungen in 1 Sam. 7.', *ZThK*, 56, 1959, pp. 253–272.
WELLHAUSEN, J., *Die Composition des Hexateuchs* (*Jahrbücher für Deutsche Theologie* 21), Berlin, 1885.
Reste arabischen Heidentums gesammelt und erläutert, 2nd ed., Berlin, 1897.
Prolegomena to the History of Ancient Israel, London, 1888 (ET).
WESTERMANN, C., *Das Loben Gottes in den Psalmen*, Göttingen, 1954.
WESTPHAL, G., 'Aaron und die Aaroniden' *ZAW*, 26, 1906, pp. 201–230.
Jahwes Wohnstätten nach den Anschauungen der alten Hebräer, *BZAW*, 15, Giessen, 1908.
WEVERS, J. W., 'A Study in the Form Criticism of Individual Complaint Psalms', *VT*, 6, 1956, pp. 80–96.
WIDENGREN, G. *Sakrales Königtum im Alten Testament und im Judentum*, Stuttgart, 1955.
WILDBERGER, H., 'Die Völkerwallfahrt zum Zion, Jes. 2. 1–5', *VT*, 7, 1957, pp. 62–81.
WOLFF, H. W., 'Hoseas geistige Heimat', *ThLZ*, 81, 1956, col. 83–94.
WOLLEY, C. L., Lawrence, E. T., *The Wilderness of Zin*, *Palestine Exploration Fund Annual* 3, 1914/15.
WRIGHT, G. E., *The Old Testament Against its Environment*, *StBTh*, 2, London, 1957.
WÜRTHWEIN, E., 'Der Ursprung der prophetischen Gerichtsrede', *ZThK*, 49, 1952 pp. 1–16.

ZIMMERLI, W. 'Das zweite Gebot', *Bertholet-Festschrift*, Tübingen, 1950, pp. 550–563.

'Ich bin Jahwe', *Alt-Festschrift* (*'Geschichte und Altes Testament'*), *BHTh*, 16, Tübingen, 1953, pp. 179–209.

Ezechiel, *BK*, 13/1 f., Neukirchen, 1956 f.

'Die Weisung des Alten Testaments zum Geschäft der Sprache' in: *Das Problem der Sprache in Theologie und Kirche*, Berlin, 1959, pp. 1–20.

ZIMMERN, H., 'Religion und Sprache' in: *Die Keilinschriften und das Alte Testament*, ed. by E. Schrader, 3rd ed., pp. 343–653.

INDEX OF AUTHORS

SCRIPTURE REFERENCES

Leviticus

Numbers

SUBJECT INDEX